THE GOOD DAUGHTER:

SECRETS, LIFE STORIES, AND HEALING

ALSO BY CONNIE SHOEMAKER

"Ma'alesh: Verses from Egypt"

*Write in the Corner Where You Are, Write in the Middle,
Interactive Techniques for the ESL Class Room*

Co-author of *Write Ideas and Inside the News*

The Good Daughter:

Secrets, Life Stories, and Healing

"Don't judge a life good or bad before it ends."

Sophocles, "Women of Trachis"

CONNIE SHOEMAKER

THE GOOD DAUGHTER:
Secrets, Life Stories, and Healing

Print ISBN: 978-0-9864253-0-1   EISBN: 978-0-9864253-1-8

Library of Congress Control Number: 2015902211

The Good Daughter™ is an Amity Bridge Books trademark.

Cover and Interior Design: Cindi Yaklich Epicenter Creative, LLC
Cover Photography: Hoffman Studios, Longmont, CO.

TO ALL DAUGHTERS WHO ARE CARE-GIVERS FOR THEIR MOTHERS AND FATHERS

This memoir spans a decade of care-giving, so some sequences of events have been compressed or changed to improve the pacing. The names of long-term care centers and some of the names of nurses, nursing assistants, and physicians have been changed to ensure privacy. Conversations with my mother are not verbatim but reconstructed from my note-taking as we reviewed her life and her own written notes to me.

My deep appreciation also to:

Those who read early drafts and offered encouragement: My daughters Sonja Tilliros and Melissa Shoemaker, and good friends Bill and Lucy Brenner, Marty Dawley and Manijeh Badiozamani, also a memoirist.

My son Troy, who often reminds me that family members sometimes have different versions of the same memory.

Dr. Isabella Morozova, who shared her research on the elderly and the meaning of "home."

My husband, who has filled my life with cherished memories.

I offer my heartfelt gratitude to my editors: Shari Caudron, who deftly led me through a personal short-course in memoir writing and encouraged me to use my reflective voice, and to Rebecca Berg, who expertly copy-edited the manuscript and offered suggestions.

I also sincerely thank my cover and interior book designer, Cindi Yaklich, for her creativity and insight into the essence of *The Good Daughter*.

CONTENTS

CHAPTER I

THE BALANCING ACT

A SIGH PUNCTUATES EVERY OTHER STEP AS I WALK DOWN THE HALLWAY TO room 214 at Ivy Manor. The door that's usually open a few inches is closed. I knock twice, but no response, so I grasp the door knob, cold and slightly sticky, in my warm hand. I inhale before turning it and slowly pushing the door open, so it won't collide with the bathroom door. My tiny eighty-nine-year-old mother is perched on the end of a sagging mattress. She's bending over a cardboard easel cut to fit an eight-by-ten piece of watercolor paper, so engrossed in the painting on her lap that she doesn't hear me enter the room. A plastic glass of water sits on my mother's medicine table next to the rainbow of paint ovals. The yellow and blue ovals, her favorite colors, are puddled with water. In front of her is the ever-present walker with the catheter bag and the pale yellow umbilical-like tube disappearing under the hem of her purple paisley skirt.

I pause just inside the door to announce my presence in a loud voice.

"Mama, my goodness, you're painting?"

She doesn't answer. I come closer and repeat my question.

She brushes back a wisp of grayish-blond hair, lifts her head slightly, and pushes up the black plastic shades attached to her glasses.

"Oh, Connie. I didn't know you were here."

She reaches for her hearing aid, puts it in her right ear and adjusts it to stop the piercing whistle.

"It's been such a long time since you painted a picture. That's wonderful."

Relief at a sign of her adjustment to Ivy Manor replaces the apprehension I feel each time I see her. Instead of constantly complaining about this nursing home, my mom is using her artistic talent to do something positive. This may be a step in the right direction.

"I'm trying to do a Viking ship, but I just can't get that cross on the sail right."

She puts her finger on the slightly crooked, dark blue cross and shakes her head. She doesn't notice the smudge of paint on her forefinger as she adjusts her glasses and looks up at me. She pauses a moment to mentally retrieve her daily list of requests.

"You're late, aren't you? Were you able to get the mashed potatoes right this time?"

The lilt in my spirits diffuses. She calls her critical attitude "pickiness." I call it downright negativity with a fatal dose of perfectionism. Although I expect it as a necessary part of each visit, the criticism makes me shrink back into the little girl who wants her mother's approval but is never quite good enough to receive it. All thoughts of my other life as an I-can-do-it-all director of an English language institute, a community volunteer, and a wife, mother, and grandmother seem worthless on my mother's scale of perfection. Before responding, I reason with myself. Should I ignore her criticism or confront her? An "I" message is a possible response, a positive technique I've tried to use in counseling my international students. I could say, "I really feel frustrated when you criticize me" or "I need you to appreciate all the things I do for you each day." But there's really no choice here. This isn't the time to challenge her. My displeasure might physically upset her, just as it did when I was a child, when I said "No, I don't want to" to an enema for *my* health or a daily nap for *her* health. She's afloat on the raft of her final years and has little control of what happens to her in this miserable little nursing home, and, as an only child, I'm it: her caregiver, her daughter, and someone who loves her in spite of the negativity. I want to give her as much quality of life as possible.

"Yes, Mama. The gravy is on the side, not on the potatoes."

I prop my blue canvas tote bag on the bed. Like a surgical nurse, I carefully place the items she has requested on the tray table at the end of her bed. Most important are the little plastic bowls of her favorite mashed potatoes and gravy—easy to eat when you have irritable bowel syndrome and very few teeth. The potatoes must be from KFC, purchased just ten minutes before my arrival at Ivy Manor, so that they will still be hot when she takes them down to the dining room. Next is the *Rocky Mountain News*, not the entire paper because she finds it too cumbersome to hold, just the crossword/comic strip section, the local news, and the obituaries. Finally, I pull out a six-pack of tapioca puddings; only Kraft brand is acceptable. I separate them, so she can easily place one in the striped bag on her walker, in case there's nothing on the lunch menu that she can eat. I roll up my tote bag and pause, an only child waiting for her Mom's approval.

She fine-tunes my efforts.

"Would you fold up the newspaper and put it on the bed instead of on the table? It gets in the way when I'm painting. And leave the door open just about a foot when you come in." Not waiting for a response, she busies herself with cleaning her paintbrush and putting away the water colors in a recycled Kleenex box.

I stuff my irritation into my emotional wastebasket, which has grown enormous after all these years of not expressing my displeasure. No confrontation means no problems. It's the easy way out. As I was growing up, I learned to attune myself to my mother's perfectionism, to try to develop empathy with her, so I could see life from her point of view. If I understood her better, I theorized, I could relate to her better. And here I am now, a sixty-five-year-old child still trying to please her mother by fulfilling all her needs.

If only I could find a balance between what she needs from me and what I need for myself. I need time for solitude and reflection; more time for my husband, kids, and grandkids; time to read, see friends, and write poems and books; time to create new programs at work; and time to soak up sunshine and beauty to restore my soul. Right now, I'm like a gardener with only one full watering can in a season of drought. Do I let some of the plants wither—even die—while others thrive? Do I give a little water to each? What if that it won't be enough to sustain any of them? What about my own thirst?

As expected, my visit is greeted with a list of complaints about Ivy Manor. Mama uses her arthritis-crooked fingers to tally up the misdemeanors, nodding her head side to side in disbelief. In order to listen in what I hope is an attitude of rapt attention, I slide the white plastic lawn chair that I've added to the room's yard-sale décor from beside the door to the end of the bed.

"What a morning this has been! Everything went wrong. The nutty lady across the hall barged into my room without any clothes on her bottom half. No diaper. No pants. After that little Indonesian aide got her out of here, he left the door wide open. And, would you believe, here comes Nurse Jessica wheeling Daddy in to see if he recognizes me. I've been here three months, and I tell them every morning. Don't bring him in here. Not in my room. I'll see him at lunch and dinner. I wish they'd just listen to me. He *doesn't* know who I am."

Her complaints seem to exhaust her. She moves her walker and scoots back on the bed. A grunt accompanies the task of lifting up her legs. She lies down with her head propped on the pillows that are stacked against the head board.

"Daddy may not know exactly who you are, but I think he has some recognition of you," I suggest. Maybe I can plant a seed of empathy in her mind. "He needs to see a familiar face. I don't think they're trying to bother you."

It's probably an illusion, but I want her to show him some love and caring that will cut through the fog of Alzheimer's. This would comfort him in the alien environment of the nursing home and, in turn, might affirm a positive role for her.

Her face still reflects only her incredulity about the morning's events. She hasn't heard a word I've said. "I just don't know, Connie. Life is so hard and sometimes *you* just don't understand." She closes her eyes and sighs.

"I try to understand, Mama, but we need to give Daddy some attention, too. Do you remember yesterday at lunch when you helped him with his bib? He thanked you and smiled."

"I don't know. I don't know," she mumbles as she drops her head to her chest.

I look up at the large black-and-white clock on the wall and discover that I have just 40 minutes before an appointment at school, not enough time to sit at the lunch table to visit with my mom and dad and get back to school. Maybe if I hurry. The tug between my two lives makes my throat constrict. My life has been thrown into complete disarray by my dad's stroke and my mom's declining health. Since returning to Colorado after four years at American University in Cairo, I and my own family have carved out fulfilling lives. My work with international students is challenging but supported by a professional faculty and staff who are also my friends. My husband just retired from a career as a communications professor and educational specialist. Our three children are in good marriages and starting families. Until now, I relegated my mom and dad's care to Sundays, when we picked them up from their downtown Denver apartment, helped them shop, and enjoyed a family dinner at a restaurant. At that point, my mom was handling medical appointments for both of them at a nearby clinic. What I failed to recognize was my dad's anger at his increasing dementia and my mom's frustration at the responsibilities that his decline added to her own agenda of irritable bowel syndrome and incontinence. The chess board of my orderly, pleasant life was carefully set up to play a game I thought I could win—until events of the last year scattered the pieces on the floor. At this point, I can't pick them all up and put them back where they belong. I've been able to deal with challenges throughout my life, but I've never felt as inadequate at balancing my responsibilities as I do now.

"Let's go down to lunch now," I say, "so I have a chance to visit with Daddy, too. Is that okay?" Even in adulthood I still call him Daddy, just as my mom does when she talks about him to me. It's a term of endearment that I hope still exists in his shrinking memory bank.

I bend over to retrieve the canvas bag and my purse, in preparation for the rush down the hallway to his room. Mama pulls the corner of the pillow up over her mouth, muffling her voice.

"I suppose so. I don't feel so well now. I'm not really hungry. Maybe I shouldn't go downstairs to lunch. I'll just eat here in the room."

"Oh, God," I mutter, turning from the bed. "Not now, I don't have time for this." If I have to gather the lunch items and sit with her while she eats, I won't have time to wheel my dad down to the lunch table and visit with him. The purpose of this visit is to sit down with both of them. I want them to have some kind of relationship with each other. I want the three of us to be together like an ideal family, healthy and supporting one another, an impossible dream but one that recurs frequently. I take a breath and compose myself, so I will sound convincing.

"It's time for the first shift at lunch now, Mama. I'll walk you down and then go to Daddy's room to get him."

She fingers the hearing aid in her left ear and shrugs her shoulders. "If I have to, I will. But I may want to leave before Daddy's finished. He's so slow."

The added fillip of criticism is typical of any concession she makes and not just reserved for my dad.

She sits up and carefully moves her legs from the bed to the floor. While she is adjusting her skirt and the catheter bag, she asks me to clear her table. I quickly move the newspaper from the table to the bed. Then I pick up her watercolor of the Viking ship for a closer look. It's all in shades of blue against the background of a pale yellow sky with tinges of orange. The waves are tipped with white foam from the wind that fills the four sails and furls the orange flags on the masts. The main sail is filled with a slightly angled blue cross.

"The cross looks okay to me, Mama. It's really quite good considering your eyesight and the fact that you don't have an easel. Would it be easier to hold your hand steady if you tried that small easel I bought for you?"

As always, I'm the problem solver, a task I was assigned by my mom when I was six or seven years old.

"I don't know what I'm going to do about Daddy," she would confide. "He just doesn't listen to me."

I never knew what to respond, but somehow felt responsible for a solution. I worried then about what I could do to make it better, just as I do now. It's finally dawning on me that she doesn't really want me to solve the problems, just to hear her complaints.

"By now you should know I can't use that wooden easel. I'd rather prop the cardboard on my lap. Anyway, I need to change the cross until it's right. It shouldn't slant on the sail like that."

"It doesn't have to be perfect, Mama. Nothing is ever perfect."

My thinly-veiled message to her is to accept my imperfections in return for me accepting hers.

She pushes her glasses up on her nose, and looks up at me. Because her neck is becoming rigid from arthritis, it's difficult for her to raise her head. Her pale blue eyes look larger through the heavy glasses, and moisture is collecting on her lower lashes. She seems to be absorbing my presence, really looking at me, as if she were measuring me with a pencil to determine perspective for a painting. No words. Just recognition in her eyes and a flicker of understanding.

"No, nothing is ever perfect," she whispers.

I nod my head in agreement, both philosophically and practically. Now I can move on to other tasks. Once my mother is safely positioned in her walker and is propelling herself to the dining hall, I hurry to my father's room. As I open the door, I automatically hold my breath to block the pervasive smell of Lysol laced with urine. I'm greeted by loud music from a Korean video of dancing ladies in bright pink traditional dresses. My dad's new roommate, Sam, is snoring in a chair. His head is propped on his folded hands, which grip the walker in front of him, just a foot from the portable TV that stands on a small bedside chest. Sam, who is developmentally disabled and speaks no English, is barely five feet tall, still muscled from farm labor but boasting a large belly that protrudes from his brown and white-striped t-shirt. He is my father's second roommate, the result of my complaint about the first one, Harold, who cursed my father whenever he tried to access their shared closet and who pulled the curtain between their beds so that my dad couldn't see the door of the room.

I squeeze through the narrow space between the TV and Sam. Daddy is sitting in his wheelchair in the sunshine of the window, his bristly chin settled on the V in his white undershirt, dozing, oblivious to the loud music. I put my hand gently on my father's shoulder.

"Hi, Daddy. It's Connie."

He opens his eyes and looks up at me, trying to focus on who I am. A twitch of a smile crosses his lips.

"Umm, oh. Is it time to go home?"

"No, Daddy, it's time for lunch."

"Here? Where am I?"

For what seems like the hundredth time, I repeat the *Readers' Digest* version of events.

"You're here at Ivy Manor. You had a stroke while you were living with Mama in your apartment downtown. You had to come to a nursing home, so you could get better care. Mama's here now, too."

I don't fill in the time between the stroke and Ivy Manor. He wouldn't understand his stay in the hospital, or his time at Briargate Care Center, where his hands were tucked under a strap at mealtime, so burly male aids could force spoonfuls of food into his mouth while protesting tears ran down his cheeks. Forget the other detail of Mama in assisted living for two years until she needed a permanent catheter in her bladder and could no longer stay there. I try to simplify my explanation with the hope that he'll understand. I try so hard.

"Mama? Where is she?"

"She's here, Daddy. She came just two months ago."

"She's not in Longmont?"

"No. Right now she's waiting for you at the lunch table. She sits right across from you. Remember that lady with the pretty blue skirt and purple blouse?"

"That little old lady?"

"Yes. That's your wife, Mildred. And my mother."

This dual role seems so simple. But I remember how difficult it is for beginning English learners to fathom family relationships. I yearn for the classroom whiteboard where I can draw a family tree with connecting lines to illustrate how one person can have two roles. And it's true that Alzheimer's has reduced my dad's understanding to that of a beginning language learner. The difference is that his understanding will never improve. It will only diminish.

The buzz of my cell phone interrupts. I fish the irritating device out of my purse. Missy, who is my daughter and who is also the foreign-student advisor at my school, Spring International, tells me that the prospective teacher I was supposed to interview is waiting for me.

"Oh, shit, Missy! I'm still here at Ivy Manor. I can't leave right now, and it takes 20 minutes to get there. Please tell her I'm sorry, and see if Cheryl can talk with her."

I use the S-word selectively in times of severe frustration but never in my mother's range of hearing. Missy is more accepting. She probably enjoys her mom's slips of tongue. The pressure of not making it to the appointment pulses in my temples. What can I do? I've always multitasked, but the "shoulds" and "want to's" of my daily life are now battling for dominance. My colleagues at work are supportive of the time I need to spend at Ivy Manor, but I'm making more mistakes in paper work and not showing the usual support and encouragement to them, a joyful part of my job that I don't want to neglect. Like a favorite shirt that's getting threadbare, my family life is fraying, too. I sound like my mother, continually contradicting my husband, Floyd, when he makes a statement that I think is incorrect. Although we see two of our children, Missy and Troy, and their spouses at brunch on Sundays, I'd like to carve out more time with them and with six-year-old Benjamin, the only grandchild here in the United States. Also, more chances to visit our oldest daughter, Sonja, and her three sons, who live on the island of Cyprus. The mantra "I can do it all" shoves work and family to the bottom of the list and drains my energy and coping skills. I try to fill the empty well with food and top it off with every ounce of spirituality I can muster. Several slow, deep breaths and a mental "Be with me, dear God" help me to pull myself into the present moment. Today, my goal is to get my mother and father together and spend a few minutes with them. "Come on, Daddy. Let's go down to lunch and see Mama."

He puts his good hand on the arm of the chair and grasps it with his fingers, ready for a trip to an unknown destination.

The aide has already taken Sam down to eat, so I can wheel my dad out the door and around the corner to the activity room, which is doubling as a dining room today because the only elevator to the first floor dining hall is broken. This is a monthly occurrence at decaying Ivy Manor. Ten tables of four each are set up in the small second-floor room. Like a fire brigade passing buckets of water, the aides are relaying the food up the stairs from the downstairs kitchen. The only people sitting at a table near the door are Mama and a resident whose name is also Mildred but is differentiated by a T after her first name. There's room for both Daddy and me.

I wheel my father to the table and remove the chair across from my mother, so that the wheelchair will fit under the table.

"Here's Daddy, Mama."

My mom pulls up the black plastic shades on her glasses, looks up, and forces a smile. "Hello, Jim. How are you doing?"

He looks at her for a few seconds but doesn't respond. Mildred T. gets up, greets him, and puts a blue terrycloth bib around his neck. She affectionately pats him on the back. My mother pushes up the glasses on her nose. She glares at Mildred T., who sits down in the chair next to my dad and reaches over to arrange his utensils. Mama moves her walker to the side and leans over to whisper to me.

"I can't believe this. Who does she think she is?" A faint hiss fans my cheek.

Luckily, Mildred T. doesn't hear. Is it possible that my mom is jealous of another woman taking over her wifely role, one she abdicated several years ago? Maybe this is a good sign. Competition could improve her relationship with my dad. After all, she is the one who should be tying his bib and patting him on the shoulder. Just the physical act of touching my dad would please him, I think, and warm my heart, too.

Daddy is already arranging his place setting. With a shaky right hand, he puts the two plastic glasses, one for juice and one for water, thickened so he won't aspirate it, on top of the plate. He carefully sets the one utensil, a plastic spork, in one of the glasses. Then he turns the other glass upside down next to the plate. He looks at his creation with a slight smile. The table setting is something he can control in the midst of all the confusion in his mind. He continues to manipulate what's around him. He picks at the end of the long, blue terry cloth bib and starts to roll it under with his hands still inside. It forms a mound around his clasped hands. He settles his hands on the flabby shelf of his stomach. Looking contented, he stops fidgeting.

My mother glances sideways at Mildred T. and decides to assert her authority over my dad.

"Jim, what are you doing with your bib? Unroll it and put your hands on top. You look like a pregnant woman," she says.

Her scolding is gentle but authoritative, a typical response to improprieties. As a child, I appreciated the softness in her voice but not the frequency of "Don't do it that way" when my actions didn't measure up to her standards.

My dad stares at her, smiles, and is quiet for a few seconds. Then he shakes his head, slumps down a bit in the wheelchair, and moves his hands over his protruding tummy.

"Oh, no, not again," he mutters. "That first baby was really hard on me."

I can't believe his mind is able to come up with this response, a glimpse at the pre-Alzheimer's sense of humor I enjoyed so much. This unexpected repartee makes me hope that a fragment of humor is still active in the twisted neurons of his brain.

The laughter at the table is his reward. He smiles and glances up at his table mates, still keeping his hands in the rolled up bib. I reach over to pat his arm but find myself clinging to his sleeve instead. I don't want to release this remnant of the father I knew.

"You are a piece of work, Jim," Mildred T. says.

She leans over to touch his knee. My mom reacts by slamming her empty plastic cup on the table. "Oh, just leave him alone. He doesn't need any attention."

Mildred T. settles back in her chair, her mouth open in surprise. My dad is oblivious to the dispute because his meal has arrived. Brian, an aide from Nigeria, is wielding a tray heavy with food. He straightens out the glasses and spork in front of my dad and puts a rimmed plastic plate with three divisions of food in front of him.

This distraction gives me a chance to change the tense mood at the table.

"What's on today's menu?" I ask.

"I think it's pork chops, apple sauce, and green beans, with pudding for dessert. You never know," Brian laughs.

Daddy studies the re-arrangement of the place setting in front of him.

"What do I do next?" he asks.

"You can eat now, Daddy."

I place the spork in the right hand of my once decisive and logical father. He slowly scoops up the pudding, smacking his lips after each bite. According to the doctor who diagnosed his Alzheimer's, he may eventually forget how to swallow his food and face the danger of ingesting food into his lungs, followed by pneumonia.

My mother interrupts my thoughts. She has pulled her walker

close to the table and is fingering the assortment of items in the striped bag that hangs on the front.

"Connie, will you take this awful food away, and get my mashed potatoes out of this bag? The kitchen knows I can't eat pork chops and green beans. When will they learn?"

I find the potatoes and pour the gravy on them, presenting them to my mom with a pudding cup from the stash of items in the walker. Everyone at the table has settled down to eat lunch. I sneak a look at my watch, put both hands on my lap and twirl my thumbs. I've spent longer than I thought, but if I leave right now, I can make it back to the office in time for an instructor's annual-review meeting. My mind goes into overdrive as I try to decide between my obligations here at least three to four times a week and at work Monday through Friday, with a spill-over into weekend schoolwork at home. The title page of a college philosophy paper from years ago trails across the bottom of my cluttered mind screen: "This is not your best work, Connie," scrawled Dr. Eddy. "Don't rob Peter to pay Paul." Good counsel if I have an established priority, but I've already committed the crime of stealing almost two hours from work, so I quickly decide to short-change my parents and try to repay that time to my job. My guilt feelings make leave-taking from Ivy Manor awkward. Graceful goodbyes are not in my repertoire. I try to quietly inch back my chair, but it makes a harsh scraping noise on the tile floor that alerts everyone who has a functioning hearing aid. All eyes, except my father's, are on me. I get up and stand by my mother's walker. She's looking at me with suspicion.

"I need to leave now, Mama. I can't come tomorrow because there's a teachers' meeting downtown. I'll be back to visit on Saturday."

The words scurry from my mouth in one breath. I'm hesitant to deliver a message about not fulfilling my duties. She purses her lips and looks down at her food.

"You're just too busy, Connie. You need to take care of yourself and not do so much."

I've heard this phrase many times since my dad's stroke. It's both a criticism and a challenge. What my mom really means is "You don't do enough for *me*," a statement that tops off the guilt I already feel. In her view, I should quit my job and focus solely on her needs. The challenge is to prove her wrong by accomplishing all the tasks in my life even if I don't do them all well.

As I lean over to say goodbye, she has the final word.

"If you have too much to do, Connie, you don't have to bother coming so often. We'll get along without you." She frowns and shrugs her shoulders.

Blood rushes to my head and my throat tightens. Underneath the surface of her words is a threat that has haunted me for years. It's as if my mother has scolded, "If you don't do it my way, I'll withdraw my love." I stumble over to my dad, put my arm around his shoulders and brush his forehead with a kiss. As I leave the table, I put my hand on Mama's arm, tell her I'll see her Saturday, and head down the stairs to the sanctuary of my car. I fasten my seat belt, place my lunch of KFC coleslaw and a piece of chicken in the cup holder next to a half-full bottle of water, and take off for the office. I should be able to get there in twenty minutes if there's not much traffic. Along the way, I'll multitask by filling my empty energy tank with food and my empty spirit with the mountains and greenery I see through the windshield. I've set a goal of absorbing five inspiring sights before I get to the office.

CHAPTER 2

HOME

IT'S THE MONDAY AFTER MY WEEKEND VISIT TO MY PARENTS. THE CLOCK ON the dash says 7:05 a.m. I make a quick left into my designated parking spot near the front door of Spring International Language Center. Grabbing my cup of McDonald senior coffee and my handbag from the passenger seat, I balance them in one hand while I open the car door. A breath of cold, dry air wakes my brain and clears my nostrils. I'm not dressed for 30-degree February weather because I'm planning on the Colorado sunshine to warm up the day. My Skechers make a criss-cross print in the skiff of snow as I get out of the car. I retrieve my briefcase from the back seat where it has sunk into the collection of canvas bags destined for the nursing home later this morning.

I'm usually the first person to arrive at school, so I have the privilege of unlocking the outside door, dismantling the security alarm, and entering my building. It isn't actually *my* building. It belongs to two of us. My friend, co-founder, and partner is Pambos, a Greek Cypriot. We planned and built the school building just a year ago. Our population of students had been growing, and the community college across the street no longer had adequate space because of renovations. Native Colorado stone trims three stories of red brick. Three flag poles boast the flags of our students' countries in addition to a large American flag on a taller pole. Because we have students from 23 countries this term, I change the flags each week to reflect the different nationalities. It's hard to believe that the second mortgages we took on our homes 20 years ago have resulted in the three English-language centers we now have on university and college campuses in Colorado and Arkansas.

My hands are full, so I push open the inside door with my shoulder. There's still a whiff of newness in the air. It's spiced by a bouquet of red and white carnations, a Valentine gift from a student from the Emirates. The early-morning light coming through the bank of west windows makes the bronze and blue-green chips in the terrazzo floor glint and sparkle. This floor is the *pièce de résistance:* its colored chips form a mosaic map of the world set off by a tiny bronze chip for the island of Cyprus, Pambos' native country. I walk across the Atlantic to the Mediterranean to see if Cyprus is still in place. My damp shoe leaves a smudge on the little island. I wipe it off with my finger. Everything is orderly and beautiful. This is my second home. My world.

Today is Valentine's day, a unique holiday for our students from the Middle East, who see love as something that may or may not come after an arranged marriage. Sweethearts exist only in their imaginations or from a photo or a clandestine meeting. For me, this day is a sad reminder of the time just two years ago when my parents' lives, and mine, were unraveled and left in a tangle of unmet needs. My agenda this morning is completing the tasks of my job, so I can visit my mother and father at lunch time. I'll get a head start here before the students' five-hour day of intensive English as a Second Language classes begins. Then a babble of languages from more than 120 students will fill the hallways.

I unload my briefcase, handbag, and coffee in my office. While my computer is booting up, I open my to-do notebook to the "School Tasks" page. I ignore the "Mama" and "Home" pages that follow. Like a Biblical list of the Ten Commandments, but with bullet points, it reminds me about the jobs I need to accomplish before classes begin: Write the daily memo promoting student activities and reminding instructors to report their attendance. Prepare transparencies for my writing class. Review resumes of three teachers who have applied for an open position. Before launching into the list, I take a quick survey of the collection of artifacts from students and my own overseas marketing trips: a framed batik of an Indonesian dancer hanging on a wall to my right, a woven tapestry of the holy places of Islam on the half-circle wall to my left. On the bank of shelves next to the door is a collection of country picture books and ESL textbooks interspersed with a Congo voodoo statue, a Russian babushka doll, and a white-faced Geisha doll. On the top shelf is a replica of a large brown Colombian beetle perched on top of a package of the actual fried beetles, way past their expiration date. This motley collection of remembrances is a daily reassurance of the joys of my job, a place where I have almost free reign to create programs and services, solve problems, teach students to write in their new language, discover their personal stories, and mentor instructors.

My role in the school has fulfilled a lifelong goal of helping people understand and appreciate each other. Two years ago, I felt that my parental caregiving and professional lives were worlds apart, but recently a beam of self-knowledge has been peeping through. In a way, my mother trained me for this job, with lessons in how to please her and instruction in sensitivity to what she required of a "good little girl." My situation was similar to our son Troy's training of his black lab, Zipper, to stay in place while he walked away. When Zip performed correctly, he received a "good dog, Zip," and a pat on the head.

When I performed well for my mom, I received the much-awaited treat of her approval, with a shared laugh over some silly pun we concocted, a special trip on the street car to the children's library, or a chocolate soda at the corner drugstore. I always knew that she was proud of the accomplishments she urged me into. The results were prizes and newspaper photos; blue ribbons in 4-H projects; crowns for being Miss 4-H, Snow Ball Queen, Dairy Princess, and organizer of a neighborhood teen canteen, and more. All the commands and rewards polished my good-child skills, ones that I use in my job: awareness of others' needs, patience, diplomacy, and the desire to solve everyone's problems. Like a GPS that loses its satellite connection, I'm lost unless I'm pleasing someone by fulfilling their expectations. Where is my place in the world if not in service to someone? This isn't as noble as it may sound. It bothers me. Is my motivation the same in my professional life as it is in my caregiving life? Do I try to meet student needs so that they will like me? I'm embarrassed to admit the selfish pleasure I feel when a homesick student says "You're like my second mother. Thanks for helping me." Granted, this gratitude is part of my motivation for addressing student needs, but it's not the only reward. Seeing a Japanese and a Korean become good friends in their American homestay, greeting visiting alums who have become leaders in their countries, and helping students to overcome their learning problems—these are my treats.

I look up from my desk to see Bader, a Saudi Arabian student and an accomplished musician, slipping quietly through my open office door. A wide smile, showing perfect white teeth, is the focus of his clean-shaven face. His eyes, listed as black on his ID card, are actually deep brown accented by long lashes and expressive black eyebrows. With a toss of shoulder-length black hair, he holds up his *oud*, an Arab lute, in one hand and a well-worn violin in the other.

"Happy Valentine's Day, Miss Connie. Which one—*oud* or violin?"

Before I can answer, he places the oud on my desk, tucks the violin under his chin, and launches into a bit of Mozart. Bader's talent is amazing; he doesn't read music but can play anything he hears. His accomplishment in spoken English is also astounding but, unfortunately, it is coupled with what I suspect is attention deficit disorder and dyslexia. The dyslexia is hard to diagnose because Arabic is read from right to left, which adds further confusion to his reading in English. Later today, we have an appointment to visit a psychologist who will test him for these disorders. Like most of the students we have at Spring International, he participates in 23 hours of classes per week and hopes to complete enough academic English to enter a university or college in the U.S. But first, he must pass the GED high school equivalency test to make up for two lost school years during which he bid his mother goodbye every morning, walked to the school yard, and then sneaked away to sit under a tree in the park and play his oud and sing.

I put down my notebook and pen and watch the smooth bow strokes and his long fingers on the violin strings. I breathe in the lilting music, and it relaxes my shoulders.

"Thank you, Bader. I always love to hear you play. Don't forget to meet me at three, so we can go to the testing center."

Like cupid, but with a bow and violin, he blows me a kiss and quietly exits.

This is my reward. He has interrupted my planning time, but his affection is a warm start to Valentine's day.

Just as I turn to the computer to begin the morning memo, Missy pokes her head into the office. My door is always open unless I'm discussing a private matter. It's not usual to share a workplace with a close relative, so Missy and I tuck away our personal relationship behind what we hope is professional decorum. No, "Hey, mom. There's a student to see you." In fact, students are always surprised when they find out that we're mother and daughter. Missy's long, softly-curled blond hair, a marked contrast to my short, darker hair, frames a face that shows concern.

She gestures to a seventeen-year-old student from Thailand, one of two brothers who have just arrived. They chose the nicknames Ping and Pong when they discovered that their classmates and most instructors couldn't pronounce their four-syllable Thai names.

"Excuse me, Connie. Pong doesn't feel well, and I can't schedule an appointment for him unless I know what's wrong," she says. "Would you give it a try?"

My "good morning" to the shy teenager is returned with averted eyes and a quiet "G'morn, Miss Connie." As a sign of respect for their elders, Thais usually kneel on the floor when they speak to an older, seated person. Since Pong looks in pain, I encourage him to sit on the chair next to my desk.

"How can I help you, Pong?"

"Doctor, I need doctor, Miss Connie. No sleep. No study."

He looks embarrassed and moves back and forth in the chair.

"Where do you have pain? Is it your head? Your stomach?"

Like any good ESL teacher, I touch my head and then my stomach in case he doesn't understand. Pong points to what appears to be his left knee.

"Is your knee hurting? Your leg?"

"Is him noise," he says pointing at the floor and continuing to squirm. He's almost ready to cry.

"'Him noise'? I don't quite understand."

Pong shifts back and forth in his chair. I begin squirming, too, hoping this condition isn't catching.

"Let me see if I can find the Thai dictionary, Pong, so you can tell me exactly what's wrong."

I search the bookshelves by my desk to locate a paperback Thai/English dictionary. I hand it to him. He seems greatly relieved as he thumbs through the pages.

"Here, Miss Connie, him noise."

I look where he's pointing his finger on the page and discover the elusive ailment.

"Aha! It's hemorrhoids, Pong. I understand now. It's not a big problem, but it's a good idea to see a doctor. I'll ask Missy to make an appointment for you."

Before the words "not a big problem" escape from my mouth, I recall the many times I've said the same thing to my mother when she recounted symptoms to me and how peeved she was with my diminishment of her aches and pains. In this case, Pong is relieved and, with a smile, he thanks me. He gets up slowly from the chair, places his hands together with a slight bow of his head, and backs out of the office.

Laughing to myself, I try to settle back into my to-do tasks. I need to finish quickly, so that I'll have time to sneak out of the building and visit Ivy Manor. My colleagues understand my daily absences, but I still feel guilty at leaving in the middle of the work day. I've tried to visit my parents in the late afternoon or evening, but it just doesn't work. By the end of the day, my mother is too tired and achy to enjoy the visit, and, most importantly, she often doesn't eat anything served to her at Ivy Manor, so I provide my daily offering of potatoes and gravy. Also, by mid-afternoon, my dad is more disoriented and restless, a condition of dementia called "sundowning." If I want to make my visits count for something, I need to come around lunchtime. Today Faizah, the activities coordinator, will have over-decorated Ivy Manor's dining room. Hearts and cupids will be hanging from the ceiling, pasted on the walls, and lying broken-hearted on the tables. Maybe the cooks will even add pink coloring to the pureed chicken. Who knows? I've become a Scrooge about this holiday.

On February 14 two years ago, my office phone rang just as classes were beginning.

"It's the worst day of my life, Connie. You've got to come right away. Daddy's had a stroke."

Her voice was loud and clear, but the message didn't resonate in my mind. Yesterday everything had been fine. Our whole family had enjoyed our usual Sunday brunch at Marie Callender's Restaurant. Our son Troy and his wife, Diana, and Missy and husband Mark were chatting, eating, and trying to keep three-year-old Benjamin in his booster chair. My parents were relishing their favorite cream-of-potato soup and biscuits. At eighty-six and eighty-seven, they were self-sufficient and enjoying a simple life in their downtown subsidized apartment. My mom had some nonthreatening medical issues—colitis and some urinary incontinence—but my dad had been diagnosed with early-stage Alzheimer's disease, which, in turn, was putting stress on my mother as she tried to deal with his misuse of their credit card and the anger he expressed at the condition that was nibbling away at his mind. He also had narrowing of the blood vessels that provided blood to his heart. He carried nitroglycerin tablets for chest pain, angina, but had needed them only a few times since the diagnosis. All of this should have been a red flag to me, but it was easy to forget when he was still taking the bus with my mother, enjoying sports on TV, and walking to McDonald's for pancakes each morning. I wasn't expecting the inevitable.

"Is he OK, Mama? Where is he now?"

Ignoring my questions, she repeated, "This is the worst day of my life."

This phrase is usually an overreaction to a series of small irritations of life, like dropping a cup, misplacing her keys, or stubbing her toe on a chair. But to hear that my dad just had a stroke stunned me. I had no response.

"When I got up to go to the bathroom at 5 a.m., I found him lying on the floor in his bedroom. He was groaning and trying to pull himself up. He kept saying, 'Help me! Help me!' so I tried to lift him up. I think I've hurt my back. It was just too hard on me."

I moved the telephone receiver closer to my ear, not sure that I was hearing my mother clearly. Did she say it was hard on *her,* not on my father? Oh, god, she's trying to bring the spotlight back on herself, just like a sibling who wants her parent's undivided attention. The acid rising in my throat at her complaint was battling the fear I felt for my father. Ignoring her comment, I repeated my original question in a husky but louder voice.

"Where is Daddy? Is he in the hospital now?"

She paused for a few seconds. I could see her blinking, shaking her head and trying to re-live the morning's details.

"I called 911 and the paramedics came right away. He's in Presbyterian St. Luke's. They told me to call in an hour to see how he is. Can you come down right away, Connie? I feel awful."

I reassured her, choked down my fear and called the hospital. The nurse on duty told me that my dad was resting comfortably. I could see him any time. Should I hurry to the hospital first or check on my mom to be sure she wasn't in need of medical attention? As always, my mom won the competition, aided by the fact that my dad was in good hands in the hospital.

I explained the situation to Missy, my backup at work in times of turmoil, and hurried out of the office. As I drove to my parents' apartment in downtown Denver, I listed in my mind the things I had to do: Confirm my mom's status and call Floyd to tell him about my dad's stroke because I'd probably need to stay overnight with my mom. That I'm-always-able-to-handle-a-crisis attitude took over. I recalled all those times in Cairo when I had to facilitate the adjustment of our three children, Sonja, ten; Missy, eight; and Troy, just two years old; or when I had to deal with Missy's broken leg, Floyd's bout of cholera, and a brief, but scary, Ramadan war with Israel. Being in charge of my family in a foreign city of 11 million people was my training ground for handling crises, an essential education because Floyd had undiagnosed Addison's disease. He had absolutely no adrenal gland function and, thus, no reactions to stress. His responses to the hassles of meeting the daily demands of a poor, aggressive, take-advantage-of-Americans populace were met with a casual "so what?" Fight-or-flight decisions became my responsibility, and for the most part I chose to fight. As I considered the situation with my dad, I told myself that I had been calm and effective during our family's crises. I pushed to the back of my mind the fatigue and loneliness I felt after the crisis was over and my adrenalin rush had subsided.

The trip between my office and downtown went by in a blue fog. I parked in the 7-Eleven lot next to my parents' apartment building, two blocks away from the busy pedestrian mall, risking a parking violation. Ignoring the usual homeless man asking for money, I took the elevator to the second floor. I expected the door to be open, as it usually was when my mother knew I was coming, but the knob wouldn't turn. I knocked several times but no response. What to do next? In the muddle of my thoughts, I remembered the key my parents had given me, that I had never used. It was in one of the pockets of my purse. But which one? My fingers felt disconnected from my mind. I rummaged through the packed handbag and finally felt the edges of the four-leaf clover connected to the key.

When I opened the door, everything in the small living room was as I remembered it, reflecting the fifteen years that my parents had called this apartment home. My dad had made two chairs from wooden barrels, painted off-white and topped with aqua pillows sewn by my mom. A small aqua-and-brown tweed sofa was next to a long bookcase holding a well-worn set of set of World Book encyclopedias, Royal Copenhagen souvenir plates, family photos, a bouquet of silk flowers, and several small framed watercolors that my mother had painted many years ago. I could see the kitchen table through the pass-through on my left. It was set with cereal bowls, my dad's favorite Denver Nuggets mug, and my mom's blue tea cup. A jar of grape jelly finished off the preparations for a breakfast that hadn't happened. I walked quickly to the open bedroom door, hoping that I could spend just a few minutes with my mom and then hurry to the hospital to see my dad.

"Mama, I'm here."

She was lying on top of the chenille bedspread with a small blue blanket pulled up to her waist. The neck of her flannel nightgown was twisted to one side. A damp white washcloth was balanced on her forehead. She was pale, but her eyes were surprisingly clear and not swollen. Her Nordic stoicism usually drew the line at displays of emotion, but something else was at work here. Instead of empathizing with my dad's situation, she had quickly turned the camera on herself and how the event affected her.

"Thank God you're here, Connie. I've had terrible diarrhea and my back is so sore. I shouldn't have tried to help Daddy up from the floor."

My hand automatically covered my mouth, so the words wouldn't escape. Oh, Mama, don't say that. Of course you should have helped him. He's your husband and I hope you love him because you've lived with him for more than sixty years. How could your selfishness be more important than Daddy's stroke? I wanted to confront her with these words, but I mentally revised them into a less offensive statement. I didn't want to upset her more. That would increase her problems and mine, too. I wanted to reassure her and head to the hospital.

"I know you're hurting, Mama, but it was a normal reaction to help him."

She removed the washcloth from her forehead and handed it to me. After pushing herself to a sitting position, she adjusted the neck of her nightgown.

"Normal? You should know that nothing's normal today."

She pushed the blanket aside, groaned, and put her legs over the side of the bed.

"Help me get to the bathroom."

I held her arm as she got on her feet. She was much weaker and frailer than I had realized. When we'd had brunch on the weekend, she told me that she had walked to the library and also shopped for groceries and brought them home on the bus. Now I needed to take her arm to help her from the bed to the bathroom. I reminded myself that, in fact, she was 87 years old. I realized then that I had been ignoring the signs of aging in both my parents because I had premonitions of how it would change this calm and productive stage of my life. Holding my arm, Mama shuffled step by step to the bathroom across the hall. She was able to finish toileting by herself. I poured her a glass of water and gave her an Imodium from the bottle on the sink. As we walked slowly back to the bedroom, she said, "I think I may need to see Dr. Hansen. My back is really sore. Daddy was lying on the floor by his bed, and I thought I could get him up, but he was too heavy. I shouldn't have tried."

The picture of my dad trying to understand what had happened to him and asking for help hit me again with a sharp pain between my shoulders. I had to see him now, to touch him, to console him. But first I needed reassurance that my mom was physically okay.

"Did you fall when you were trying to lift him?" I helped her onto the bed again. She closed her eyes and drew the blue coverlet up to her chin.

"No, but I did strain my back. And, of course, my stomach is all twisted in knots from the stress. I need the doctor."

As I had suspected, she was okay, except for the diarrhea. This was the permission I needed. "Let's wait to call the doctor until I've been to the hospital to see Daddy and talk to his doctor. Is that okay?"

A long sigh ended in a soft whine. "I suppose so, but you'll hurry back here, won't you?"

I reassured her, helped adjust her pillows, and put a glass of Gatorade next to her bed to help rehydrate her.

Distracted by a headache and tension in my shoulders, I drove in circles until I finally located the hospital parking lot and Daddy's room in the ICU. The door was open. A heart/blood pressure monitor was blipping, but there were no other tubes or machines. My dad was awake and lying on his back with the sheet thrown to the side. His right hand was tugging at his diaper. His left hand was lying limply at his side. A surge of sadness swept over me. I had never seen him so helpless, so hopeless, and I was empty, devoid of power to change his condition. I bent down close to his head, so he could see me.

"Hello, Daddy. How are you doing?"

I pulled the sheet up to his chest and held his right hand in both of mine. He had trouble focusing on my face because his cloudy brown eyes kept looking from side to side as if he expected something to jump out at him.

"Huh? Wha's happening? Wher'm I?"

He'd suddenly been set down in a foreign country with no recognition of the terrain, the people or the language. I wanted to be his guide and comfort, but I didn't know the lay of the land any better than he did. This was a role I had never assumed with my father. It was always my mother who needed comforting, never my father. An overflow of tears made my vision as cloudy as his. I mustered what I thought was a logical explanation.

"You've had a stroke and now you're here in the hospital. You'll have to be here a few days."

He didn't seem to understand, so I repeated what I had just said.

"I dunno. What'm I s'posed to do?"

He was asking for directions and trying to find his way home. My heart was aching, but I didn't know how to help him. He had always given me subtle directions in my life by asking rhetorical questions, like "So, you'd like to do this secretarial job rather than going to college?" In his condition, he wouldn't even be able to understand a direct question.

My only response was, "You don't need to do anything, Daddy. Just get well."

A green-scrubbed intern with a bad case of acne interrupted us and asked me to come into the hallway. He gave me a memorized speech. My father had suffered a CVA, a cerebral vascular accident. An artery that supplies blood to the brain had burst, causing a "brain bleed." As a result, the part of the body controlled by the right side of the brain couldn't function properly. The left side of his body was partially paralyzed. I asked him about the effect the stroke would have on my dad's mind, which already showed the ravages of Alzheimer's in short-term memory loss, disorientation, and flares of anger at his diminishing abilities.

"We'll just have to wait and see. He'll begin physical therapy tomorrow, and then we can transfer him to a nursing home for additional therapy and long-term care. The social worker will talk to you about placement at Briargate at Dr. Hansen's suggestion."

These facts were colliding in my mind as I returned to my dad's room. How would my mom react to this change? Would a nursing home really serve my dad's needs? What would my mom do if she had to leave the downtown apartment that she loved? How would I arrange all of this? I was it. No sisters or brothers to assist me. I had never resented being an only child. In fact, I had no idea of what it would be like to share attention or responsibility with a sibling. I had always relied on myself, but a seed of resentment was growing in my mind. I tried to erase it and replace it with my mantra, "I can do it." But a question kept nagging: "Can I really?"

My dad was sleeping soundly now, the sheet pushed away from his body again and the diaper pulled down below his hips, baring his flaccid penis. I had seen him naked before because he had never been terribly modest and had slept in the nude, but I had never touched his lower body. I hesitantly adjusted the diaper, my fingers lightly grazing his cold, damp skin. I covered him up and kissed him on his prickly cheek. I didn't want to wake him.

When I got back to the apartment two hours later, my mother was still in bed, eyes wide open, waiting for me. I propped myself on a stool near her bed, barely catching myself from falling. I shared the information about Daddy, but she shook her head as if to dismiss it as unimportant. This wasn't the response I wanted. I need you now, Mama, I thought, as a mother to me and as a companion to my dad. Assure me that you're concerned about him and that everything will be okay. I want you to remember the love you felt for him when you offered small acts of kindness and caring: preparing his meals, reminding him of medications, and playing his favorite pieces on the organ. But her response to my hospital visit told me it would take time for her to focus on my father's situation.

"Connie, would you call Dr. Hansen now? I think I may need to go to the hospital because of my back and the diarrhea. I don't think I can make it here. Daddy's stroke was just too much for me."

I could feel the tearing of my emotional fibers, like ripping a piece of cloth apart. A ragged half of me was worried about my father's hopeless future. The other half was troubled about my mom's physical state and her history of dehydration from diarrhea, caused by what doctors in the past had diagnosed as nervous stomach, colitis, and ulcers. I was also gulping down an emotional cocktail of anger at my mother for demanding attention equal to what my dad needed for his situation and despair that she wasn't considering the tasks and decisions that I was dealing with.

"Please, Mama, give me time to digest all of this. I can't handle everything at once."

She turned toward me, opened her eyes, and stared.

"What? I didn't hear you."

"I'm having a hard time with everything that's happened. Just be patient," I pleaded. "We'll talk to the doctor tomorrow morning."

I convinced her that she could make it through the night and promised that I would be there to help her to the bathroom whenever she called. Exhausted and overwhelmed with what I needed to do, I decided to lie down in my dad's bedroom, where I could easily hear my mom. The small room barely had space for the large electric organ my mom had won in a contest, my dad's desk, and his single bed. My mother slept in the other bedroom, so that she wouldn't be disturbed by his snoring. His desk was cluttered with dog-racing books and yellow legal tablets with the mathematical calculations that would help him determine the winner. A computer that I had given him several months ago was sitting on the floor. His failing memory had made it impossible to master the new technology. A green velour blanket was pulled halfway off the single bed. He must have grabbed it trying to get up from the floor. I discovered that it had torn away from several large safety pins that he had used to secure it into a kind of cocoon. I didn't have the energy to unpin everything, so I just pulled it back onto the bed and lay on top, fully clothed and emotionally bare, open to the mosquito bites of fear, doubt, and insecurity. An orderly, comfortable life pinned securely together, like my dad's blanket, can be pulled apart in an instant. No matter how hard I might try, the frayed and torn fragments could never be made whole again.

As I curled up on the sweaty-smelling blanket, I remembered the musical Valentine card and stationery gift for my parents, still sitting on my desk at the office. What a change of plans for this day! The blinking 7-Eleven "OPEN" sign outside the window, the whir of traffic on the street, and thoughts about the decisions that confronted me kept me awake until early morning. Could my mom live by herself in this apartment? If not, I'd have to find a place for her, and as soon as my dad finished his therapy, I would need to decide on a nursing home for him. Would Medicaid cover these living situations? Would Floyd and I have enough money to help them in two different places? I reflected on decisions I had made in the past: choosing a college major, marriage, having children, adoption, moving to other states and countries. These were good decisions made with adequate time to consider information and feedback from others. But I was going to have to decide about my parents' lives under the pressure of limited time. I realized that I had a short history of bad decisions shrouded in pressure and made in haste. "Just decide and take the easy way out" does not always produce good results. An episode from our life in Egypt flitted through my mind. The preface to this story seemed to be: "a lesson to be learned."

During our second year in Cairo, I had to dispose of two young dogs that were born to Snoopy, a mother dog who inhabited the garden of our villa. We loved and cared for all the stray cats and dogs that were part of this university home, but the barking of the six-month-old pups was disturbing everyone, and I was afraid the Egyptian soldiers who patrolled the street at night would shoot the pups if they were outside our fenced walls. A Turkish neighbor told me about the British Royal Society for the Prevention of Cruelty to Animals (RSPCA). They would pick up the dogs and take them to a no-kill shelter. Because my Arabic wasn't up to par for this detailed

telephone call, I asked Salim, our cook, to call them. On the day
the RSPCA was to come, I was bicycling home from a friend's
house with our four-year old son Troy in a seat on the back. About
half a block away, I saw a police truck outside the villa with a man
yanking one of the dogs up into the truck by a noose tied around its
neck. This couldn't be the RSPCA. With a feeling of panic, I turned
the corner and rode around the block. Luckily Troy hadn't seen the
truck. I just couldn't deal with using my limited Arabic to face the
men in the animal control truck, so I ignored what I had seen and
turned on the road to our villa. I wanted to be finished with the
problem, just one of the many responsibilities I faced on my own in
this demanding culture.

When Troy and I came back to our gate, the dogs were gone, and
the irate Turkish neighbor was shouting at me.

"You sent your dogs off to be shot. What did you think you were
doing?"

Evidently Salim had called the local animal control officers, not
the no-kill shelter. As an animal lover, what had I done? I was crying.
Troy was crying.

"I want the dogs back, Mommy."

In this case, I was offered a second chance. I could take a taxi to
the other side of Cairo to retrieve the dogs. It took more than an hour
to find a taxi driver whose cab was dilapidated enough that he didn't
mind putting dogs into the trunk. Troy had to be my accomplice in
this act of penance, because no one was home to watch him. When we
reached the rambling mud-brick building near the Muqattam Hills, I
told the taxi driver I would give him *baksheesh kwayiss*, a large tip, if
he would wait and take us back. A guard in a rumpled khaki uniform
took me to a police captain who spoke some English. He laughed at
me, an *Amrikani* who loved dogs, but he was won over by Troy who
firmly told him, "I want my dogs!"

He took us to a round enclosure with blood-spattered walls. Our two dogs were cowering near a low door.

"Madame, go! Get your dogs," the captain said.

Troy and I crawled into the foul-smelling pit. The dogs came to us immediately. We managed to get them out, with ropes around their necks, into the trunk of the taxi, and home to our villa. With the help of the Turkish neighbor, we found homes for the pups. I'd been able to reverse my decision, and the ordeal was over.

"Connie, I need you," my mother called from her bedroom. As I mustered the energy to get out of my dad's bed, I realized that I couldn't ride my bicycle around the corner to avoid the present crisis with my parents. The experience from my Cairo past was a hand on my shoulder cautioning me to consider all aspects of my mom and dad's situation before determining their future. I needed to take a deep breath. Take my time. Seek counsel from the doctors and other caregivers who have been through this experience. And not make a hasty decision I would regret.

CHAPTER 3

MULTIPLE CHOICE QUIZ

IT'S STARTING TO SNOW AS I PULL UP IN FRONT OF IVY MANOR THIS February 14. Before I go into the nursing home, I always try to sit, for a few minutes of attitude adjustment. I crank up my Little Mary Sunshine attitude, a moniker a high school friend gave me when my excessive positivity irked her. It's a trait that's also irritating to my mom and, on occasion, to my husband, whose cup is often half empty, but it's an attitude I developed as a child to balance my mom's negativity. Looking for the best in almost every situation keeps me sane. It may be simplistic, but I believe that problems have solutions, that every person has some innate goodness, and, in general, that life is good.

In the spirit of this hopeful attitude, I ask myself what has been accomplished since the stroke that uprooted my parents. I've mastered the complicated Medicare/Medicaid bureaucracy; I have filled out the forms and made the phone calls that have enabled three different institutions to receive the money needed for my parents' care. First, there was Briargate, where my mother convinced her doctor to place her for just a week, so that she could receive the same attention as my dad. Then there was assisted living near my school, when she and I decided she couldn't live alone in their apartment. This was followed by my father's abuse at Briargate and the need to quickly retrieve him from that situation and place him in a safer nursing home. It took more than fifty frustrating hours to find a decent facility in the area that accepted the small Medicaid payment of $800 per month and still treated its residents with respect. After a month of surveying homes that looked like Southern mansions or Italian villas and required private pay rates of at least $5000 a month, my list was down to just three within a fifteen-mile radius of home and work. Ivy Manor won the competition, and a year after my father was admitted, my mother joined him because she needed nursing care for her permanent catheter.

As I look through the snowflakes, the exterior of Ivy Manor looks attractive. It's a small two-story, red-brick building with two white gazebos on each side of a curved concrete walk. The flower bed between the two walks has been neatly trimmed for winter. A squirrel is raiding the brass bird-feeder that hangs outside one of the resident's windows.

I remember how relieved I was when my search led me to Ivy Manor. I was greeted there by Raheen, the activities coordinator, a slim, smiling, dark-skinned lady in a bright blue dress and high heels. She welcomed me with a slight Pakistani or Indian accent and a comforting friendliness. We sat down in the small reception area facing a large glass cage filled with yellow and orange canaries. The twittering of the birds contrasted with the words that tumbled out of my mouth and the unexpected tears that wet my cheeks.

"My father is in a terrible situation at another nursing home. I need to get him out of there as soon as possible, and he has no income other than social security, which is going to my mother who is in assisted living in Littleton."

"No problem," Raheen said.

She must have come fully prepared for near-the-edge emotions. A Kleenex box appeared from nowhere. She reassured me that there would be a room for my dad since only sixty-nine of the eighty-one beds were full, and almost all of the residents were in the same financial straits as my father.

I started choking up again when I asked the most important question on my mind.

"My dad has dementia, so Briargate restrains him in his wheelchair and puts him at a feeding table, and the aids are force-feeding him. He can feed himself. He doesn't have to be restrained with a belt. What are Ivy Manor's policies on restraints and feeding residents with Alzheimer's?"

I sounded as if we were making a matter-of-fact business deal instead of a quality-of-life decision about my father. *Policies. Residents.* A month ago, I wouldn't have had the vocabulary. *Restraints. Force-feeding.* And even now I can't believe that my dad is belted into a wheelchair like a death row prisoner restrained for execution.

"No feeding tables here," she reassured me. "Residents are encouraged to feed themselves with the help of special plates and utensils. Then if it's necessary, a caregiver will feed them individually. Respect for each person is really important at Ivy Manor."

She explained that restraining belts were used only with permission of the family, to keep a resident from sliding out of his wheelchair. I liked Raheen. She seemed honest and concerned. A huge weight was slipping from my shoulders. Ivy Manor was the support system I needed. I was so relieved that I didn't pay much attention to information about the food, shared rooms, nurse-to-patient ratio, and activities. I might have kept looking for another situation, but I had made up my mind. This was going to be the end of my search. My dad's safety would be taken care of, and I could close the lid on the Pandora's box of stolen hearing aids, dirty diapers, restraints, and disrespect. I had fixed the problem, at least temporarily.

A quick decision about Ivy Manor placed me here, two years later, in front of the nursing home of my choice. It's time to walk through the dusting of snow to the automatic doors. I've inappropriately called this place a nursing home. Nursing, yes, but it will never be "home." Homes are familiar, predictable places, full of memories that mark the continuity of one's life. A care center provides assistance with getting in and out of bed, bathing, and dressing, plus a high level of medical care. It is not a home, no matter how hard the staff works at making it "homey."

With my canvas bag in hand, I walk through the doors decorated with cupids. Raheen, red high heels matching the red stripes in her Sari-style dress, greets me. She is the queen of hospitality at Ivy Manor. In fact, her job depends on the participation and good cheer of the residents. She wishes me a happy Valentine's Day and gives me a morning report.

"Your dad is so funny, Connie. Every time I say 'Hello, Jim' and pat him on the shoulder, he gives me a little pinch with his good hand. It's usually on my arm, but today he found my fanny."

That information buoys my spirits. Although he never would have done this before Alzheimer's—broken the barriers of propriety—he used to enjoy making funny, slightly sexual comments. Maybe the holiday celebration has cleared away some cobwebs.

"Sorry about that," I say. "Maybe you're his sweetheart of the day."

"I hope so." She laughs and ushers me into the open elevator. "He always goes with my program and seems to enjoy the music. And some of the games we play. He won a candy bar at our Valentine's party this morning. But of course he could choke on it. So I just gave him a cupid pin and a hug. I'm worried about your mom. She doesn't think of Ivy Manor as her new home. She just stays in her room and doesn't want to join in any of the activities."

Raheen is rightfully proud of her activity program and strongly believes every resident should do the chair exercise, the craft activities, and the games. This is not my mom's cup of tea, but I know Raheen won't give up on her. Her reputation depends on total participation from nursing home residents.

I explain that my mother isn't comfortable with big groups of people, leaving out her statement that "the patients here are half-dead and demented." She is starting to paint again, I tell Raheen. She writes several letters a week and does a daily crossword in the *Rocky Mountain News*. I'm proud of my mother's ability to do these activities and encourage them with praise and the materials she needs. She did the same for me as a child. She pushed me to achieve by providing me with arts and crafts projects, taking me on trips to the library, and, sometimes to my dismay, signing me up for 4-H competitions, beauty pageants, and spelling bees. As I think back on our lives together, I focus on the opportunities she gave me. I downplay the daily irritation of not meeting her standards.

A visit to my dad is first on the agenda today. It's difficult to sustain more than fifteen minutes with him because he doesn't have much response to conversation. So I usually satisfy my mother's needs first, one of those childhood habits. My quiet, unassuming father was never demanding and always remained in the background.

Daddy isn't in his room. Only Sam is there, awake and watching the same Korean video. Jenny, one of the assistants, pokes her head in and tells me that my father is in the middle of a bath.

"I think Jim would take three baths a day if Cindy would give them to him," she says.

Yes, he probably would. He enjoys being naked and having a woman bathe him. So now he has two conquests, Raheen and Cindy, to bring pleasure into his life.

As I move on to room 214, I find the door wide open, an unusual occurrence. My mother's instructions are that it be left ajar by no more than a foot. Mama is sitting back against the pillows on her bed, her eyes trained on the door. A blue and white lap robe is pulled up to her chin.

"Thank goodness you're here! I called your office three times. I'm freezing. Can you believe that the furnace isn't working in this wing? Victor, the maintenance guy, tells me it went out last night. They've called a repair man, but who knows how long that will take. Ivy Manor is the pits!"

She's shivering and on the verge of tears. I get a larger blanket from the closet and replace the lap robe.

I'm not ready for this, another complaint that I need to lodge with the director. Last week the elevator wouldn't work. Now there's no heat. Before I can respond, she adds a third complaint.

"To top it off, I'm getting a roommate this afternoon. They've already moved my bed over. They're putting in a lift to get her from the bed to her wheelchair. I never had much room, but now I won't have any."

Her frustration adds a flush to her cheeks and volume to her usually soft voice. I open the curtain between the beds and inspect the large metal hydraulic lift that's used to hoist a heavy person into a wheelchair. The space for each resident is already limited and this will take at least a foot from my mom's side of the room. Not to mention the fact that the closet next to my mother's bed has to suffice for two people, and a wheelchair cannot fit in the space. Why couldn't they have put this new resident in a larger, three-bed room? I'm on my mom's side here.

"You're right, Mama. That doesn't leave you much room. Maybe I can talk to Oscar. See if they can place her in another room. I should be able to do something."

With a huge sigh, expelling the last shred of positive energy from my body—along with Mary Sunshine—I drop the canvas bag on the floor by the bed and prop myself up against the closet door facing my mother. I'm not certain that complaining to Oscar, the boss, will do any good. When I requested a room change for my dad to get him away from his angry roommate, Oscar didn't comply until I sent a letter to Ivy Manor's management company. Because my complaint made him angry, he probably won't want to hear me knocking on his door again when I ask him to remove the resident with the mechanical hoist from my mom's room. The caregiving accomplishments I was reviewing in the car are worthless now. I'm not ready for this today, but I tell myself I'll do it anyway. I push away from the closet door and straighten to my shrinking height of five feet two inches.

"Let's worry about the heat first," I say. "I'll go to the basement and ask Victor if he has a small heater. That might help."

"There's no room for a heater. Where would you put it?"

"On the little chest of drawers."

"It might fall off."

"I think it would fit there."

"I don't want you to move the photos and the sewing kit."

"It's just temporary, Mama. We can put things back when the furnace is fixed. Let me go talk to Victor and see what he can do. In the meantime, I'll get you that sweater I gave you for Christmas, so you'll be warm enough to go down to lunch."

"I don't like the sweater, Connie. The sleeves are too tight over my blouse. And I'm not hungry. I'll just stay here and eat the mashed potatoes. You can get me a glass of Lactaid from the refrigerator in the activity room."

I can feel my already high blood pressure rising ten notches. It's been fifteen minutes since I arrived, and I haven't sat down yet. But now I have to or I'll keel over with no place to land except on top of my mom's walker.

"It'll be hard for you to eat with a blanket pulled up to your chin."

"Oh, just forget it, Connie. I won't eat then. You just don't understand how hard life is."

The "you don't understand" phrase always catches me off guard. I've tried so hard to be empathetic, to put myself in my mom's place, but her negativity fires the first shot, and I respond with a volley of positive problem solving when what she really wants is to be heard. I feel the same way when my husband doesn't listen and empathize with me when I share a frustrating event at work or at Ivy Manor. Instead he answers with a solution prefaced by "You should do...." At the end of my tether, I sit back in the chair and take a hard look at my mom. Her heavy glasses have slipped down on her nose as she peers over the edge of the blanket. Arthritis has twisted her head slightly toward her right shoulder. Her skeletal fingers, knotted and permanently stiffened, are grasping the edge of the blanket. Blue veins run like ropes across the backs of her hands. My frustration starts to unravel. I take a few deep breaths and try to relax my shoulders. I do love her. She's my mother. Good daughters honor and love their parents. And I see her suffering through the last years of her life. I want something better for her, but what can I do?

"I'm so sorry, Mama. It must be really difficult to be in such a bad situation. Maybe I can find a better place than Ivy Manor."

The minute these words are out of my mouth, I realize that I don't mean them. What I really want is for her to get over it and adjust because this is the best I could find. Before I visited Ivy Manor, I had checked out every nursing home in this part of town, but there weren't many choices since we didn't have money for private pay.

"Moving again isn't what I want. That would add to my troubles."

"It would add to my troubles, too. We can talk about this later, but how about some of your mashed potatoes and some hot tea? Then I'll go downstairs and talk to Victor about the furnace to see when it will be repaired."

She pushes the heavy blanket down and puts her arms over it. She has stopped shivering. She pulls the tray in front of her, so I can put the mashed potatoes and gravy on it.

"Don't forget to complain to the director about the lady taking up all the space in the room," she says, "and leave that door open about a foot."

Why do I try to do all of these things and expect to do them completely and perfectly? Why do I always say yes when sometimes I want to say no? And why don't I ask for help when I'm snowed under? I should have addressed these questions in my early twenties, the period of life designated for "finding yourself," but here I am asking the same questions almost fifty years later. In my simplemindedness, I've never acknowledged that I have an addiction, and not to alcohol or drugs. I'm addicted to pleasing people. I think I was born wanting to please, which led to my being a wimp, which in turn led to me being led around by a solid gold nose ring. To be truthful, pleasing has its rewards. People *like* me. My mom is starting to like me more. My friends sometimes take advantage of me, but they like me, too. My husband, my children, my colleagues, my students, and the people I supervise like me because I try hard to please them and fulfill their needs. But my god, does it take a lot of energy. It's draining, and it's increasingly hard to fill that empty cup again.

I'm almost seventy, and it's about time to start pleasing myself. How do I get out of this abyss—or do I want to? My first reaction is to defend my approach to life. I realize that it began in childhood, not unusual for an only child. As I psyched out my mom's needs, I developed the ability to put myself in other people's shoes, a kind of sensitivity to their problems that extended to other relationships in my life. I see this as a good trait. In fact, today I bought a GED high school study guide for an eighteen-year-old who had to drop out of school to have a baby. I meet her at the drive-through window of McDonald's several times a week when I get my breakfast coffee. She tells me her story in snatches each time I see her. She's desperate to finish school and change her life, so I want to encourage her. Helping others is a goal I set for myself in childhood, and it probably stems from my desire to please, but it's an important part of my life and one that I enjoy. I get love, approval, self-esteem, protection from being rejected. These are good results, but I'm never quite satisfied. I continue to need them in even greater quantities, so I expand the circle of people whose needs I try to meet. The more I do, the more people expect me to do. Then, I have to admit, I feel resentful, though I try not to show it. Showing it just wouldn't be nice. So far, I haven't been able to step off the merry-go-round of this addiction.

CHAPTER 4

PATERNAL RESPECT AND MATERNAL BLACKMAIL

TWO WEEKS HAVE PASSED SINCE THE FURNACE FIASCO AT IVY MANOR. My morning cup of coffee is empty and just a few crumbs of baklava left over from our twenty-third annual International Dinner dot the shiny top of my desk. Neither one has relieved the tightness in my neck and shoulders. I pull my to-do notebook from my purse and thumb through three pages of tasks. What to do first? Does it matter? I rip the pages out, crumple them, and throw them into the wastebasket under my desk. This act of defiance doesn't diminish the list of work, home, and Ivy Manor tasks, but it gives me a sense of control. Now if I just had someone to throw the wads of paper at, one of the ways our family relieved stress when we were fed up with the craziness of living in Cairo. We would crumple up pages of the *Egyptian Gazette* and bombard each other with them until we were exhausted and laughing. I'm on the edge of exhaustion and ready for some laughter.

A small box on my desk is filling up with funny examples of student mistakes, proof of the difficulty of learning English. I sort through the note cards. "One of my friends is coming back for the foul semester." "Parts of the verb to write: write, wrote, wrotten." "American cooking is different from Japan. Much Americans don't absorb grease." "Every Friday we bray at the mosque." That one is an example of first-language interference: no P sound in Arabic. "He is the best couch of the team." And on the final card: "I watched the super bowel last night." It occurs to me that my mom might enjoy these sentences, especially the last one, since "bowels" loom large in her list of concerns. Puns and word play were central to her winning 25-words-or-less jingle contests back in the 40s and 50s. Maybe sharing these would lighten her up for an announcement I need to make. I've signed up to attend an Educational Exhibition in Brussels, Belgium. My colleague Pambos has focused on marketing trips to Japan, South Korea, and Taiwan and has encouraged me to travel to Latin America, Europe, and the Middle East in order to recruit students for our intensive language program. The Educational Exhibition in Belgium would give us access to a new market in Europe, one that has not been much represented in our student population. It sounds like a refreshing break from my tasks at Ivy Manor, but I'm apprehensive about my mother's reaction to my leaving for two weeks.

This event is coming up in just six weeks, so I need to make airline reservations soon. I haven't taken a marketing trip since my dad's stroke more than two years ago. Floyd recently retired from his work as an educational specialist at the Federal Emergency Management Agency. He'll be teaching a class at Denver University, but he won't begin until the winter quarter. He could travel and work in the booth with me. We could have a much-deserved vacation, visiting a country that's new to us. My dad probably wouldn't miss me, but what about my needy mother and flaky Ivy Manor? Can I trust the nurses and aides to take care of her? I know Missy would pay attention to both of them and bring my mom her lunch necessities. I'm always at a crossroads, not sure which direction to take. As a caregiver, I probably should choose to stay here, but job-wise I need to take the trip. Then, too, getting away from the all-consuming tasks of my life might make me a better caregiver. A breath of relief comes with this thought. Maybe, just maybe, it will work. I'll try to broach the subject with my mom when I visit today.

After two days of repairs, the ailing elevator at Ivy Manor is working. As I step out on the second floor, I'm expecting the usual crowd of wheelchairs and walkers; instead I see a spiky, red-headed nurse humming and boogying around the nurses' station. She hurries to greet me, green eyes peering over the rose-colored spectacles perched on her nose. Her energy slices through my apprehension.

"Hi, I'm Olivia. I bet you're Connie, Mildred and Jim's daughter. Right?"

She extends her hand and pulls me closer to her heart-adorned scrub. I peer at an assortment of pins clustered on her shoulder: a butterfly, a daisy, a rhinestone stethoscope, a Colorado flag, and a Denver Broncos logo.

"Don't mind me. I'm a little zany, but I have fun. Your dad's a sweetheart and your mom, well, I'm trying to get on her list of good nurses."

Mama's habit of ranking caregivers seems to be common knowledge among the nurses and assistants. Mama doesn't write her rankings down; she just introduces them into any conversation with an Ivy Manor employee: "You're pretty good, Emily, but that guy Joe is a disaster." Olivia's fun-loving frankness may push her toward the top of the charts—as long as she doesn't make any mistakes. So far, no nurse has made it all the way to the top. Some infraction always moves them to the bottom. No one ever ends up in the middle, either. If I'd had siblings, I probably would have been at the end of the list, too.

I turn to the south corridor to walk to my dad's room first. He's a stark contrast to my mother: no complaints, no demands, no tallying up of good and bad caregivers. I'm tired of this pattern of conversation with my mother, but any of these reactions would be welcome from my father. Then I would know that he was still mentally alive. I've brought along a photo album to stimulate his memory, but the room is empty. I check the planter box of red geraniums I've put next to the window. The plants are drowning in water. He loves to putter, so he probably has watered them several times today. When my parents were living in their downtown apartment, he filled the balcony with geraniums and petunias, but back then he remembered when he had last cared for them.

Cynthia pushes open the door with a wheelchair bearing my smiling father. He's clean, wide awake, and wrapped in a white terry cloth robe. She says hello, pats him on the back, and tells me she'll come back to dress him for lunch after we visit for a few minutes.

I move the wheelchair over to the bed where I can sit and talk to him. I brush the damp, gray hair back from his forehead. "Hi, Daddy, it's Connie."

I always remind him of my name with the hope that he'll remember it. He hasn't called me by name since his stroke. I'm pleased to see a shade of recollection in his eyes and a smile on his lips. Maybe today will be one of those few times of clarity that he experiences.

"What's the program today?" he asks. I can tell he's circumventing his failing memory of my name and who I am by generalizing his greeting.

I can guess what's underneath the question. He would love to go out to Furr's cafeteria, a familiar place to bring the whole family together for Sunday lunch. We try to do this once a month, but it's becoming increasingly difficult to transfer him from his wheelchair to the car and to situate my mother in the backseat with her walker. It's also necessary to take a packet of liquid thickening agent to add to my dad's drinks. He can easily aspirate liquid or food into his lungs because, as a result of Alzheimer's, he has difficulty swallowing, Evidently swallowing is a complex function of the brain, which sends the message that food, drink, or saliva needs to be swallowed. This message may not get through the tangles of his brain, and, thus, the sequence of muscular movements and contractions may not get the mouth working and the fluid or food may not get moved over the upper airway and into the esophagus. In spite of these difficulties, he relaxes at the cafeteria table, enjoys the sound of conversation among the adult grandkids he doesn't fully recognize, and slowly relishes the mashed potatoes, gravy, chopped up fish, and chocolate pudding.

"We're not going out today, Daddy, but I came to visit you and show you some photos."

I offer him a small brown album with some old black-and-white photos from his past and more recent color photos of family events at our house. I've labeled each print with names and places, hoping that they might re-charge the memories that Alzheimer's disease has stolen. In a Pac-Man scenario, I visualize protein fragments in his brain gobbling up the synapses that connect nerve cells—cells that are essential to storing memories, processing thoughts, and planning and ordering how he moves his body. Maybe all hope of stimulating his memories is lost along with the synapses. Daddy's hand is trembling too much to hold the album, so I turn the pages for him and recite what each picture is. He seems interested but doesn't respond. When I come to a photo of his last birthday celebration at our home, his finger stops me from turning the page.

"Birthday? How old am I?"

"You were born on January 21, 1911, so that makes you almost ninety years old," I explain to the man who used to be a mathematician and the valedictorian of his class. He shakes his head in puzzlement.

"Are you sure? I thought I was a hundred."

"No, Daddy, just eighty-nine."

"No," he counters angrily. "I'm sure I'm a hundred. I want to be a hundred."

"Well, if you subtract 1911 from 2000, you get eighty-nine, Daddy. But that's a good age."

I quickly realize that I shouldn't have responded in this way.

Giving him an arithmetic problem just emphasizes his inability to process numbers. It's better to agree with his wish. He pushes the photo album away just as Cynthia arrives to dress him for lunch.

"OK, Daddy, you can be a hundred. We'll celebrate that big birthday in just a few months. You'll be a century old."

His anger subsides. I give him a peck on the cheek, tell him I'll see him at lunch, and head down the hallway to Room 214.

Olivia is in my mom's room replacing her catheter, so I lean against the guide railing on the wall outside the room and turn the pages of the photo album. My father when he graduated from high school. A handsome eighteen-year-old with thick, dark-brown hair, a high forehead, and a determined jaw. I study his eyes and see depth, inquisitiveness, and kindness, a sad contrast to the vacant quality they now have. My dad has never talked about those days, but I remember looking at his 1929 high school yearbook, the Longmont High Trojan, which detailed his achievements: editor of the yearbook, debate team member, glee club, annual play, operetta, student body vice president, and valedictorian. Not the quiet, introspective, and outwardly unemotional father I knew. A classmate wrote, "I tell you, Johnson, you have a good 'bean,' but don't be afraid to use it. The idea of working while you work and playing while you play is a good one. Mixed is bad."

Using his "bean" garnered my dad a scholarship to Antioch College in 1929. He had saved money for his living expenses from his work at the Kuner Empson canning factory throughout high school. In the fall, he set out on the bus to Yellow Springs, Ohio, with his savings and the scholarship letter. In a motel along the way, someone stole the envelope of money he had carelessly laid out on the dresser. He made a life-changing decision to hitchhike back to Colorado to attend Colorado State Teachers College in Greeley, where he would study mathematics with the goal of teaching and where he would meet my mother. Flipping the album page, I focus on my favorite photo, one that encapsulates the conclusion of their college careers: my mother in a long coat with a fur collar holding a bundled-up baby in her arms and my father with his arm around her shoulder, smiling at the camera. They had met at a fraternity party during her senior year, married and conceived a child. Without the money needed to finish college and take care of a family, my dad dropped out of college before his senior year. Did these circumstances shatter dreams he'd had? Were there goals he never reached? I wish I had asked him these questions when he was able to answer me. The responses might have explained his retreat into himself.

The Great Depression hampered his choice of jobs, so he returned to the canning factory to work as an accountant for six years. Then he took a civil service exam and found employment as a clerk at Fort Logan, south of Denver. We lived on Sunset Ridge just outside the Army Base until World War II was declared and he joined the Merchant Marine to work in the recruiting office in downtown Denver. His childhood record of rheumatic fever made him exempt from any other military service. We moved four times in Denver during the war and, finally, after peace was declared, moved to our long-term home in West Denver as my dad found other jobs that led him to his work as a radio and TV broadcast engineer.

I don't recall him playing with me as a young child, probably because my mother kept me busy as her companion and confidante. However, a photo in the album reminds me of some special times we had when I was growing up. In the little black-and-white snap shot at frozen Evergreen Lake, I'm about eleven or twelve years old. Daddy is holding my hand as I push off on my first pair of ice skates, purchased from a pawn shop on Larimer Street. I remember that he even flooded part of our side yard during the winter, so that I could practice skating.

We also worked together on my prize-winning 4-H Victory Garden in the backyard, planting and tending unusual crops like Swiss chard, strange-shaped gourds, and huge field pumpkins in addition to the common vegetables. I'm certain now that these efforts were part of the focus-on-Connie plan when my parents decided not to have more children. Those times brought my father and me closer together and balanced the time that my mother needed from me.

The photo album also has a picture of my dad and Gene Amole, well-known *Rocky Mountain News* columnist and KMYR radio announcer and station owner. I guess Daddy did sometimes mix work and play. He spent 30 years working as an engineer for radio and television stations in Denver. Many of those years were spent in solitary jobs at foothills transmitters for KMYR and later KOA. He kept himself alert during those tedious hours, many of them at night, by creating an electric piano/organ for my mom, by designing a mathematical scheme to "figure the winning dogs" at the Mile High Dog Track, and by thinking up jokes to "break up" the announcers, proof that he liked to mix work with play. Amole was the frequent object of my dad's practical jokes. On my parents' sixty-sixth anniversary, Amole sent me an e-mail: "I was your father's greatest fan, even that day he painted his toenails red and operated the controls with his bare feet." I can sometimes see this humor peeking out of the Alzheimer's mask in the playful stacking up of his eating utensils and the pinches on Raheen's bottom. All of the I-wish-I-had's come out of hiding in my relationship with him now. I wish we had shared hugs and kisses and confidences, so I try to show him physical affection, rubbing his shoulders, holding his hand, kissing him on the cheek. Even though he doesn't respond, I talk to him about what's happening in my life and what his grandchildren are doing, and I tell him how much I love him.

I close the photo album when Olivia opens the door to my mom's room and welcomes me inside. Her wide grin is balanced by the pink eyeglasses that have slipped down on her nose.

"C'mon in. Mildred's all finished. She's a bit uncomfortable, but we've formed a real bond. She even sang me a little song as a thank you for doing the catheter."

I can't believe my mom sang to Olivia—a song she used to play on the piano: "Why do I love you like I do? I don't know why, I just do." A warm relief relaxes my shoulders. Maybe Olivia's attention will diminish what my mom needs from me. I tuck the photo album into my bag along with memories of my dad. I'm so relieved that Olivia has risen to the top of my mom's list of good nurses and has been rewarded with a musical "ditty," as my mom would put it. God bless Olivia.

This visit should be more successful than the last. My mom called me at five this morning, her usual time to wake up. When the phone rings that early I think of strokes and heart attacks, but she had some rare good news. She has heat in her room and no new resident requiring a huge lift to take up space. Evidently, the room will remain empty until a more suitable roommate emerges.

Mama is dressed in the purple blouse and blue paisley skirt that has become her uniform. I can't convince her to wear more than one or two other outfits in spite of the many clothes in her closet. She's sitting on one side of the bed with her tray table pulled up in front of her. My usual inquiry about her health produces a "so-so."

"Did you bring the stamps?" she asks. "I wrote a letter to Sonja this morning and want to do one to Linna in Denmark."

I admit that I've forgotten the stamps she asked for in the early phone call this morning. I promise I'll put stamps on her letters and mail them from my office. She hands me the two envelopes addressed in her almost perfect cursive style, the writing that won her a prize in elementary school. Sonja, her oldest granddaughter, lives in Cyprus. Mama writes her once a week. At least once a month she also writes a letter in Danish and English to Linna, a distant cousin in Denmark. It's another good sign. She's trying to fill her time at Ivy Manor productively.

I go through the routine of mashed potatoes and gravy, a pudding cup, and pieces of the Rocky Mountain News.

"I already have a glass of Lactaid," she says, "so I think I'll eat in the room today."

I'm tired this morning, so I don't try to convince her that it's better to eat in the dining room. I put the meager offerings I have on the tray table. Because of her lack of teeth, her tastes, and the stomach problems that plague her, it's almost impossible to get food she can eat from the kitchen, except for Jell-O and cake. We've tried scrambled eggs, but they arrive in an unappetizing microwaved square. I help her get settled on the edge of the bed with the tray table holding her lunch. Then I pull up a chair to visit while she eats. I'm surprised when she smiles, showing the dimples in her still smooth cheeks. She seems eager to share some positive news.

"We had a new aide today," she announces. "His name is Kingsley, and he's from Ghana. I told him I knew Ghana was in West Africa. He was surprised. Then I asked him if he was from Accra, the capital. He almost dropped the blood pressure cuff. 'Miss Mildred,' he said. 'How do you know these things?' I told him I've always liked geography."

She sits up straighter than usual with a proud look on her face.

While she eats, we start naming the other certified nursing assistants and their countries. Juanita is from Mexico; Brian from Uganda; Auggie from Guatemala; Lenny, Joe, and Victor are Indonesian; Jo Ann is from Vietnam; and Jeannie is from the Philippines. The only assistant from the U.S. is Kendra. My mom knows the capital cities of all their countries and something about their geography. When she doesn't know something, she asks me to get the almanac from the third drawer of the dresser, so she can use her magnifying glass to retrieve the information, a lifelong habit that she passed on to me along with her interest in geography, her mother's favorite subject.

"If you don't know something, look it up," is advice that has stuck with me from the days of my childhood *World Book* encyclopedias to my habit of researching subjects on the internet today.

This conversation presents the opportunity to slip in the possible marketing trip to Belgium. I hope she doesn't sense the hesitation in my voice.

"Pambos and I talked today about a language exhibition in Brussels. We'd like to get more European students to come to Spring School. Floyd and I could go. It's next month, so I'd be gone about ten days."

My mom stops drinking her Lactaid, puts the glass down, and shrinks into a slump. She's gritting her teeth, trying hard to think of an appropriate response.

"I'm sure you want to go, Connie, but I hate to see you leave. I've been feeling so much worse lately. What will I do when you're gone?"

This is déjà vu. Damned, devious, debilitating déjà vu. I draw my breath in through my teeth and cross my arms on my chest. She's using her ailments to control me, just as she did when I was a child. The worst example of this was when I had just graduated from high school. I was dating Floyd and was very close to his family. They asked me to take a road trip to Washington, D.C., with them that summer. His brother Rollin was going to the White House to receive a 4-H Leadership award from President Eisenhower. We would be treated to tours of the White House, the FBI, and all the historic sites in the capital. I told my mom and dad that I really wanted to go with them. My dad thought it would be a good experience, but my mother disapproved.

"I've had lots of health problems lately, and I'm afraid if you go, I may get even sicker than I am now," she argued in a voice that weakened as she spoke.

Blackmail of this sort had been used several times before to exert control over me. That was the first time I stood my ground. It was a once-in-a-lifetime trip, and she survived with no ill effects.

Soon after we returned, Floyd's mother gave me a letter that my mom had sent to her while we were in Washington. Mama had written that I was a very selfish daughter who wasn't concerned about the health of her mother. That I had disobeyed her and left when she needed me most. After reading the letter, I tore it up and threw it away. I was hurt and angry. What made her say those things about me? Was she jealous of my relationship with Floyd and his family? What would Floyd's mother think of me, and what would she think of my mother? I should have confronted my mom. Instead I destroyed the letter and made a commitment to myself that this was the end of doing everything she asked. I needed my freedom. Luckily, when I went just sixty miles away to university, she turned to my father with some of her needs. She started to rely on him, and he welcomed her attention. They talked more and started to develop common interests in local basketball and football and home improvement projects they could work on together.

My marriage to Floyd provided the biggest break from her emotional ties to me. We married during our senior year in university. As editors of the biweekly student newspaper, we received enough money to manage food and a one-room apartment. My mom responded to the impending wedding with more bouts of illness, but once the ceremony was over, she realized the need to establish a closer relationship with my father. We left Colorado after graduation, moving to the University of Missouri, back to Colorado State, on to Michigan State, and ultimately to American University in Cairo. Physical distance helped us establish an adult mother-daughter relationship and, most importantly, it forced my mom and dad to find ways to enjoy more activities together and to appreciate each other.

Unfortunately, the initial stages of Alzheimer's began to weaken their tie. My father answered "yes" to every sales call and sweepstakes letter. He bought magazine subscriptions, cheap jewelry, anything that promised a fortune if he'd just buy something in order to enter a sweepstakes. My mom couldn't control his spending, so their lone Visa card built up an impossible balance that didn't mesh with their $1100 monthly income and the $300 I added to it each month.

It was pancakes at McDonald's, a two-block walk from their downtown Denver apartment, that triggered the official diagnosis of Alzheimer's. My dad enjoyed the $2 breakfast every morning at 8 a.m. On this particular morning, he finished his pancakes, stood up, walked out the door and lost his bearings. Where was he? Which way was home? He wandered down the Sixteenth Street Mall and sat on a bench for more than two hours until a shop keeper talked to him, found the ID card in his pocket, and called my worried mother to retrieve him.

Now my parents are together again, but they have only a thread of a relationship left. My dad doesn't recognize my mom, and my mom limits their contact to an across-the-table lunch that I have to arrange each time I visit Ivy Manor. If I leave on this marketing trip to Brussels, their contact may diminish to nothing.

Mama has pushed the pause button on our Belgium conversation by closing her eyes. I wait with the hope that she'll reconsider. She clasps her hands to her chest and opens her eyes. "Could you postpone the trip, Connie? Maybe I'll feel better in a month or two."

I explain that this specific Brussels Education Abroad Exhibition is held only once a year, so the opportunity is now. "Missy will come to see you several times a week, and she'll check in on Daddy, too. I'll leave Lactaid with her, and she'll buy the mashed potatoes each time she comes. And I'll ask Olivia to pay extra attention to you."

"I know, but it's just not the same. You're the only one who knows what I need. I have a little bit of happiness when you come to visit."

Am I really the only person who supposedly can bring pleasure to my mom's life? This statement burrows into my psyche like a tick. I want to get rid of it, but it's painful to dig out. Do all female only children have this complicated attachment to their mothers, or am I the only one who has allowed it to progress this far? I sometimes feel like I'm struggling for breath in these conversations with my mother. I'm reminded of the strangler tree that fascinated the kids when we were in Egypt. As we taxied to American University, we passed the famous hundred-year-old banyan tree almost daily on the corniche, a stretch of grass and trees that divided the main boulevard in Cairo. Its branches arched several hundred feet across the sparse grass and concrete that ran along the Nile, almost touching our little Fiat taxi. Hundreds of gnarled roots appeared to be hanging loose from the tree, but on closer observation, you could see that each root had firmly attached itself to the mother tree, criss-crossing the trunk and each other like bulbous veins and arteries, all competing for the light. As the tree had aged, its aerial prop roots grew into thick woody trunks that had become indistinguishable from the mother tree. I don't want to be one of those roots. I need light and freedom from fulfilling my mom's every whim. Yet I'm the only one she has. I miss having brothers and sisters more at this point in my life than I did when I was a child. It would be so comforting to share burdens and decisions with someone else.

Mama is quiet. I can tell she's turning over the problem of my absence in her mind. No frowning, no shaking of her head. She's trying hard to be positive about her granddaughter caring for her. "You know I love Missy, and it's nice of her to visit me if you go on that trip. But you're so good to me and you know just how I like things. After all, you are my only child."

"Yes, I am your only child," I affirm, "but I need to make this trip. I'll do everything to make you comfortable while I'm gone." She turns away from me and tells me she's tired. I give her a pat on the shoulder and leave.

That evening, when I'm soaking away the day's concerns in my nightly bubble bath, I visualize my mother wrapping a long rope around her waist, handing one end of it to me, and jumping off a bridge into the water below. Her life, her happiness, is in my hands. She needs me, or so I have thought at certain points in my life, to fulfill the demands that will provide her with a satisfying life. And I, too, have a need to please her in every way possible to gain her approval. Can we both change and take responsibility for our individual happiness? It's not too late for me, but it may be for my mother in this last sliver of her life. If I release the rope now, she may die an unhappy death. What can I do? My hands are raw from all the years I've clung to the rope, but as I grow older my strength is ebbing. I need to let go.

I scoot down in the scented water, letting it cover my shoulders, liquid that can soothe, bless, or drown a person. I speculate on my relationship with my own three children. I feel responsible for the quality of my own life, but I also recognize that I have frequently felt responsible for my adult children's happiness, just as I have in my mother's case. No mother wants to see her children unhappy, whether they are toddlers or adults. I also realize that at times Floyd and I have responded to our children's problems by helping to solve them rather than letting them struggle. Am I deluding myself by thinking this action has helped them rather than enabling them to ask for more? I've learned from these last few years with Mama that there's a hair's breadth between fulfilling a need out of love and enabling a person to continue being needy.

Brushing the remaining bubbles from a body that's gained

twenty pounds in the last twenty years, I note a few familiar scars, reminders of breast cancer and a knee replacement. I pat the loose belly folds, a remnant of three full-term pregnancies, including two beautiful daughters and one stillborn baby. The scars and bumps aren't reminders of pain and injuries. They are proof of healing and a full life with a good husband and three children.

Sonja was our first child, born a year after I lost another baby girl whose Down syndrome caused a heart attack in the ninth month of pregnancy. When Sonja was born we were overjoyed with the gift of a healthy, beautiful, blond, blue-eyed daughter, her name and face a credit to my mother's Danish heritage. She grew from a one-year-old who talked to everyone she met in the supermarket to a shyer and quieter little girl whose passions were books, ballet, and playing school with her little sister Missy. Seven family moves between Sonja's fifth and fourteenth years made her cautious about making close friends; it hurt to lose them. In Cairo, she discovered her passion for other cultures and languages. When we returned to Colorado, she decided to spend her senior year of high school in Venezuela, learning Spanish. By then, she found American guys boring. She began dating students from other cultures, got an M.A. in bilingual/bicultural studies, married a Greek Cypriot, and ultimately moved to the island of Cyprus to make close friends among the expatriate wives and to have three sons, much to her Greek husband's delight. Sonja is a creative, accomplished instructor of English at European University in Nicosia, Cyprus. Her measured thoughtful way of speaking emphasizes the serenity that she projects. No ropes here. She has carved out her own bicultural life and is responsible for her own happiness.

Our middle daughter, Melissa—"Missy"—is just a year and a half younger. As a child, she was a beautiful, bubbly, blue-eyed blond. She cultivated friendships as we moved from Colorado to Michigan to Cairo, Ohio, and back to Colorado. No family or friend's birthday was, or is, ever forgotten, no thank-you neglected. When she was in elementary school at Cairo American College, she and best friend Elinore formed their own pretend detective agency, scouting out errant Egyptians at the local sporting club and looking for mummies in the Egyptian desert. This may have led her to choose a degree in criminal justice. Diagnosed with Type I diabetes when she was 17, she has boot-camped, bicycled, and controlled her diet to prevent the disease from controlling her life. When she was twenty-two, she married Mark, whose family had emigrated from Great Britain when he was a child. Because of her diabetes, they decided to adopt a son, Benjamin, from the same agency that Floyd and I adopted our son, Troy. Missy worked for her own spending money during high school and college, later worked as a juvenile counselor, and then joined the Spring International staff as international student advisor. Both my daughters share my quirky sense of humor, but Missy sometimes extends it to practical jokes. In the last ten years, not only has she developed strong physical muscles, but she has also gained strength in facing challenges and has independently carved out her own happiness.

When our daughters were five and six-and-a-half, we decided to adopt a son rather than having another biological child. We believed, like many young adults in the sixties, that adoption was one of the solutions to the population explosion that had begun after World War II. Most importantly, though, we wanted to complete our family with a third child, possibly one with Native American heritage, to honor the Cherokee blood of Floyd's father and his continuing interest in this cultural heritage. After searching and applying at several agencies, we completed the lengthy process at Lutheran Services in Denver and were presented with a three-week-old, five-pound, brown-haired and green-eyed baby boy who had been given up for adoption by his Alaskan Inupiat mother. As was typical of 1968 adoptions, only a few details were provided: his biological mother was eighteen and beautiful, and the granddaughter of a tribal elder in a village on the Kobuk River. That was fine. All we needed to know was that Troy James was truly our son, adored by his mom and dad and the sisters who mothered him throughout our moves to Michigan and Cairo. As a child, he loved the outdoors and all kinds of animals, and he revered his grandfather, who taught him to ride horses on his Black Forest ranch, shoot a rifle, and work harder than he'd ever worked. From the time he was five or six, Troy could put together any mechanical object without directions, glean information and facts by just listening and watching, and add sparks of hyper energy to any occasion. In Egypt, he sat in the kitchen with Soliman, our cook, drinking tea with milk and lots of sugar, and tore around our garden on his Big Wheel, horrifying the gardener by hitting the huge pots of geraniums. Although he was just two-and-a-half when we arrived in suburban Cairo and not quite seven when we left, he was my GPS, always knowing which way to turn as he sat behind me in the basket on my bicycle. When we returned to Colorado, via a year in Ohio, he quickly made school friends, although dyslexia challenged his reading skills. As a handsome, six-foot-two-inch teen, he worked to earn his spending money and to buy his first car. As an adult, he can bargain successfully for almost any purchase and relishes discovering new places, doing new things, and talking to strangers. He's an affectionate adult who cherishes his wife, Diana, his family, and his home in Colorado.

I attribute the closeness of our family to Floyd's strong family life and to lessons I learned with my own parents. Although their marriage was far from perfect, my mom and dad remained committed through more than sixty-five years of marriage. I learned my best lessons from observing their mistakes. I was determined to love my children unconditionally. I did not want to satisfy my needs for approval and achievement through them. It seems to have worked.

Chapter 5

Mama's Secrets

Six weeks later, it's time to start organizing the bags I'll take to Brussels. Our departure is in two days. I've already packed the brochures and banners for the booth at the educational exhibition; they can be sent ahead. But I still need to pack my personal items. I've taken my large bag out of the closet, sticky-rolled the cat hair off the top, and placed it on the bed, open and ready to receive two pairs of shoes, when the phone rings. It's Florence, the head of nursing at Ivy Manor.

In a staccato voice, she announces, "Your mother fell in the bathroom about thirty minutes ago. She's conscious but in pain. Possibly a broken bone. We don't know yet. The ambulance is here now to take her to the emergency room at Swedish."

Without asking questions, I tell her that I'll go to the hospital right away. I slump down on the bed next to the empty suitcase. Our cat, Xena, jumps up next to me, curious about the open bag. Instead of reacting immediately to the call, I start petting her. As always, her soft black-and-white fur and responsive purr help me to pause and contemplate. Here I am again with another crisis to pack into an already full bag. I've heard all the stories about broken hips leading to an elderly person's death. Did Florence say it was a hip or her leg? I don't remember. Whichever it is, I can't imagine deserting her while she's in the hospital. I'll need to be with her, trip or no trip. It's clear to me that Belgium isn't as important as my mom's situation. Then a whisper from the past reminds me of my mother's threats when my plans didn't agree with her wishes. "I don't feel well now, and I'm afraid that I may get really sick if you do this." Surely she wouldn't fall just to keep me here. I try to rub away the memory, but it's like a sticky spot on the kitchen counter that can't be cleaned off with just one swipe. I'll attend to it later.

Xena climbs into the suitcase and curls up, leaving wisps of fur on the zippered edge. I let her stay, pick up my car keys, and head for the hospital. My mother has already gone into surgery, I'm told, where a pin will be implanted to repair a broken femur, not her hip. I wait in the quiet, powder-blue family room, praying silently for help in making decisions that may result from her injury. Will she be able to stay at Ivy Manor for therapy? Will she walk again or just give up? She would never adjust to a wheelchair like my dad has. I need to be here to make those decisions and to ease her back into life at Ivy Manor.

When the green-scrubbed surgeon meets me in the family waiting room, he reports that the operation has gone well, although a minor heart attack accompanied her fall. She'll remain in the hospital for a few days, but he predicts a good recuperation with the help of physical therapy back at Ivy Manor. If the therapy is successful, she will be able to return to her walker, no wheelchair necessary. His report is perfunctory but hopeful. I stay with my mom in the recovery room until she comes out of the anesthesia. Then I return to work to cancel the Brussels airline tickets, hotel arrangements, and participation in the event. I'm disappointed but certain that I've made the right decision. There will be other educational exhibitions in other countries, and they may come at a more appropriate time.

The next morning on my way to the hospital, I visit my dad at

Ivy Manor with the impossible hope that I can confide in him the news about Mama's broken leg. I can't find him in his room, and all the nurses and CNAs are at a meeting downstairs. I look into the activity room and see him through the doors to the upstairs patio. He's all by himself, slumped in his wheelchair in the direct July sunshine. Rivulets of sweat are running down his red cheeks and his eyes are pinched shut. I touch him on the shoulder.

"Daddy, are you okay?"

He tries to open his eyes against the bright sun.

"Mmph, hot," he mutters.

"I can't believe they've left you out here in the sun—and for how long?"

He doesn't answer and wouldn't be able to tell me anyway because the concept of time truly has flown from his mind. If I had the aide who left him here on the patio, I would shake him by the shoulders and scream, "Why aren't you doing your job?" Instead I feel my heart beat faster, an accurate barometer of my blood pressure. Tears of frustration fill my eyes as I wheel him quickly to his room, dampen a washcloth with cool water, and dab at his face and forehead. I look for the thickened water that is supposed to be by his bed, but no cup is to be found. As the meeting downstairs breaks up, the assistants and nurses begin to come upstairs. I grab the first person, a new nurse whose name I don't know, and ask her to come into the room to check out my dad. My voice is shaky and louder than usual.

"How long was your meeting?" I ask.

"More than an hour—too long for me. I'm not used to staff meetings."

This casual answer raises the pressure in my temples. I take a step closer to her.

"Are you the nurse for this wing? You must be new. I don't know your name."

She backs away from me and hesitates a moment before answering. "I'm Debby. I'm a substitute for Janet. She's sick today, so this is my wing. Is something the matter?" She glances over at my dad, who's holding the washcloth over his mouth and breathing heavily.

"Someone left my dad on the patio in the sun before your meeting and completely forgot him. He's sunburned, he's hot, he's tired, and I'm tired too. Tired of the shit that goes on here." I've finally expressed my frustration, and I'm glad.

Debby's mouth opens, and she shakes her head. She quickly moves over to my dad, feels his forehead and takes the washcloth from his hand. His eyes close and his head nods down to his chest. Fatigue takes over, and he needs to sleep.

"I'm so sorry. I didn't know he was outside in the sun. We'll check his vitals, cool him off, and get him in bed."

Debby's chin is quivering as she rushes out of the room. She's either afraid of what might happen to her or truly sorry that she forgot my dad on the patio.

I put my arm around his shoulders and gently rub his back. I can feel his muscles relax as he begins to breathe more deeply. Then I remember where I was headed when I stopped by Ivy Manor. My mom. In the hospital. I wait until Florence, the head nurse, has heard my complaint and apologized profusely. She wakes him up, takes his vital signs, and determines that he's okay. I leave when they put him in bed to give him a sponge bath. What a way to begin the day! The anger that I seldom show outwardly is eating away at my insides. I'm queasy, weak-kneed, and drained of energy, not ready for the real crisis of the day: my mother in the hospital with a broken leg.

Ready or not, here I am at the hospital. I find Mama tucked into the white sheets of her hospital bed like a letter in an envelope, only the top half of her head showing above the open flap.

"Wondered … where you were," she whispers. "Glad you're here … not Belgium. I fell. A big bug on the floor scared me."

Looking like a boxer who's lost a fight, she exposes the empty space where her front tooth was knocked out by the anesthetist.

I pull the sheet down a few inches, so I can touch her pale cheek under the oxygen tube that's threaded into her nose and behind her ears. Her right eyelid is drooping more than usual. I wonder if she might have had a slight stroke.

"How are you feeling now, Mama?"

Her voice quakes. "I'm so cold, and I don't like this place. There's nobody around at night except a big black man who's on duty. He just stares at me when he comes into the room. I'm afraid he might do something to hurt me."

This is the first time I've heard my mom express fear of a caregiver. Before I can respond, she continues.

"I'm afraid I'll have another heart attack, and no one will be here to help me."

I show her the call button pinned next to her pillow and reassure her that a nurse is nearby to help her. She doesn't seem to notice. Her eyes are darting around the room instead of focusing on the button.

"Missy brought me that huge vase of flowers. They're too big and have a strange odor. Take them home with you when you go."

A medium-sized turquoise vase is filled with purple iris and white daisies, flowers that Missy knows are her grandmother's favorites. Mama's paranoia surprises me. This is more than her everyday complaints and pickiness.

"I'm afraid of the darkness in that corner of the room. Open the curtains just a little bit."

My usual response is to make a positive comment for each of her negative ones, but I'm speechless at this flood of fearful statements.

Maybe it's a typical response to surgery and anesthesia. Or it could be the result of a new medication or the lack of an old one.

I pull out the list of her medications from my handbag and take it to the nurse in charge, a gray-haired woman with a frazzled twitch in her right eyelid. We compare my list with what the hospital has been giving her. Three of her medications have been dropped: Synthroid, a thyroid med; Ativan, an anti-anxiety drug that she has taken for the past two years; and Trazodone, an antidepressant. When I question the missing meds, the nurse glances at the paper as if it were an outdated grocery list.

"Sometimes we don't get the full information from these Medicaid patients, but I'll check with the doctor."

She turns on her heel to leave, but I touch her arm.

"Please do! She needs those medications." I raise my voice a notch. "And by the way, it seems to me that a Medicaid patient should be treated as well as any private-pay patient."

The nurse whirls around and disappears behind the glassed-in counter. I'm gaining confidence in my confrontation skills—first at Ivy Manor and now at the hospital. I exhale my anger, square my shoulders, and stride down the hallway to assess my mom's situation. She has pulled the sheet over her nose but seems to be asleep. I walk to her bedside and move the sheet down below her chin and tuck it around her shoulders just as I used to tuck in my own children. She's breathing through her open mouth but sleeping soundly. "Sleep tight, Mama," I whisper and lift Missy's flowers off the shelf to take them home.

Two days later, checkout day, the charge nurse steps inside the room to tell me that my mother "has had all the meds you asked for, and more." I resent her tone of voice. She may have had her medications for the day, but they haven't changed her mood. Her eyes are half closed, her lips turned down, and her hands nervously fingering the edge of the bed sheet. I can feel the weight of her depression as I pack the small tote bag in preparation for the ambulance ride back to Ivy Manor.

"You'll be in a first-floor room while you have physical therapy, Mama. Olivia and all the aides have been asking about you."

"I don't care. I probably won't be there long," she responds.

A tear struggles down her cheek. In my emotional math, tears produce empathy, but I've heard her use illness so many times to get her way that it diminishes my empathy for her. She opens her eyes as wide as the droopy lids will allow and beckons me to move closer. I sit on the end of her bed and lean toward her.

"There's something I need to tell you," she whispers. "I've done some bad things in my past. I don't know if God will forgive me."

My mind is grabbing at an explanation. My mother is telling me she's done bad things, but why? This must be the life review I've heard about. Helen, my colleague at work and a former social worker, has told me that this is common in patients who think they are dying. As they develop a sense of their own mortality, they are motivated to look back and reassess their lives. Psychologists say this is a normal developmental task of old age, an integration or reorganization of personality. A step toward accepting death. My mom is laboring at this task.

"Daddy wasn't the only man in my life. I had other men, many of them." She bites her lip and lowers her eyes. Her hands are clasped now and fingers entwined.

All I can do is blink and stare at her face. Is this my mother speaking? Surely she hasn't slept with other men. I don't remember her even sleeping in the same bed as my father. She takes a deep breath and spills out the rest of her confession.

"I never should've married Daddy, but I got pregnant soon after he gave me his fraternity pin at Teachers' College. I knew Papa would be angry. He wanted me to stay single and become a teacher, so we got married secretly and then I told my mother, who waited several months to tell Papa."

She sneaks a glance at me and then looks down at her hands. My voice is silent, but my mind is brimming over with questions. My mother didn't choose to marry my father? She had to get married? It's not a big deal today, but what a shameful situation in must have been in the 1930s. A pregnant, unmarried daughter could be disowned by her family or sent away to have the baby in secret. It was an era when families were encouraged to protect their secrets. Secrets were dirty laundry. In an a-ha moment, I put a missing piece into the puzzle. An unwanted pregnancy had shattered my dad's goal of a university degree, prevented my mom from pursuing a teaching career, and provided a shaky foundation for marriage.

I regain my voice and, thinking about the sixty-six-year anniversary we celebrated in April, can't resist asking when they were married. She doesn't answer for a few minutes but seems to be searching her mind for events of almost seventy years ago.

"We were married on July Fourth, soon after my graduation. But Daddy persuaded the county clerk to put April 29 as the date of the wedding. That's why I kept asking you not to do anything special for our anniversary. It was the wrong date. I should have told you the truth."

I try to keep an impassive face and nod my head encouragingly, but gulping down her revelations has clogged my throat and slowed my breathing. Surely she's mixed up the facts or imagined events that never happened. I can't believe she's telling me the truth. Excusing myself to use the bathroom might provide me time to digest what's happening. I start to stand up, but Mama seems compelled to continue.

"I didn't have any experience with sex, but Daddy had visited one of those ladies in Longmont. I wish I had known more about it. Then I could have said 'no.'" I had a terrible pregnancy. I was sick and even fainted once when we were living in a hot upstairs room above his aunt's house. I remember the night you were born. He wanted to do something sexual then. Maybe that's why I had such a terrible time with your birth. You just tore me apart."

I'm shocked. My mom never had the sex talk with me, but now she's revealing something about her own sex life.

She stops, wipes her eyes, and shakes her head. "I've done such bad things."

She seems so tiny, so vulnerable, and so hurt. By admitting her weaknesses, she is trusting me with a part of herself she has never shared with anyone else. Claiming ownership of her story has been difficult for her after all these years of hiding her secrets, but it opens the door to a deeper love for her. I reach for the hand that's grasping the sheet. She turns her hand palm up to meet mine. It's warm, sweaty, and trembling as I wrap it in mine, trying not to hurt her twisted arthritic fingers. A wave of tenderness envelops me. The words come easily.

"Everyone has things in life they wish they hadn't done, Mama. That's just being human. It doesn't change the way I feel about you. I don't love you any less because you've made mistakes. I love you now just as much as always."

Something about her vulnerability also lifts a burden from my mind. I recognize her physical losses each day as she ages, but I've never before noticed the cracks in her I'm-always-right armor. When she admits her imperfections, it helps me to relate to her in a more equal manner. I may not have been the perfect child she wanted, and she may not have been the perfect mother, but here we are. We're both human, with all the failings that go with that condition. I don't have to work so hard to please her. I can choose to love her no matter what her past includes. This is powerful. I'm in control. If I forgive her for any hurts I've suffered, maybe she can forgive me for my hurtful and disruptive entrance into her life.

I often reflect on my mother's lost dreams, the ones she shared with me, when I was growing up. "If things had been different," she would begin, and then recite the might-have-beens of staying single, becoming a respected artist, learning to pilot an airplane, traveling by ship to the Scandinavian countries, continuing her studies for a higher degree. In the thirties, married women stayed at home with their babies and forgot the dreams of their single lives. Besides, giving birth to me had been an excruciating process. I was guilty of inflicting this pain. She has frequently recalled the story of my birth. Her story has always ended the same way the revelation of her secret ends: "You almost tore me apart. I've never felt such pain."

I don't remember how old I was when I first heard this story, but I do recall taking the mother from a paper doll family, creasing it between my fingers, tearing it down the middle into two pieces, and unsuccessfully trying to fit it together again. Even though I know I'm not guilty of any misdeeds regarding my birth, I have tried to make up for destroying my mother's dreams. The process of confession, acceptance, and forgiveness that we've both emerged from today may help me to paste together the pieces of the paper doll of my childhood.

The muscles of Mama's face relax, and her hands unclasp. She sighs with what seems to be relief. My mind is crowded with amazement and questions. Could it be as easy as this? Do relief and comfort come from simply revealing secrets, apologizing, and receiving acceptance? Would our relationship have changed if she had brought these hidden revelations to the surface earlier in our lives? Will she ever refer to them again? She turns her head toward the pillow and puts her arms under the sheet.

"I'm so tired, Connie. You'd better go now."

I smooth her rumpled hair and kiss her forehead. She mumbles a soft "thank you."

"I'll see you tomorrow, Mama. Remember, I love you."

As I drive home, I sort through the events of the past hour. At the top of my mind is gratitude for my mom's gift of her vulnerability and trust. I cherish it because it brings the hope of a warmer and more loving relationship. Bubbling underneath this feeling is the shock and surprise of her revelations. The change in wedding dates and my "early" birth don't bother me. But sex? My mother? And with other men? I suppose it's always difficult for a child to even imagine her parents having sex. Maybe adolescent children hear a rhythmic thumping at night in the bedroom next door and, with distaste, guess at what's going on, or they see their dad give mom an affectionate pat on her butt or a tight hug and recoil with embarrassment. But I don't remember seeing any hugs or kisses between my parents. I always thought this was just the Scandinavian way—very few expressions of affection, and I knew that they never slept in the same bed. So, was she really telling the truth or was it the shock of her broken leg, the missing anti-depressants that caused her to fabricate a story?

I search my childhood memory for clues. I'd never seen my mother with other men. She probably was flirtatious. She'd been pretty, even beautiful, and she'd often talked about high school friends and even a boyfriend, who was the son of a Lutheran pastor. The photos in her albums show a smiling, dimpled Danish blonde with high cheekbones and hair marcelled in perfect waves. Her dresses stopped just at mid-knee to reveal light stockings and strapped high heels. In her later life, she loved face-framing hats. My favorite professional photo of her was taken by Cesar Morganti, a famous Denver photographer. She was wearing a wide-brimmed dark hat that curved around her face on one side, framing the dramatic cheekbones and the blond hair. She had won the photo in a contest. Yes, she was sexy, but that does not necessarily equate with having sex.

I'm wondering what my father was doing when my mother "had other men." I do recall a time when my mom told me Daddy had a girlfriend. It was in 1940, just a year before the war. We had moved from Longmont to Fort Logan; Daddy had a position as clerk-typist at the base, where recruits for all branches of the Army were processed. For me, it was an exciting time. I rode the army bus to second grade in Englewood, played with my first real friends, and roamed the gullies and prairie outside the base. It wasn't a happy time for my mother. After school each day, we would have a glass of milk and a cookie and she would share her problems with me. I was both pleased that she was talking to me like an adult and puzzled about what I should do. She thought my dad had a girlfriend he had met at work. At that point in my understanding, girlfriends were truly pals, very important when you had just moved to a new place, so I wasn't sure why my mother was so "worried sick," as she frequently put it.

One night after I was in bed, I heard them arguing in the kitchen, a fight that probably went something like this: "You've got a girlfriend, I *know* you do. Myrna next door told me to keep a close eye on you. She saw you outside the payroll barracks sharing a cigarette with some woman. Is that who you're spending time with?"

"She's just a co-worker who likes to talk to me. Just a friend." My dad continued to speak in his quiet, even voice, but my mother's voice escalated into a loud whine.

"Does she work overtime, too? Does she go home late at night to her husband?

At that point, my mom went into the bathroom, slammed the door, and locked it. I could smell the smoke from my dad's cigarette as he lit up, took a drag, threw open the back door, and went out into the yard.

I remember slumping down on the bed. My shoulders ached from propping myself up on my elbows, so I could hear what my parents were saying. I turned on my side and covered my head with the pillow. Was this going to change our lives? My life? Was my mom going to get sick and have to go to bed again like she did in Longmont when the peeping tom scared her and she stumbled over a chair? Was my dad so unhappy that he'd leave us?

A few days after the argument, there was a change in our lives. My dad started coming home on time, and my mom started leaving the house several times, taking the long taxi-and-streetcar trip to the excitement of downtown Denver.

"Today I'm going to get some watercolors and paper at Meininger's art store, so I can start painting again," she would announce to my dad and me at breakfast. Or "I'm going downtown to meet my high school friend Mabel for lunch." Sometimes on the days when she went to the city, she wasn't home when I got off the army bus. I knew that I shouldn't go out to play unless she was there, so I would cuddle up with Tiger, the stray cat we had adopted, or turn the radio to music, so I could dance around the house without anyone watching me.

One Saturday, Mama invited me to come downtown with her. I remember that she had me put on a dress I usually wore only to birthday parties, and she wore her prettiest Copenhagen blue dress and took special care with her make-up. I enjoyed every minute of the taxi ride to Englewood and the streetcar trip to 16th Street in downtown Denver. We went to Meininger's Art Supplies to meet a very nice man. He looked like the artists in my picture book of France, although he was taller and had broader shoulders. He had friendly brown eyes, a tiny moustache above his lip, and black hair.

"You must be Miss Connie. It's a pleasure to meet you."

He gently took my hand, bent down, and brushed it with his lips. I giggled and quickly pulled it away.

"Your mother is a very lovely and artistic lady," he said. "I always enjoy talking to her." He was looking at her, not at me. I imagine my mother smiling and blushing. He said, "I just got some more tubes of that indigo blue that you wanted, Mildred. You might want to go in the storeroom to look over the paint supplies while I wait on another customer. I think you know where everything is." Then in a whisper, he told her: "Take whatever you'd like and find something special for Connie, too."

We walked into a small room lined on one side with shelves full of watercolor and oil-paint tubes. The tubes were arranged according to color, and there were colors I'd never heard of, like burnt sienna and Antwerp blue. On the other wall were tablets and rolls of special paper, brushes of all sizes, charcoal and pastel crayons, and books that showed beginning artists how to sketch and paint.

"Did he really mean that we could take something and not pay for it?"

"Yes, I know he did. Why don't you pick out a sketch pad and some colored pencils. I'll get my indigo paint."

We made our selection and went back to where he was thanking a customer for her purchase.

"Well, now, let me put those supplies in a bag for you. I'd like to see your sketches, Connie, when you come back again."

Mama and I both said "thank you" at the same time. He laughed.

"I'd like to see you, too, Mildred. I hope you can come back during the week. We'll have more time to talk."

My mother smiled, said goodbye, and turned toward the door, towing me behind her. I remember thinking that this man might be the friend she needed to confide in. For the rest of our stay at Fort Logan, there was peace in our house and my mother seemed happier. She continued to go to the big city and the art supply store at least once a week. Maybe this gentleman was one of those men she felt guilty about. Or maybe he was just a friend to talk to.

The unwanted pregnancy and hasty marriage are among my mother's regrets because they resulted in setting her dreams of a career aside. Being thrust into marriage must have made her more cautious about taking risks, both emotional and physical. She didn't want to risk having another child because of the pain of my birth. She was afraid to learn to drive and feared that I would drown if I got near deep water or would be injured if I participated in sports. Even little pleasures, like her love of cats, were pushed aside because she hated the emotional upset and, in turn, the physical discomfort that resulted from their ultimate demise. Does she regret not having engaged more fully in life? Or did she replace taking risks with other interests? More importantly, would she share her view of life with me so I could understand her better and, hopefully, learn more about myself? Sharing dreams, hopes, and feelings is something we've never done. If we could do this, it would bring us much closer together, a childhood desire that has gained momentum in these last years of my mother's life.

As I age, I realize that the things I regret are the things I haven't done. Although I'm an emotional risk taker, I've avoided the excitement of physical risk taking. I live in Colorado but don't ski. I learned to swim but don't enjoy it. I've never done any sports with my family but wish I had when my kids were young. These are mini-regrets. My major regrets—trying to please everyone, not having boundaries, and not expressing my love as often as I'd like to—are ones I've been working on, and I am starting to see results. Oh, yes, and a final regret that's receiving attention right now is not spending enough time on my lifelong passion of writing. Hopefully, at the age of 72, I have some good years left to turn these regrets into joys.

As I walk out the door of my mom's hospital room, my mind is spinning. Instead of finding my way through the maze of corridors by focusing on the footsteps printed on the floor, I'm in a fog trying to sort out the details of the hour I just spent with my mother. It's easy to accept pregnancy before marriage and changes in dates, but the trust involved in telling me the secret about other men has changed our relationship for the better. I'm wondering if she has other secrets or regrets. Should I pursue more of her memories? I wake up to the fact that I'm lost when I come to a locked door with a flashing red light: "No admission. Clearance required." I shake the fog from my head and follow the black footprints back. They are a reminder of the ones in my dad's old Arthur Murray dance book. Finally I come to the exit and the parking lot. A deep breath of crisp April air and the warmth of the sunshine revive me. I'm happy to be back in the present, not rummaging in the past.

Floyd is surprised when I share my mom's revelations with him.

"I can't believe she slept with other men," he says.

Missy has a different reaction when I call to tell her.

"Hey, Mom, if you're hiding any secrets, please tell them to me now. Don't wait until you're in a nursing home."

Fortunately or unfortunately, I can't think of any secrets to reveal.

CHAPTER 6

ENOUGH ALREADY

"MY GOD, WHAT'S THAT?" I MUTTER.

In the chair that blocks my way into my mom's room, a plastic, suntanned leg is suggestively pointing its pink, sock-covered toes at the ceiling. It's actually a pleasant change from the dull view that usually greets me at the door. I sneak a peek at my mom, dozing on top of the blue bedspread, glasses slipped down to the tip of her nose, and her blue-flowered blouse pulled out of the gaping waist of her skirt. She's lost weight, I think, from her usual 105 pounds. Instead of waking her, I take this once-in-a-lifetime opportunity to examine a prosthetic leg. I start at the top, feeling the clump of toes under the sock before running my hand over the slightly nicked surface of the calf, and then proceeding to the smooth, un-muscled thigh. I'm surprised by its lightness as I lift it off the chair.

"Would you get rid of that horrible thing, Connie?"

My mom's voice startles me. I fumble with the leg, almost dropping it. Then I lean it carefully, right-side up, between the two small chests of drawers on the opposite wall.

Mama is struggling to push herself to a sitting position on the bed without using her broken leg in its black Velcro thigh brace. I offer to help, but she shakes her head, pushes her glasses up on her nose, clears her throat, and issues a command.

"Do *not* set it there. Put it on the other bed. It belongs to Phyllis. I don't know why they put her in my room. This place is such a mess."

Evidently Phyllis, a fifty-some-year-old amputee, will be sharing the room with my mother while she has therapy to adapt to her secondhand prosthesis. She told my mom that she was homeless until recently when she was taken in by her new boyfriend, a man in a wheelchair who lives in a motel on Santa Fe Drive.

"Where is she now?" I ask.

"She's probably down the hallway in her wheelchair. Hopefully, she won't be here long. She told Cynthia that I'm not friendly. I guess she doesn't like me." She pauses, shakes her head, and mutters under her breath: "I don't like me, either."

My back is turned as I put the leg on Phyllis's bed, so I'm not sure I heard her right. Is she referring to the secrets she told me in the hospital or just saying she doesn't like the condition she's in, broken leg and all? It has been a week since she returned to Ivy Manor, and she has never spoken about her hospital confession.

"What is it you don't like, Mama?

"Oh, never mind. My life just seems worthless. What have I done with all these years? I just don't know."

This is a surprise. I've never heard my mother reflect on her life, except in her hospital confession.

"I think you've achieved many things in your life. You graduated from college with honors, you're creative, you...."

"Forget it, Connie. I don't want to talk about it. Did you bring me the cushion I wanted for that chair?"

Before I reach for the pillow in my bag, I tell her I'd like to talk some more about her life. I put the flowered cushion in the visitor's chair and lift the chair up so my mom can see it. She scrutinizes it carefully and shakes her head.

"It's a nice color, but I don't think it will work. It's too thick to sit on."

I ignore the comment, sink down in the chair, and wiggle around a bit to demonstrate how comfy it is.

Mama has turned away from me and is concentrating on her fingernails, rubbing them back and forth over the bedcover. "You need to cut my nails again. They catch on the spread. You didn't file them down last time."

Whoops! Something else I didn't do. My good humor is slipping through my fingers. The back of my neck is tightening, and the twitch in my eyelid returns. I wish she would join the group of women for their weekly manicures, but "I don't want Raheen trying to cut my nails, and I don't want that ugly red polish," she has told me before. So the task falls to me. It's not one I mind carrying out because it gives me permission to hold her hands, touch her, and have a physical connection, an action she usually shrinks from. What I don't like is fulfilling orders when I've just arrived for a visit.

"Let's take first things first, Mama. I'll do that after you have your lunch. Let me empty the bag."

She nods okay.

"I have some special things for you today to celebrate your return from the hospital. Some broiled salmon, a piece of the cake you like, some new watercolor paper, and a picture book of ships that you can paint."

"I don't want anything but the cake—without the frosting. Did you forget my Lactaid?"

"A loaf of bread, a glass of Lactaid, and thou," I joke. "You're hooked on it, and since Ivy Manor can't keep it in stock, I'm your drug dealer."

Mama looks up at me, perplexed. "What are you talking about?"

"Just trying to be funny. Never mind."

Like many of my efforts to raise my mom's spirits, today's goody bag is descending into failure while my frustration is quickly ascending. I try to rub the twitch away, take a deep breath, and move the tray table near the bed.

"Can I help you swing your legs over, so you can sit up at the table?"

She opens her hands in my direction, as if to say *duh*. "There's no way I can do that. Don't you remember that I broke my leg?"

A bug bite of sarcasm. Yes, I do remember the broken leg, and I remember canceling my trip to Belgium, and I remember all the failed times I've tried to please her. The swarm of failures engulfs me. I mimic her open-hands gesture, look toward the ceiling, and step back from the table. My voice slices through her deafness with a hiss.

"Mama! Enough is enough already. I don't need any more criticism."

She touches the ear with the hearing aid and looks up at me. Her jaw has dropped, and she's squinting through her glasses. My eyes are welling with tears and my hands are clenched. I start to back away from the bed to the door.

"What? What was that?"

The disbelief in her voice makes me turn around and take a step toward her. My eyes meet hers in a steady gaze. Her hands are pressed to her lips.

"I've just had it with the criticism. This is too much. I try so hard to take care of you, to bring you what you want, to make you happy, but all you have for me is constant criticism and not even a thank you."

There. I've said it. An economy of words but ones that sum up my feelings. This is one of the few times in my memory I have confronted her. Maybe this rehearsal will make it easier in the future. I relax my shoulders and stretch out my fingers. Mama has scooted down on the bed and pulled a corner of the top pillow over her cheek. She's sniffling and reaching for the Kleenex box. This confrontation will increase her stomach pain and make her sick, an expected reaction. I don't regret my words, but I don't want her to suffer more because of them. I move close to the bed and put a hand on her shoulder.

"I'm sorry to upset you, but I need to let you know how I feel."

She takes off her glasses and dabs her eyes with the Kleenex.

"Oh, Connie, I don't know what I'd do without you. I *am* thankful. I'm sorry that I'm so grumpy and complaining. It's so hard to be here—in this place."

Her words surprise me. Such a quick reversal from demands to apology and gratitude. If it's this easy to tell her how I feel, why haven't I defended myself before? It's that old childhood fear of not being liked, not being loved, or, in one case I vividly remember, a fear of being beaten up. That eighth grade memory flashes through my mind. I'm being pinned up against my locker by Genevieve Garcia, her fist under my chin and her tattooed arm pushing on my shoulder. Her best friend had just lost the class presidency by seven votes—to me.

"You're too good, bitch! I wanna hear you say some dirty words."

I turn my head away. "I'm not mad at you," I whisper. "Why are you mad at me?"

"Mad? Shit. What are you scared of? Me needing to teach you bad words?" She hisses between her teeth. "Talk, damn it, talk."

"Shit. Damn. Fuck ... fuck you!" I repeat in a whisper.

She laughs and lets me go. "I'll see you tomorrow, shithead."

I straighten up from leaning over the bed and pull myself up to my full height, five feet two inches at last measure. It's as if a clean, cool breeze has swept through the room, even though the only window is stuck shut. I've confronted my mom and nothing terrible has happened. No collateral damage to me but some to her tormented bowels, for which I'm sorry. But if I don't defend myself now, I'll never do it. We'll see if there's a lasting effect.

Mama stops rubbing her tummy, and, in a small voice, says, "I think I need something to drink now. Please."

I refill her water glass and offer it to her. She reaches to take it, with a "thank you," but the third finger of her arthritic right hand pops back an inch making it impossible to grasp the glass. I take back the glass while she massages her hand. I've noticed the beginning of the same finger quirk in my own hand. I hurt along with her as I struggle to accept the infirmities of aging.

"Just put it on the table where I can reach it later, Connie. I need to close my eyes and rest for a while. Will you come back tomorrow?"

I take the glass, place it on the table, and learn over to kiss her forehead.

"I'll always be here when you need me, Mama, but I have needs, too. I have to catch up at work, but I'll come the day after tomorrow."

She nods and closes her eyes. A single tear is drying on her cheek. Her right hand continues to massage the cramps in her stomach.

CHAPTER 7

LIFE STORIES

CATCHING UP AT WORK MEANS DIVING INTO THE PICTURE PUZZLE OF scheduling instructors, classrooms, and six levels and multiple sections of students for the winter term, keeping in mind the instructor requests for specific classes and subjects they would prefer to teach. I push back from the computer to shuffle through a manila file of teacher requests. Under the instructor forms, I discover a paper-clipped stack of in-class compositions that I should have graded yesterday, so final grades can be tallied this morning. These essays, usually a pleasure to savor, are now a hasty priority.

I glance through the pages to see what the sixteen students have chosen to write about the topic "A Major Turning Point in Your Life." Most have detailed the changes in their lives when they came to the U.S. Natasha, a Russian woman who met her American fiancé on the sexy Russian Desire website, confesses: "Husband is not important to me, but is turning point for my son, who will get a good education in America." Tareq, an air force officer from Kuwait, tells about the first time he had "flown his plane against an enemy." "The US troops rescued us. Their strength made me want to train in America." The only immigrant in the group is Anh, a Vietnamese woman improving her English to enter a nursing program. "I was only three when my parents had to leave Vietnam in 1974," she explains. "They made turning point and saved my life and my brother. I am lucky for school here. They are sad because they miss home and language and good job." Each student has a unique and moving story.

Perusing the student essays makes me pause to consider the secrets my mother revealed to me several weeks ago. These are just a few threads of a larger narrative that she might enjoy telling me. Searching her mind for turning points in her life could show her that the years she has lived are worthwhile. I can benefit from her life stories, too. As I've lived through the ups and downs of caregiving, I've been journaling, writing some poetry, and composing scenes that I don't want to forget. As a child who didn't have siblings to talk to, I always wrote my anger, happiness, and sadness on the lined pages of a red Big Chief tablet and later in a diary that my mom unlocked and read. Rereading my entries helped me to see where I was stuck in my life, where I didn't want to go, and what possibilities were out there in the future. It was good therapy.

Now my journals are hardcover composition books that I fill with entries about the difficulties of caregiving, notes about insightful moments in my relationship with my mom, a few poems about the characters who inhabit Ivy Manor, and thoughts about the imbalance in my life. I've left many pages blank, hoping they will be filled with more details about my mother's childhood, the happy and sad times in her life, her marriage, her regrets, and her achievements. I also wonder if my mother remembers times that she hurt me and times that she helped me. Basically, I'd like to understand her better. Those pages can be filled if she will agree to help me write the story of her life. I'll be the facilitator, and she'll be the narrator, the one in control of her own story.

The accomplishment of work tasks has calmed my stress and prepared me to introduce the idea of the writing project to my mother. On the following day, I go to Ivy Manor with an old photo album that I retrieved when I cleaned out my parents' apartment. Interesting photos have always been the trigger for writing ideas in my ESL textbooks. Maybe this photo will hook Mama into a story.

After joining my dad at lunch to share bites of the lemon meringue pie I've brought him, I wheel him back to his room for naptime. Mama wasn't at the lunch table because she's on a tea-and-toast diet today for her stomach problems, a possible result of the confrontation we had two days ago. Olivia has helped her to sit upright at the tray table with an extra pillow behind her back. She looks half-ready for bed in a blue button-down duster and slipper socks. Everything about her is droopy today: hair that needs a shampoo, cheeks that are sallow and concave, and dry, turned-down lips. This may not be the best time to introduce my idea of writing her life story. She manages a half smile when she sees me, prefacing the list of her complaints with a much appreciated "I'm so glad you came."

I sit where she can see me over the tray table.

"I'll visit with you while you drink your tea, Mama."

Her only response is the measured sips she takes from the cup on the tray.

"I have an idea that you might like. You've told me some interesting things about your life, but I'd like to know more about your parents and your childhood and all the contests you won. I think your memories would make a good story or even a book. What do you think?"

She puts down the cup and looks across the table at me, blinking to clear her eyes. I can hear the crack in her neck bones as she tries to move her head side to side to emphasize a phrase I hear more often these days. "I don't know, Connie. I just don't know. Life is too hard."

"I know it's difficult right now, Mama, but you have a story that your grandchildren and future great-grandchildren would enjoy reading."

She puts aside the cup, places her hands one on top of the other, and looks down at them.

"I can't write much with this crazy finger," she says as she rubs the ring finger on her right hand.

"You can talk and I'll do the writing. We'll just spend ten or fifteen minutes whenever you feel like reminiscing. Okay?"

She looks up at me and pauses for what seems like several minutes. After a deep breath, she measures her words into phrases. "Maybe that would work. You'll let me read what you write, so I can check it out, won't you?"

I reassure her that she'll have the final say with permission to correct my version of what she tells me. Control has always been essential to her and even more now, when she can't control her bowels, her bladder, her arthritic fingers, the assignment of roommates, or almost anything in her life. This is the time to record her stories— while she still has her sharp memory for details. Her mind will never be as blank as my father's, but surely it will dull as her body weakens in these last years. I reach over and give a few pats to her bare arm. Too many touches, I know, and she'll pull away.

"You're not feeling well today, Mama, so let's wait to begin your story until you're better. I found a photo of you as a little girl. You might think about that time in your life, so we can write about it. It was in an album I saved from your apartment."

I hand her the square, black-and-white photo of a six-year-old, tow-headed Millie (her nickname) in a long-sleeve dress with a bib collar. She's wearing light-colored stockings and shoes and affectionately tugging her Mama's elbow close to her cocked head as she smiles at the camera. Her mother's face is obscured by a shadow, but one can see her heavy, dark hair, twisted into several rolls around her face, above a dark, V-neck dress. She's pointing at a low, wide sign in front of them: "Don't pick flowers or fruit. Don't tie horses to trees. Please." Next to Millie's mother is Papa, about the same short height as Mama, looking very formal, dark hair parted in the middle, sporting a bow-tie, a light-colored shirt and an open suit jacket. Hat in his hand, he's leaning slightly forward on the sign. In the background is a two-story brick building with awnings reaching out from the windows. Penned across the border of the photo is the date, 1917.

"What's this?" She hesitantly takes the photo and holds it close to her eyes. Her glasses are in the empty Kleenex box where she stores important items.

"Oh, my goodness, this is Eben Ezer. I remember that dress. It was pale yellow, and Mama was wearing navy blue with her mother's gold pin at the neck. There's Papa with that old brown hat. What a wonderful time that was!"

Her positive reaction brings a smile to my lips and, as usual, tears to my eyes, a salty mix of joy and sadness. In spite of her aching stomach, she's excited. The photo has worked. We haven't done a project together since I was in junior high school, when she couldn't resist adding those finishing touches that would bring me an A. This time the goal isn't a high grade but a closer relationship as we work together on her life story and, I would guess, a better understanding of my own life as it relates to hers.

"Put the album in the bottom drawer of my dresser," she says, "so we can look at it tomorrow. I'll write down something for you after my nap today. I don't have the energy right now." After a short visit, I take my leave, pleased.

She is ready for me when I sit down with her the next day. She hands me a pink note card and two lined stationery pages full of descriptions of Eben Ezer, the TB sanatorium in Brush, Colorado. When I glance through the notes, I'm astounded at her memory of colors, smells, and names. I've inherited some of this detailed memory, but it doesn't equal hers.

She still looks pale but has combed her hair today, put on her glasses, and turned up her hearing aid. The paisley skirt, blue blouse, and green slipper socks provide some color against the washed-out blue of the bedcover. The Velcro brace was removed from her leg this morning during a therapy session in which she used the walker. Propped up in her usual position on the bed, she launches into her childhood story.

"I started remembering things about Mama's tuberculosis, Minnesota, and the trip to Brush. Some of it's there in my notes, but I need to tell you more. Where do you want to begin?"

I settle into the cushioned chair and fish my notebook and pen out of the bag, ready to begin my role as ghostwriter. "I don't know much about your early childhood in Minnesota. Why don't you start there?"

She closes her eyes and unbuttons the top of her skirt, so she can fold her hands under the belt and over her stomach while she talks. She tells me about her grandmother, Maren Olson, a Norwegian immigrant, who contracted tuberculosis and died in Cedar Falls, Iowa, at the age of forty-seven, leaving her only daughter, Bettie, who was twenty-two, to remain with her father and older brother. The deadly disease spread to Bettie but wasn't diagnosed until after she had married Danish immigrant Jens Grondahl and had given birth to my mother. When my mom was three years old, Bettie was sent to a sanatorium near Lyle, Minnesota, where the family moved so that they could be near her. But her TB, fueled by the Minnesota cold and dampness, continued to progress.

I pause in my note taking to consider the impact that TB had on three generations of women, my great-grandmother, my grandmother, and my mother. My mother developed some faint scars on her lungs but never had an active case of TB. Even so, the disease changed her life. I can see now that my mother's fear of illness and her focus on bodily functions, both hers and mine when I was a child, must have stemmed from living under the threat of TB for more than half her life. This insight is put aside as Mama gains momentum in her story.

"The doctor in Minnesota said mama would die if she didn't go west to a higher and dryer climate. That's how we ended up in Colorado. I was only five years old when she left all by herself on the train to the Danish Lutheran sanatorium in Brush. I didn't understand why we couldn't go with her, but Papa said there was no work there and told me she would be back in a year. I remember saying goodbye to her at the train station in Lyle. She was crying, and all she could do was pat me on the head. We couldn't kiss or even hug because of the TB. She always had to hold a white handkerchief over her mouth."

"Reason for aversion to hugging and kissing?" I scribble next to the details I'm recording in my notebook.

Mama puts her hand up to her mouth and is quiet for a minute. It's my guess that she's considering the empty spot in her life when her mother left. In fact, judging from all the restrictions TB imposed on the family, she must have missed the kind of care that healthy mothers could give their children. My perspective of my mother is becoming more objective as I drop the day-by-day baggage of my efforts to meet her demands at Ivy Manor. I'm more the reporter now, not the daughter, asking questions of an interesting person and looking for the lead for my assigned story. Mama hugs herself with her arms folded across her chest.

"Goodness sakes. She was so sick. I don't know how she ever made the trip by herself."

She closes her eyes, and continues. After six months, the doctors at the sanatorium sent good reports of her mother's progress toward health but cautioned the family not to move her back to the harsh Minnesota climate. The decision was made. Her father sold their few possessions, packed their clothing and other necessities, and bought their train tickets for Colorado.

"I was so excited. I was going to see Mama. I was going to take a train. I was also a little scared, because my friends Lloyd and Katherine told me there were coyotes and rattlesnakes everywhere in Colorado."

She recalls keeping her face pressed against the train window looking for wild animals while Papa Jens despaired of the lack of trees and grass as they crossed the dry prairie of Nebraska. My guess is that he always missed the lush greenery of Denmark. He'd left in 1908 at the age of 24 when a schoolmate, Sigurd Kaer, wrote to him about the wonderful opportunities in America and encouraged him to farm with him in Cedar Falls, Iowa. When I think about how hard it is for the foreign students I work with to temporarily adjust to American culture, I realize how difficult it must have been for my grandfather, even though he settled in a heavily Scandinavian community. He didn't speak English and probably realized he would never see his family again. Although he had been well educated in Denmark, he worked at physically taxing jobs in Minnesota: unloading coal, bailing hay, delivering furniture, and any other task that would provide some income.

Mama rubs her left eye, trying to get the lid to open wider.

"Would you put some drops in it, Connie?"

I hold the lid open and squeeze in a few drops of lubricant. Then she dabs the eye with a Kleenex.

"We can do this tomorrow, mama. I know you're tired now."

"No, while I'm thinking about it, I want to tell you a little bit more. I can see in my mind just what it all looked like."

She easily retrieves the visual details from her memory bank and smiles at the memory of seeing her mother for the first time in more than a year.

"When I got off the train in Brush with Papa, I couldn't see her anywhere. I worried that she was too sick to come. Then I saw two strange women in long, black dresses and little white capes. They had these funny white pleated caps tied under their chins in big bows and there were white crosses around their necks. It was Sister Sine and Sister Ingeborg, two women I'll never forget. Then I saw this short, smiling woman in a navy-blue dress and coat. It was my mother, but she looked so different, so healthy. I started to cry when she said, 'Here I am, Millie.' That was her special name for me."

"Having your mother back must have been a turning point in your life," I interject. I'm hoping for some introspection about the reunion, but instead she raises one eyebrow and gives me a sidelong glance.

"Well, I don't care about turning points. I just know I was happy. I guess I hoped she would pick me up or hug me, but then I remembered the TB restrictions and just hid my face in her skirt." She looks at the old photo again and puts her finger on the sign over the entrance. "I remember it so well. As we drove up to the gate in the horse cart, Sister Sine put her arms around me and told me I would be special because I was the only child at Eben Ezer."

"Inside the gate, it was like a fairy tale. The grass was turning green, and the mulberry and linden trees were just leafing out. There were all kinds of flowers: tulips, daffodils, and crocus. Oh, yes, and a pretty white gazebo. I can see all those colors in my mind. I'd like to try painting the gazebo when I feel better."

She reaches over to the old tissue box she has outfitted with her paints and brushes, just to check that they're ready and waiting. Being able to touch the tools she needs seems to comfort her. Her optimism at wanting to continue painting in spite of the crooked fingers and the droopy eyelids makes me appreciate her determination. I sense that she's feeling real joy in taking me along on her journey through this happy childhood memory. Although her voice is softer now and she's a bit hoarse, she continues.

"I remember the kitchen so well. The patients' meals were served in Bethesda, where Sister Ingeborg did all the cooking, baking, and canning for the residents. In a pantry off the kitchen were hundreds of jars of canned rhubarb, gooseberries, and other fruits and vegetables from the gardens. I loved the smell of the brown bread baking in the oven, and I'll never forget that little elevator that carried food upstairs to the dining room."

Evidently she was fascinated by the dumbwaiter with its rope pulleys. I can see that Sister Ingeborg was like a second mother to her, one who gave her special privileges.

"She let me help her pull on the rope that sent the trays upstairs, and she always gave me a cookie from the dessert tray. It was our little secret."

She scoots up higher on the pillows and takes a few sips of water. I don't want to dilute the "happy" in her memory, but I wonder what effect the atmosphere of illness and death may have had on her. After all, she was only a child.

"Was it difficult to be around so many sick people, Mama?"

"Well, there were lots of rules. Papa and I weren't allowed to go into any of the rooms in the hospital building, where Mama was when she was contagious. Everyone had to take afternoon naps in the wooden tents with the canvas flaps open, so sunshine would make them healthy. I remember seeing patients in the gardens carrying a little flask that they had to spit into when they coughed because using a handkerchief might spread the TB germs. In fact, if anyone used a handkerchief, they were told to burn it before it dried. To kill the germs, I guess. I know some patients died because I heard their names in the Sunday service in the chapel. I remember Mama checking to see if my hands were washed and my bowels were regular. That was a very important."

Now I get it. That must be where my mother's appreciation of enemas originated. When I was just a toddler she would threaten me with an enema when I didn't produce the right quality and quantity of "little fishies," as she called them. I'll never forget the wooden potty chair in the dark, damp bathroom of our first house in Longmont. Although it had a decal of a smiling bear on the back, the tight arms and the brown leather strap turned the chair into a trap and a test of my ability to please my mother. Hanging next to the potty was a red bulb syringe with a black nozzle, the punishment for constipation. Every day after breakfast, Mama made me sit in the chair with the admonishment of "Do your best, but don't take too long." I would grunt and groan for what seemed like fifteen minutes. Then I'd look in the bowl. If I had produced quality "fishies," I could breathe a sigh of relief. If instead, the result was a hard brown lump, I would sneak one of the hairpins from the cupboard next to the toilet, cut up the obstinate "fishie" into a small school of amphibians, and arrange them into a pleasing pattern in the white ceramic pot. I would sit back down and shout, "I'm done, Mama. Come and see." She would wipe my bottom and remove the bowl for a look. "Good job, Connie, no enema today" was like an announcement that I had won the lottery. It was also the beginning of a bit of trickery that was useful in the future.

When I stop taking notes, I look over at Mama. Her eyes are closed. Her mouth is open, showing the missing front tooth, but her lips are turned up in a half-smile. She's snoring softly. My guess is that she's back in the sanatorium reliving that happy time with her mother and all the attention she received from the sisters. Lately, she has been living more in her daydreams than in the reality of daily life. Part of this is the decline of her physical body, but her mind is as strong as ever. I need to capture her memories while I can. Exploring her life is starting to open up a review of my own life, providing insight into who and why I am. It's like watching a movie I've seen many times before and suddenly having an a-ha moment the third go-round.

I gather up the notes I've taken and pull up the patchwork quilt from the end of the bed to cover her as she sleeps. I slip quietly out of the room. As I walk down the hallway to check on my dad, I think about my mom's experience with TB and the strong influence that this life-threatening disease had on the generations of women in my family. My forebears were women who had to be isolated from their families, women whose daughters learned to fear illness and adapt their lives to prevent it. My own mother learned all the previous lessons plus the skill of using sickness as a way of controlling those around her. As a fourth-generation daughter, I need to consider this legacy and how it has affected me and my daughters.

Chapter 8

Back Together Again

It's two in the morning. Floyd and I are sleeping soundly in our upstairs bedroom. A squeaky, metallic noise wakes me slightly. I turn over to face the side of the bed and pull up the covers, ignoring the sound. It's probably just the cats having their nightly romp, I think, because we forgot to close the bedroom door tonight. I doze off again until I feel the covers being pulled off my shoulders. I look up and see the blur of a figure standing over me. Before I can move, my legs are pinned down. Someone is sitting on them and a cold hand is pressing on my outstretched arm.

"My god, who is this?"

I check to see if Floyd is still on his side of the bed. His rumbly snore confirms that he is. I pull away my leg and kick at the dark form that is starting to put a leg up on the bed. Then I recognize the night visitor. It's Floyd's father, teetering on the edge of the bed, trying to get his balance. "Whoops!" he says. I grab a handful of his flannel pajama bottoms and tug him back onto the bed. Floyd jumps up, disoriented and ready to fight the intruder. His dad is settling back into my side of the bed when Floyd realizes who it is. He comes around the bed and helps his father stand up beside his squeaky walker and leads him back to his bedroom across the hall. My fear quickly dissolves into laughter. Even dementia has its moments.

This is Sunday of a weekend caring for Floyd's 90-year-old father, who has Alzheimers but, unlike my father, is not relegated to a nursing home. He lives with Floyd's brother, Forrest, and his wife Ginger, so we try to give them a break from their round-the-clock attention to his needs by inviting him to our house two weekends each month. He recognizes family members, but he continues to ask about his wife Harriet, who also lived with Forrest and Ginger before she died of cancer a year ago. Adjusting to our house is difficult because he doesn't remember where he is after a two-week absence.

I'm still chuckling the next day as Floyd and I walk through Ivy Manor's automatic doors to attend a quarterly care-conference for both of my parents. We take the elevator to the second floor to sit at lunch with my parents before the conference, and I think how much better it would be for my dad if he could have a situation like Floyd's father. If he lived with us, he could enjoy our garden, pet our cats and our basset hound, be surrounded by people who love him, and have Floyd, someone he's always liked, as part of his life. Reality sets in when the elevator door opens. Living with us is impossible because of the limitations of our house, because of his wheelchair, his bathing needs, his incontinence, and, of course, the fact that I'm still working.

Floyd hurries down to my dad's room to wheel his chair to the dining room, and I go to the opposite hallway to retrieve my mother. She is already navigating the hall in her walker, with the striped bag full of snacks in case lunch is unpalatable. When she sees me, she stops and lifts the black shades attached to her glasses. "You're later than usual, aren't you?"

I ignore the mild scolding and explain that Floyd and I have a conference. She nods and we walk together in slow motion to their assigned table. I start to pull out one of the four chairs for her, but she stops me.

"Don't give me that chair, Connie. It's wobbly and they haven't replaced it even though I told them it was broken."

When I press down on the back of the chair, one of the back legs wobbles and creaks. I can imagine the rickety chair toppling over and throwing a resident to the floor, an invitation to a broken hip. I sometimes ignore Ivy Manor's failings out of sheer frustration at the difficulty of correcting them, but not this time. Lack of maintenance is added to my list of concerns for the care conference. I push the wobbly chair next to the wall and pull out a different one from the table for my mother just in time for Floyd to push my dad's wheelchair into the empty space. Floyd and I sit down in the two remaining chairs designated for the tardy table mates, Gladys and Francis.

"Hi, Daddy. It's nice to have all four of us together at the table."

He has a confused look in his eyes when he surveys the group, and one corner of his mouth is turned down. I notice that bits of fuzz from his blanket are stuck to his unshaven cheeks and his hair is uncombed. Evidently he hasn't been shaved today, and his face probably wasn't washed. My vision of a happy family has been replaced by anger at the caregivers and guilt at not advocating strongly enough for my dad's care. I've been ignoring his needs while attending to my mom's.

"Four? Who's here?" he asks.

With a sinking feeling, I run through the cast of characters at the table, pointing to each one.

"There's Floyd, my husband. Mildred, your wife, and my mother. And," putting my hand on my chest, I say with emphasis, "me, your daughter."

I instantly regret defining "Mildred" with two relationships—wife and mother. I can't get out of the habit of trying to help him understand who we are and how we're related. He stares at Mama and narrows his eyes to see her better.

After arranging the blue bib on her lap, my mother takes off her glasses for a minute and looks over at him. "Hello, Jim. How are you?"

He blinks a few times but doesn't respond, busying himself with his meal-time routine. He fingers the bottom of the blue terry cloth bib that Floyd has tied around his neck, puts the spork in the brown plastic coffee cup, and fumbles with the two plastic glasses, placing them awkwardly in front of him.

Mama sighs, puts on her glasses, and adjusts her walker by folding one side in close to her knee.

His pre-lunch routine finished, Daddy looks up at her again and responds to her previous greeting. "I'm okay, I guess." He keeps his eyes on her face, tipping his head to the side.

Gladys comes shuffling up to the table, dragging her oxygen tube behind her. I give her my chair and help her get seated. Floyd gets up, so there will be a place for Francis, who's just coming into the room in her wheelchair. My mother greets Gladys and hands her a bib. My dad doesn't acknowledge any of the changes at the table but continues to look at my mother. Floyd and I spend a few minutes chatting with my mom and her table mates. Daddy has stopped fumbling with his table setting and is staring at Mama. The aids pull the food service cart up to our table.

"We need to let you get on with lunch," I explain, "and it's almost time for our care conference."

"Will you be back after the conference?" my mom asks.

I reassure her that we'll return, give her a quick kiss on the forehead, and head around the table to my dad. As I start to kiss him on the cheek, he puts his hand on my arm. This is the first time in years that he has reached out to touch me. I respond with an arm around his shoulders. I can feel the warmth of his body and a slight tremor from his hands to his arms. He moves his normally bowed head to look up at me.

"Thanks for bringing my wife back to me," he says. "It's been a long time."

I can taste the sweetness of this lucid moment and the hope of a loving relationship between my parents. I glance at my mother who is busy looking for a pudding cup in the bag of her walker. She hasn't heard my dad. I wish that he would repeat those words loudly, so she would know that he cares. The tears that well up in my eyes are for both the hope that my parents will re-connect with each other and for the larger possibility that it's too late. Always embarrassed by the attention tears bring, I give my dad a hasty peck on the cheek and head for the door with Floyd behind me. He grabs my hand, and I know he shares my feelings.

It's difficult to leave the sentiment of our lunch meeting behind to face the stark reality of our purpose in being at Ivy Manor today: to speak for my father, who cannot speak for himself, and to support my mother's welfare. When I think about it, this isn't an unusual role for me. I've had lots of experience being an advocate. In my professional life, I enjoy supporting faculty and staff members who have suggestions and ideas for our programs. When the case is a sound one, I champion the cause of a failing student who's slated for dismissal but has the potential to succeed, the new instructor who has potential but weak evaluations, racial and ethnic minorities, the homeless, abused animals, the person who's losing an argument: "But what about her side of the story...." Effective advocacy requires empathy, a response that must have been fine-tuned by my relationship with my mother but an attitude that is not always beneficial to a relationship. I frustrate my husband when he states a strong opinion and, rather than hearing what he says, I quickly contradict it and present the other side. Even simple circumstances can develop into an I'm-right-you're-wrong scenario. For example, "That stupid driver is tailgating me," is answered with "Yes, but he sees you going thirty miles an hour in a forty-mile zone." An occasional comment from a friend or colleague, "You're always supporting the underdog," is a warning sign that I've carried empathy too far.

To be fair, I need to champion my mother's good qualities. I often become frustrated at her self-centeredness, but I recognize that she has been my advocate, too. She encouraged every shred of childhood talent I had, partly because she enjoyed living her dreams through me but also because she cared about me. She pushed me to enter school competitions from third grade on. I still have the six-inch-thick scrapbook she created to record newspaper articles and photos from the *Denver Post* and *Rocky Mountain News*. The scrapbook begins with a ten-year-old me dressed as the Lady of the Lake in an altered Goodwill gown: "Fairmont Schoolgirl Wins Book Week Competition." Mama grilled me on spelling words to prepare for the state spelling bee; enhanced class projects by "helping" with fancy posters she outlined and I colored; encouraged me to enter a radio Quiz Kids contest; and started a 4-H Club to help me socialize with other kids, give me opportunities to win blue ribbons and trips to Chicago and Washington, D.C., be crowned Denver 4-H Queen, and ultimately win a scholarship to college. She called the local papers when some neighbor kids and I wanted to turn an unused fire station on our block into a teen canteen. A photographer took our picture, with me standing on the hands of my buddies, peering into the dusty window. We didn't get the firehouse, but the need was recognized and resulted in use of another building.

My mother wasn't alone in her cheerleading. When I showed interest in playing the marimba, my dad built one with used pieces from a music store and spent the little cash he had on lessons. He encouraged baton twirling lessons so that I could perform for special events and lead the high school marching band. He always applauded the results of my efforts and backed up my mother as part of a pact they had agreed to when I was eleven years old. Not knowing she was pregnant, my mom suffered a traumatic miscarriage. This led her to talk to the doctor about not having more children. My dad went along with her in the decision. Instead of enlarging the family, they agreed to "just put all our efforts into Connie," as my mother recently put it. Like most kids, I didn't fully appreciate their efforts at the time, but, achievement by achievement, I grew to like the spotlight and to set goals for myself, without my mom's efforts. Being forced out of my quiet, only-child shell helped me to develop confidence and leadership skills and encouraged me to take the risks of competition—because I just might come out on top. It's important for me to repay my parents' support and encouragement during my childhood with the best care and attention that I can offer them in the last years of their lives.

In that spirit, I put on my advocacy hat, and Floyd and I take the Ivy Manor elevator down to the quarterly care-conference. This meeting marks the third anniversary of my dad's life at Ivy Manor and two years for my mom. The small conference room barely allows space for the chairs placed around the slightly dented mahogany table. I sit down at the foot of the table with Activities Coordinator Raheen on my right and Social Worker Sandy on my left. Jessie, the new head nurse, is ensconced at the head with a heavy-duty grey binder open in front of her. Her red hair is pulled into a knot at the back of her head, emphasizing her no-nonsense, professional authority. Floyd is squeezed in behind me to observe the proceedings, hoping he won't have to participate. He's had enough this year with the death of his mother and his own father's increasing dementia.

Jessie begins the meeting with a thump of her clipboard on the table.

"Thank you for coming today, Mr. and Mrs. Schuman."

"It's Shoemaker," I respond. "I think this is the first time we've met."

"Oh, yes, yes. Shoemaker. Sorry. Anyway, let's get down to brass tacks here. First, your mother, Mildred, seems to be holding steady health-wise."

She quickly reports on my mom's weight, blood pressure, oxygen levels, and catheter, with a brief comment on her poor diet. I've slipped into mentally replaying my dad's recognition of my mother at lunch and not paying attention to Jessie's rapid summary of my mom's stats. I wake up when Raheen suggests that my mother needs "the social life" that she would gain by participating in chair exercise, crafts, and other activities. I remind her that my mother isn't a very social person but enjoys her own activities of painting, writing letters, and studying geography and Danish in her room. I'm fully aware when Jessie begins my father's report. Armed with some real concerns, I try to be patient as we go through a printed set of questions regarding his thickened liquid and pureed food diet, the steady progression of his dementia, and affirmation of the no-resuscitation directive that both of my parents signed many years ago at the senior clinic.

"Do you have any questions, Mrs. Shoemaker?" Jessie asks.

I move my chair closer and lean forward with my folded hands on the table.

"I don't have questions, but I do have some complaints."

A deep breath puffs out of my mouth—the cloud of complaints that I've stored up during the past few months.

"I'm tired of seeing my father's cleanliness neglected just because he can't care for himself. He needs to have someone assist him in washing his hands before and after meals and after he has had a change of diapers. I replaced the pad in his wheelchair because it had a bad odor, but now it's missing. I checked with the CNAs and laundry and they don't know what happened to it."

The back and forth tapping of Jessie's pen on my father's record book interrupts my list of concerns. She straightens her back and raises her chin.

"I'm sorry about that. The CNAs should be seeing to his personal hygiene each day."

She writes a few words in the book and turns several pages to a new divider. I surprise myself by quickly confronting her.

"Yes, the CNAs do the work, but you're the one responsible for making sure they follow through on instructions. There hasn't been one day when I visited that his hands were clean and his face washed."

My voice quavers and I can feel a rush of blood to my head. Jessie is giving me her full attention for the first time. She's learning forward as if to shrink the distance between the two ends of the table. Her dark eyebrows form a straight line across her brow emphasizing her penetrating stare. The thought of my nice, no confrontational self flits through my head, but I glance at Floyd and he nods his head, half in surprise, and half in support. It's enough to spur me on.

"He needs at least three baths a week and, if possible, when he is particularly dirty, a fourth one. If this is an extra service, I'd be happy to pay."

I know this is an insult to their claim that "we care for all the residents' needs."

In chorus, Jessie and Raheen chime in, "Oh, no, that isn't something you'd have to pay for. It's part of the care at Ivy Manor."

"Yes, it should be, but it's not."

I pause for a moment to clear my throat. My mind is replaying a scene from last week. I see my dad slumped in his wheelchair, nose running into the unshaven stubble of his upper lip and trying in vain to wipe it away with his crippled right hand. A spurt of energy strengthens my voice.

"This can't continue. These are simple solutions, like giving him a tissue to blow his nose. I bring Kleenex and hand wipes to him regularly, but they disappear. Also I don't think anyone is helping him to brush his teeth. I asked to have the visiting dentist come four months ago, but nothing has happened."

Jessie remains immobile and silent. My frustration and anger start to spill out in tears that I'm afraid will weaken my protests. Raheen leans over and pats my back. My elbow is on the table and my head is resting on my hand. I need to turn this recitation of complaints around. Maybe an unexpected remark might diffuse the tension and gain support. I lift my head and temple my hands together under my chin.

"Look, guys. I know you're all hard-working and underpaid. I also know that your hearts are in your work and you do your best to care for my mother and father. From my perspective, Ivy Manor has very little support from the parent company, money-wise and management-wise. That's where the problem is. It's not your fault."

Raheen starts to agree but looks quickly at Sandy, who raises her eyebrows. Jessie stares at both of them, makes a few more notes, and slaps shut the notebook.

"We've noted your concerns, Mrs. Shoemaker, and will address them immediately. Thank you for bringing them to our attention." She summarizes my complaints, and apologizes again for the lapses in care.

Then my husband remembers another important question. "What does Jim do when he needs a drink of water? I know that his water has to be thickened, but I've never even seen a pitcher or a cup next to his bed."

It's unusual for him to enter into any conflict, so I welcome his support more than he knows.

"He should be offered water several times a day," Jesse says. "We'll check on that, too." She makes a few notes, gathers up the notebook and the clipboard, a sign from her point of view, that the conference is over. Raheen nods and smiles at me as if to say "It's okay, Connie." My throat is constricted and I'm sweating as I get up from my chair.

Floyd joins me at the door. "You forgot about the broken chair," he says.

"Later," I say, "when we go to maintenance in the basement. I don't want to go back in there now."

I'm drained of energy. I question whether the complaints will change my dad's situation, but at least I've gained experience in confrontation and will use it to fulfill my role as his advocate. It might have been more convincing if my father were able to complain himself, but his dementia closes him off from the day-to-day routine. He is unaware of the missing care he should receive. If today's complaints don't work, I'll continue to the director of Ivy Manor and then, if I get no result, to the corporate management, with a call and a letter. Many residents of Ivy Manor don't have any advocates, nor even any regular visitors. Florence, my mom's newest roommate (the previous one graduated with her prosthesis), has two sons, one in Alaska and one just minutes away from the nursing home. The Alaska son sends regular cards and flowers on holidays, but the son living nearby comes only once a month. When he comes, Florence cries so much she can hardly speak to him.

My dad's needs are different from my mother's. At this point, my mom cares for herself quite well, including changing her own Depends, washing her face, combing her hair, brushing her teeth. She doesn't trust the nurses to give her the correct medication, so she jots down her meds on a note card and delivers it to the nurse's station twice a day. "Mildred's little love notes" are a cause for humor among the nurses, but she has managed to catch a number of mistakes when pills were delivered by new nurses or subs on the weekend.

When we stop by my mother's room to say goodbye, she is standing by her dresser, looking in the top drawer for the *World Almanac*. She locates the book, closes the drawer, and turns her walker toward us. Her eyes are on the floor in front of her, a cautionary measure after the fall that broke her leg.

I knock on the inside of the open door, so we don't surprise her.

She looks up at us and measures her steps to the bed, where she can sit down. "Well, what happened at the conference?"

I haven't had time to sort through the events scattered throughout my mind, but I force myself to give a quick summary. "I guess we did the best we could, but I'm still worried about Daddy's care. It's so frustrating because it takes so long to resolve problems, little things that are just basic needs."

Mama shrugs her shoulders and declares in a louder-than-usual voice, "I suffer every day in this crazy place, Connie. That's just how things are. Accept it."

I'm surprised at her vehemence. Is she angry because I haven't included her in my worries, only my dad? Has she accepted the weaknesses in care at Ivy Manor? No way! Complaints are still part of her daily routine. If I took her advice to just accept it, my parents would no longer have anyone to support their welfare and the lapses in care would continue. Mama has placed the almanac on her bedside table, re-arranged the bed pillows, and managed to get both legs up on the bed, so she can take her after-lunch nap. She whispers "thanks," and Floyd and I say goodbye.

As we go down in the elevator, I rotate my head to relieve the tension in my neck. Floyd greets the other occupant, Joe, an eighty-year-old who always wears an orange Broncos shirt. I don't speak. I just want to get out the door, but a resident in a wheelchair is blocking our way. As I walk up beside her, I see that it's Mabel, a woman I always say hello to but who seldom replies. Her hands are clutching the wheels of her chair and rolling it back and forth a few inches on the wood floor at the edge of the green welcome mat. She's straining forward against the pull of her widow's hump, like a runner waiting for the starting gun. In spite of my rush to get out of Ivy Manor, the nicer part of me decides to speak to her. I take a step forward and bend down so she can see me.

"Hi, Mabel, how are you?"

She turns her head slightly toward me, pain narrowing her eyes. "How d'ya think I am?" She scowls and inches the wheels back and forth again.

"Are you waiting for someone?" I ask.

I can hear her neck crack as she tries to look up at me again. "What the hell does everybody in this place wait for?"

Her bitterness invades my body, rooting me to the floor. I want to move around her, but I'm stuck in place, staring at her bowed head. I want to say "I'm sorry, Mabel," but I can't. What would I be apologizing for? The fact that all life ends in death? That this place is not the best waiting room one can find? That I'm incapable of making it better? That neither my parents nor I could afford a good nursing home? That I'm an only child who's burdened with my parents' needs? I yearn for someone to care for me, to engulf me in his arms and console me, but I would have to ask. And I'm not in the habit. My nose is running, and I lick at the salty tear that has reached the corner of my mouth. I move Mabel's chair back a few inches and walk across the welcome mat to the door. On my way to the car, I recall my mother's bit of advice: "That's just how things are. Accept it." I don't often heed her advice, but there is a note of wisdom here. There are many things I cannot change: the fact that my parents are near the end of their lives and, by the way, that I'm not all that far behind them. I try to see every day of my life as a gift, but because of their situation, each day can bring more pain for them, more loss of control, and more time for me, unfortunately, in a two-star nursing home, battling the substandard conditions that make their final days more difficult. I feel as if I've put in eight hours raking leaves and the wind has just blown them back in my face. My shoulders ache, and my neck is stiff from fighting for the simplest things that my parents require.

CHAPTER 9

ACCEPTANCE

It's 2001. Almost three years' worth of quarterly conferences have come and gone. My father turned ninety-one in January and my mom will be ninety-one in June. Floyd and I have just returned from thirteen days of celebrating our September 11 wedding anniversary — the longest break I've had in these four years of caregiving. The horror of the World Trade Center tragedy on the actual day of our anniversary has blotted out our memories of beaches, volcanoes, warm trade winds, and tropical sunsets. The travel ban delayed our return for four days. I'm happy to be home but feeling a bit apprehensive about my parents' well-being even though Missy has been visiting every other day.

Olivia welcomes me when I step off the elevator at Ivy Manor. She lifts the cuff of her blue scrub to reveal a pink rose just above her ankle.

"What do you think of my new tattoo? I told your mom about it, and she thought I was crazy. I guess tattoos on women weren't common in her day. By the way, she did just fine while you were in Hawaii."

I thank her for the extra attention she has given my mom. In fact, she has become my mom's staunch supporter, her defender, her confidante, and someone who is better than I at tolerating her pickiness and cajoling her into a better mood. Before I left for Hawaii, my mom gave me a full report.

"Olivia worked two shifts yesterday," she said. "She works too hard. I'm afraid she'll burn out so fast that she'll leave Ivy Manor."

Evidently Olivia is trying to make extra money, so she can take time off to study for the registered-nursing exam. Her dream is to become a visiting nurse and take jobs at hospitals in different states. She's never had the chance to travel because she was married at sixteen and had two children. When her children were just six and eight, her husband died, and she raised them as a single mother while studying to be a licensed practical nurse. Several years later, she remarried and had a son who is now an accomplished pianist and a straight-A college student.

She puts a hand on my arm as I turn to go to my mother's room.

"I'm not your dad's nurse now, but I could hear him coughing this morning. Take a good look at him when you visit and talk to Edefina, who's the nurse in that wing."

I hurry down to my dad's new three-bed room at the far end of the north wing. His new roommates, Walter and George, are at lunch, so the room is empty except for my dad. He is slumped in the wheelchair, head on his chest, with a tray table in front of him. A Sippy cup of thickened water and a container of strawberry yoghurt are on the table, but the spoon has dropped out of his hand onto his lap. His eyes are closed. A glob of yoghurt is nesting in the stubble on his chin. The striped shirt he's wearing used to be his dress shirt. The top button has been placed in the second button hole. Panic rises in my throat as I move close enough to see if he's breathing. I can barely hear the ragged breath catching in his congested chest. I have the sudden urge to cradle him in my arms and, if I were strong enough, steal him away from this place. All I can do is touch him gently on his shoulder.

"Daddy, it's Connie."

No response. I repeat my announcement in a louder voice.

He opens his eyes and slowly raises his chin. When he opens his mouth to speak, all I can hear is a ghostly rattle. I rub his back in little circles. A tear runs down his cheek.

"I love you, Daddy. I'm sorry you're sick."

He takes a deep breath as if to respond, and then the coughing begins. I pat him on the back and try to give him a sip of thickened water, but he's unable to take a breath. I can't do anything to help him, so I hurry out the door and find the only person in the hallway, Brian, one of the assistants. He comes quickly into the room and lifts my dad under his arms, so that he's sitting up straighter in the wheelchair.

"Just take it easy, Jim. Try to breathe. Relax."

When the coughing eases a bit, Brian's able to give him a sip of thickened water.

"Dr. Terry is in the building today," Brian says. "I'll get her to come and take a look at him."

A down-to-earth, upbeat physician, Dr. Terry was assigned to my parents by Evercare, a health care company that provides medical benefits and care planning to nursing home residents, hospices, and other long-term care facilities. Cost of the care is paid for by Medicaid. She is more than a physician; she is a friend. Early in my mom's stay here, she asked a psychologist to visit with her to help her adjust to living in the nursing home. My mom wasn't warm to meeting a psychologist. She finally agreed that he could visit, "but just for ten minutes." The psychologist asked her about her life and her talents in a conversation that lasted for thirty minutes. He suggested that she start painting again because, my mother reported, "he was certain I had talent." Within a week Mama had requested that I buy watercolor paper and paint. After that Dr. Terry shared photographs of ships and scenery for my mother to use for her painting, patiently listened to her complaints, and appreciated her quick mind and active memory.

Dr. Terry, slim, fifty-ish, and dressed in creased jeans and a blue, checked shirt, strides into the room, greets me, and talks quietly to my dad. She gently massages his back and holds his hand. Then she takes his temperature and spends several minutes using her stethoscope to listen to his heart and lungs.

"He has congestion in his lungs and a fever, Connie. I'm afraid it's pneumonia again."

My father has had two bouts of pneumonia, the last one just three months ago. At that time, I was asked whether they should treat it with antibiotics or "let it take its course." I didn't have to think very hard about my decision then because Daddy still had those lucid times when I saw the real father behind the blank mask of Alzheimer's. I immediately agreed to medication, and it worked, at least for a few months. Since then my father has slipped more deeply into the quagmire of dementia. His swallowing reflex is barely functioning, and he doesn't respond to words, only to the touch of someone's hand.

Dr. Terry sits on the edge of my dad's bed and pats a place next to her for me to sit down. Daddy's attention is focused on trying to breathe. His eyes are shut.

"You know, Connie, pneumonia is both the friend and enemy of Alzheimer's patients."

I want to clarify Dr. Terry's statement, but panic constricts my throat, and all I can do is swallow repeatedly. I know that I'm going to again face the decision to treat the pneumonia or to let it result in my dad's death. I wish I could escape to the safety of my home or to the office, where I can easily make decisions about everyday matters. But here, as the only caregiver, I've been painted into a corner. The decision is a monumental one, and it's all mine.

I clear my throat. "Do you mean that pneumonia is a friend because it can ... take them before they suffer too much?" *Take* is an awkward word choice, but *kill* seems too brutal.

She removes her glasses and wipes them with a Kleenex from the bedside table. "Yes, that's one way to look at it. It's an enemy because so many Alzheimer's patients suffer from aspiration pneumonia. It's just part of the natural history of severe dementia, and the major cause of death in these patients."

I raise my eyes to look at her face. She looks older today than her fifty-some years. Her short brown hair is lightened by strands of gray, and the curved smile-wrinkles around her mouth have deepened. I can feel the warmth of her empathy.

"What about my dad? Can you treat him with antibiotics again?"

She shakes her head and sighs. "It's hard to predict whether antibiotics and hydration would stall the pneumonia for a while or if these would be futile treatments. Sometimes antibiotics don't cure, but they reduce the symptoms, so the person doesn't suffer so much."

I have a picture in my mind of my dad groaning and gasping for breath with pain made even worse because he doesn't know what it is or why it's happening to him. I remember a friend telling me that pneumonia felt like an elephant sitting on her chest.

Dr. Terry knows what I'm thinking. "Pneumonia can be painful, Connie, but if you choose not to treat your dad, we can keep him comfortable. Antibiotics don't make much of a difference if a person is near death. What they do is prolong the time until the next bout of pneumonia."

Those words "near death" are chilling. Somehow I've expected the routine of visits to my parents to continue without change. I'm not prepared to begin a new chapter in my life with the death of a parent. Dr. Terry and I sit silently for several minutes.

Then I stutter my fears to her. "It's so hard to say ... don't treat him. I'm afraid to make that decision."

Dr. Terry gives me a hug and tells me to take my time. She suggests that I talk to my mother and see what she thinks and to consider what my dad, if he could, would decide. I don't know about my mother, but I do know my matter-of-fact father would stick out his chin and say, "Let's get on with it. I don't want to live like this."

She stands up to resume her rounds. "It's good to consider what you believe he would want, and you and your Mom's thoughts, too. No matter what you decide, we'll start right now by making him more comfortable."

I continue to sit on my dad's bed and reach out to hold his hand. The coughing has stopped, but not the heavy breathing. He opens his eyes and looks across at me. I show him the cup of water and hold it up to his mouth, but he turns his head away. Nurse Edefina comes to administer a medication and get him into bed. I kiss him on the forehead and tell him I'll be back.

I just can't make myself go directly to my mother's room to give her the news. It will blot out her life stories that I recorded before we left for Hawaii. Instead I go to the car, where I call Floyd and tell him about the decision that has to be made. He immediately reacts by saying that I can't let my dad die.

"I don't want him to die," I counter, "but he has so little quality of life now and I hate to see him go through bout after bout of pneumonia. It's hard for him to swallow food without aspirating it into his lungs. I just don't know."

Floyd doesn't respond. I know that when faced with his father's death, he and his brothers decided to continue hydrating him intravenously until the very end. I also recall how much he hates making decisions about euthanizing pets. I'm usually the one who has to decide. He offers to leave work and meet me at Ivy Manor, but I decide my mother would be more upset by the impending event if both of us walk into her room. I sit in the car, for ten minutes, close my eyes, and pray for guidance. Then I go back through the doors of Ivy Manor.

I find my mother awake and sitting on the side of the bed. She's holding a small sketch pad on her lap on which she's beginning a drawing of a sailboat and a lighthouse. She greets me with a smile and a sigh of relief as I put my arm around her shoulder.

"You're finally back, Connie. I'm so glad you're here. I was worried about you when you couldn't fly home on time." She puts down her drawing and picks up the newspaper she saved from September 11, emblazoned with "Our Nation Saw Evil" above a color photo of the fragile twin towers engulfed in angry red flames and spewing gray and black smoke. "I didn't know if you'd seen this or not. It was so terrible. What about your students from the Middle East?"

We have many students from the Middle East, and young men and women from more than eighteen countries, many of whom will be fearful of studying in a country attacked by extremists. The result will probably be a huge drop in enrollment, larger than the one that occurred after the Columbine high school tragedy, when Asian parents, in particular, feared exposing their children to the violence in Littleton, Colorado.

I say, "I'm sure we'll lose many students, but we'll get through it." It's an offhand response that gives me time to think. How can I tell her about Daddy's pneumonia and the decision we have to make? I go through the routine of emptying my bag on to her table tray, acknowledging her new drawing, presenting her with a picture book of Hawaii, and listening to her account of the good and bad events of the past two weeks. She moves the newspaper and her drawing pad and pencil to the side of her bed and pulls the tray across her lap to take a bite of cake. Sitting in the chair near the middle of the bed, I try to de-stress by circling my head and rolling my shoulders. I don't want to infect her with my own anxiety.

"I just came back from visiting Daddy," I say.

She stops eating and looks up at me. "Is he okay?"

I shake my head. "Not so good.

She leans forward with a blank look in her eyes.

I repeat what I've just said.

She responds shakily. "Oh, dear, not again. Not pneumonia." She pushes the tray table aside. "Pneumonia. Pneumonia." She's whispering, hugging her arms across her chest with a slight shiver.

I move my chair closer to the bed and put my hand on her arm. We share the silence for a few minutes.

I say, "Dr. Terry says she can make Daddy comfortable if we don't treat the pneumonia and just let it take its course. She suggested I talk to you about it and consider what Daddy would want. What do you think, Mama?"

When I listen to my own words, it sounds as if we're making a studied decision about which model of car to purchase. So simple and so callous. The word "death" is hanging unspoken between us. Mama pulls her arm away from my hand, sinks into the pillows and turns her upper body toward the curtain that separates her bed from the one next to her. If the catheter tube didn't limit her, she would be curled in a fully fetal position. I lean closer to her, but I can barely make out her response.

"Oh, Connie, I don't know what to do. Talking about this upsets me so much. It makes me feel sicker. You make the decision. I don't want to."

I knew that asking her would upset her, but I was hoping for some support in making the decision. I feel the pressure of pneumonia in my own chest, inhibiting my breathing to prevent me from saying "don't treat him." Although I don't have my mother's opinion, I believe in my heart and mind that it's the compassionate decision, one that my father would agree with. I consider calling Dr. Terry now, so Daddy won't have to suffer any longer, and my selfish side encourages the same decision for a different reason: "Decide, and you won't have to suffer about the decision any longer." I step into the hall, pull out my cell phone and call Dr. Terry. I ask her to make my dad as comfortable as possible but not to treat the pneumonia with antibiotics.

Chapter 10

The Cardboard Box

Nine days have passed since my decision. The phrase "let nature take its course" keeps surfacing in my mind as I place my trust in what I hope is a kind Mother Nature. But of course Mother Nature inflicts pain and death. When a student from China asked about my father this morning, I used the nature phrase, an idiom she recognized from her reading. She nodded and said, "Yes, yes. We say that in Chinese. It's *wu wei*. No need to do anything." Only two syllables. So short and simple in Chinese and somehow easier to accept because it implies that I've turned over my responsibility to a natural force; what will be, will be, without human intervention. Interpreting my decision in this way takes away some of the anxiety I feel.

When I saw my dad yesterday, he was stretched out in bed, several pillows behind his head, oxygen tubes threaded behind his ears and into his nostrils. His lips were dry and cracked and I could hear each breath sucked through the thin plastic tubes. I expected some groaning or other expression of pain, but his body seemed relaxed, no movement in his arms or legs, no struggling. Five days ago, he refused or wasn't able to take thickened liquid when it was offered to him. I asked about an IV for hydration, but Dr. Terry told me that this treatment can prolong dying for weeks and may actually decrease the person's comfort because it promotes excessive respiratory secretions, making it even more difficult to breathe. Evidently dehydration is part of the natural process of dying. I've never had the experience of sitting with a dying person, but it seemed natural to stroke my father's sweaty forehead with a cool washcloth, one of my mom's favorite comforts, and to tell him I was there with him and that I loved him. His eyelids fluttered slightly in recognition of a human voice and touch. I sat by his bed for about thirty minutes, running my hand in light circles on his arm, and talking to him about times we spent together hoeing weeds in the victory garden, ice skating on the lake, playing Rook on the kitchen table. I hoped he could hear my voice even if the words didn't make sense.

Mama has been in to visit him each morning for a few minutes, but she spends the rest of the time in her room, taking her small meals there.

"It's so difficult to see him there," she says. "I just can't stay very long."

My colleague Pambos and I are sitting at my desk discussing the impact of September 11 on our student population of Muslims. Today is the first day of Ramadan, the Muslim holy month of fasting, and we have only four Muslim students instead of the usual forty or fifty. The call-transfer buzzer on my phone interrupts us. Like a thump on the head that I've been half-expecting, I wake up to the fear of what this call may mean. Without a hello, my mother says, "Daddy died about an hour ago."

The reprimand in her voice triggers the slow drip of guilt in my veins. What am I doing sitting here in my office talking to Pambos about the downturn in students when I should be at Ivy Manor? Why didn't my mom call me sooner? Daddy has lingered for almost ten days with oxygen, pain killers, and the relative comfort promised by Dr. Terry. I should have realized that he was close to death. I've been hiding in an emotional fog, talking about world events in order to avoid the eventual death of my father.

"Mama, I'm sorry. I'll come right away."

"He suffered so much, Connie. You should have been here."

I cringe as if I've been struck by the back of her hand. Then I pull myself together and tell Pambos and Missy the news. They both offer condolences and embraces that trigger my tears and gratefulness for their support. I call Floyd and ask him to meet me at Ivy Manor.

As I drive to the nursing home, the events of the last three years crowd my mind. My father's memory withered by the onset of Alzheimer's. A stroke that placed him in the abusive Briargate, and then his escape to Ivy Manor. My mother's move to assisted living, and the necessity of placing her, a year later, in Ivy Manor with my father. Her fall and broken femur. His decline into the pit of Alzheimer's. And, finally, my decision to not treat his third bout of pneumonia.

During these years, the fluctuations of my inner life have been background noise to the actions taking place in the real world. My emotional pendulum has swung between one extreme, frustration at my mom's demands followed by my too ready response to meet them, and the other extreme: joy from the intimacy and insight I gain when Mama and I work together on her life story. I seldom cried until I began caring for my parents, but now I always seem to be on the verge of tears, sometimes happy tears at the sparks of love I've encountered in my mother, other residents, and the staff, and sometimes tears of frustration at not being able to solve all the problems of life at Ivy Manor. Hopefulness and hopelessness seem to go in tandem. With my father's death, time has run out on my hope that living in the same nursing home would bring my parents together, but I still believe there is time left for my mom and me to establish a closer relationship as we work together on the story of her life. The true point where the pendulum has come to rest between these extremes has been the comforting regularity and joy of my family and work life grounded by my belief in the goodness and love of God, the Spirit of Life, Allah — the terminology isn't important.

As I pull up in front of Ivy Manor, I picture the dark-haired, handsome, intelligent man I knew as a child. This is the image I want to remember when I think of my father, not the ninety-year-old manikin that wore my father's striped shirts and gray pants but had no memories of the past, no knowledge of the present, and no idea of the future. In spite of the changes in his personality and his ability to communicate, he was still my father, and I should have been with him when he died. Somehow I think he would have known I was there and that I loved him.

I'm greeted by Floyd's welcome presence and a sunny bed of pink impatiens at the front entrance. Behind the automatic doors is the interior of the nursing home. Cramped. Aging. Dingy. When we reach my father's room, the door is closed. His roommates, Walter and George, are dozing in their wheelchairs in the hallway. We pause, unsure of what to do. Floyd lets me take the lead. Dutifully I tap on the door, as the nursing home requests. I'm rubbing my throat and chest, and I can feel the thumping of my heart. If only this would be a bad dream. If only my dad would say, "Come in." But there is no response from inside. When I open the door, I see Daddy lying on the bed by the window. The blue bedspread is pulled up to the middle of his chest exposing the top of the white hospital gown. His arms are under the spread.

Floyd and I stand next to the bed. I stroke Daddy's cold cheek. I can feel the three-day growth of bristly hair on his chin. Someone has closed his eyes but hasn't bothered to close his mouth. It's open in a last gasp for breath or maybe a cry of pain. Or even an expression of surprise. I kiss his cheek and brush back the thin strands of gray hair stuck to his forehead.

"I'm sorry, Daddy. I wanted to be here."

My guilty mind replaces "wanted" with "should have been." My grammar-teaching background tells me that "should" is a conditional verb indicating duty, obligation, or correctness. This word occurs frequently in my vocabulary. It was my duty to be at my father's bedside when he died. It's what a good daughter should do. It was expected of me, and I've always tried to meet other's expectations. Another "should have" is to have told my father, when he could fully understand me, how much I loved him. Just as I don't remember my father ever saying he loved me, I never expressed my love in words until his memory was tarnished by Alzheimer's. Did he know what "love" meant when I ended my visits with "I love you, Daddy"? Or was it simply a sound that was lost in the twisted fibers and plaque of his damaged brain?

Olivia, who has been on duty throughout the night, comes into the room and hugs me so hard that my chin is indented by the pin collection on her shoulder. She shakes Floyd's hand. "I'm so sorry, Connie. I stayed here this morning, so I could talk to you. Jim died a peaceful death. Your mom comforted him when she could, but her stomach was bothering her so much that she couldn't stay long. Walter held his hand through most of the night."

"Thank you, Olivia. I didn't think he was so close to dying. I wish someone had called me earlier."

"I wanted to call, but your mom didn't want to disturb you. She's in her room resting."

The fact that my mom was with my dad reinforces my feeling that she has been emotionally reconnecting with him in the last few months. In her more frequent visits with him, I've seen her lovingly patting his hand, wiping his chin, and talking to him, but I can't believe that she didn't want to share the burden of his last hours with me. I don't understand her reasoning. Maybe she was protecting me.

Yet she scolded me: "You should have been here." A toxic mix of anger at my mother, sadness, and guilt is bubbling up in my throat. Feeling nauseated, I ask Olivia for a drink of water. The paper cup of cold water cools my throat, but it doesn't quell the acidic emotions. Olivia puts a stamp of finality on our conversation by reassuring me that the mortuary will pick up my father's body this morning and follow the prior arrangements that I've made for cremation.

I smooth my father's hair and kiss his cold forehead one last time, take Floyd's hand, and walk toward the door. I try to prepare myself for our visit to Mama's room. I already know from previous emotional events that she will be physically debilitated by my father's death. She loved him in her own way, but she will also see his death as a boldface sign that her own mortality is just around the corner, and she may not be able to endure the impact this will have on her. I believe that sixty-eight years of marriage, living together in the same house (though not the same bedroom), caring for and respecting each other, and seldom having arguments qualifies as love. After all, there are many definitions of the word.

As we leave the room, Walter wheels over to us. He sits tall and straight in his chair, a gentle man with a shock of wavy gray hair and a small gray moustache. His blue eyes reveal the vacant look of dementia and a stroke that has affected his speech. He takes my hand in his bony fingers and squeezes it. He doesn't say anything, but his face shows his concern. I put my arm around his shoulders and thank him for comforting my dad. The warmth of his body releases a flood of tears as my dad's death becomes a reality to me. How I wish that I could revive the father of ten years ago: smart, funny, interested in the world and, yes, a man of few words and few shared emotions. That father died then, but the memories of his presence in my life throughout the years surfaced again today when I said a final goodbye.

The door to 214 is ajar. Mama is lying on her bed with a washcloth over her eyes. When I touch her arm, she pushes the washcloth up on her forehead and tries to lift her droopy eyelid, so she can see us better.

"Oh, my," she says. "You're both here. This is terrible. I've had an awful time. My stomach hurts so much. And Daddy suffered all the time."

She hands me the washcloth and pushes herself to a more upright position on the bed. I reach for her hand, but she joins both hands on her chest.

"I'm sorry I wasn't here," I say. "I just didn't think he was close to death. No one told me, not even Olivia."

Mama shakes her head in slow motion accompanied by a long sigh. I interpret the movement as "I don't believe it," a typical response to excuses I offer. She says, "I knew you were at work and I didn't want you to come earlier than usual."

I'm speechless, but I wouldn't confront my mother now if I could. I'm still weighing the reasons for not being present. Was my mom responsible for me not being here or was it my choice because I was afraid to see my father die? I do know that I would have come immediately if I had been called. I also know that I was avoiding the uncomfortable, taking the easy way out by not keeping a vigil with my dad.

Mama is sighing and repeating the phrase I've just said to myself: "I don't know, I just don't know," over and over again as she rocks her shoulders back and forth.

I have a strong desire to wrap arms around her, so we can comfort each other. She isn't physically able to do this and probably wouldn't allow it if she were. If she would cry, I would cry and we would share the moment of sorrow. I could say that I'll miss the father I knew before his illness or that he was such a good, kind person. But I know any expression of feelings might trigger my mother's chronic stomach pain. My words and tears need to be in private. We end our visit according to routine, as if nothing untoward has happened. I adjust her pillows and brush my lips across her forehead, in much the same way I kissed my father.

"You need to rest, Mama. Olivia said she would give you some extra Ativan and something for your stomach. I'll come back this afternoon."

She turns her head away from me toward the pink curtain that separates her bed from the bed of her roommate, Beth, who is snoring peacefully in an afternoon nap.

As we walk down the hall to the elevator, Raheen and Cynthia hug me and express their sympathy.

"I loved your dad's sense of humor," Raheen says. "He always used to flirt with me and blow me kisses."

Cynthia adds that she was his favorite bath aide; he asked several times a week to have her give him a shower. I smile at this remnant of my dad's sexual humor.

When we leave the building, sunshine and blue skies reassure us that there's a world outside of Ivy Manor. I blink my eyes and stand for a minute on the sidewalk near the gazebo. For the last few months, this care center has absorbed all of my attention. Now I realize there is another life outside those doors, one filled with the tasks related to a death in the family. As soon as I'm in the car, I pull out my to-do notebook and begin to list the tasks involved in my father's death. This is a way of controlling the cascade of events. I need to check with the mortuary where I have already paid for a cremation plan. Prepaying for cremation was a way of disposing of one of the pressures as I tried to balance dealing with two parents in a nursing home, maintaining my job, and planning for a new English project in Cyprus. What comes next? Tell the children and the few friends of my parents who are living in Colorado. My dad's only other relatives are a stepbrother in Oregon and some nieces in California. Arrange for a memorial service at our church. Create a memory folder with photos and text about Daddy's life. Inter the remains in the cemetery in Longmont where there are two plots with headstones already engraved, minus the dates.

What else do you do when a parent dies? Gather the women in the family and wail in pitched screams like the female mourners did when our family lived in Cairo? Search my closet for black clothes to wear for the rest of my life like the widows in Cyprus? Neither of these options appeals to me. My wardrobe is devoid of black dresses because they attract cat fur, and I'm too embarrassed to wail, although these emotional options might ease the pain of loss. In typical fashion, I decide to immerse myself in the tasks I have listed.

Cremation is the most difficult assignment to wrap my mind around. Daddy told me many years before his death that he didn't want "that ridiculous embalming."

"Just be practical and get rid of the body," he said.

I was never sure if he was an agnostic or an atheist, but I'm certain that his skepticism didn't allow for a belief in an afterlife. After years of fascination with varied religious beliefs, from Buddhism to Judaism to various Christian denominations, I share his doubts about any kind of eternal home in the clouds. Following his wishes, I arranged for a prepaid cremation plan a year ago, so I don't have to make a choice about embalming or caskets. It will all be taken care of. Now I'm wondering what "taken care of" includes. My mind perseverates about the steps that will lead from the nursing home to cremation. A car from the mortuary will take his body out on a gurney. Or maybe it will be an ambulance. There is only one elevator. How can they get the body to the ambulance during the daytime without alarming the residents? If the mortuary uses an ambulance, the residents may think it is just an illness that requires a trip to the hospital. If there is a sheet over his face, they will know it is a death. Or will they put his body in a body bag like we see on TV? Then everyone will know that someone has died, a fate hovering over each resident of Ivy manor.

Although I try to stop this flood of disturbing images, the final picture fills the big screen of my imagination. My dad's flabby body. Naked in a cardboard coffin. On a slab shaped like a huge pizza spatula. A decisive shove into a flaming oven. Was cremation the right choice? Maybe if I'd had siblings, we would have argued about the decision and settled on embalming and a casket, a fitting way for most Americans to deny the finality of death by viewing a lifelike, cosmetically decorated corpse. Or we might have chosen to have a closed casket that was surreptitiously taken from the funeral home and buried in the cemetery.

I work to control my imagination during the next few days, as I try to calm my mother and keep her from being too sick to come to the small memorial service I'm planning. "This is just too much for me" is her daily lament. I try to involve her in the plans, asking for choices of hymns and what she would like to have said at the service. She covers her eyes and bows her head like a child blocking out a scary part of a movie or maybe a frightening part of her own future. I suggest having a friend of mine sing "Amazing Grace" and "A Closer Walk with Thee," but she doesn't respond.

"I just don't know if I can even go to the funeral," she says. "I may not be able to walk."

I'm not going to accept this excuse. I'm determined that she come to the memorial.

"That's OK, Mama. You can use a wheelchair. You don't have to use your walker."

"How can I get out of the car and into a wheelchair? That's too hard."

"Floyd and I can help you. You've always been able to do that when we go out to eat."

My mother squints at me with her one good eye, mouths a soft okay, and sighs. It lifts my spirits to have won this round.

When the morning of the memorial comes, Mama is dressed in the best choice in her limited wardrobe: a lavender jacket with a purple scarf and a navy blue skirt. The wheelchair and the walker are loaded up, just in case. She settles into the car with the catheter bag dressed up in a blue canvas sack on her lap. I am praying that all will go well with her and my own presentation about my father.

The next two hours pass as smoothly as the finish on the new oak pulpit. Mama takes careful steps into the church with the support of her walker. She nods her head in time with "Amazing Grace," sung by one of my fellow teachers. She sheds tears when I speak about my father. She is proud of the memory folder of photos and text that I have prepared. After the service, she is comforted by the people who have come to commemorate my dad's life: Missy and Troy (our daughter Sonja is unable to come all the way from Cyprus), Floyd's two brothers and their wives, my fellow teachers and colleagues, a few of her remaining friends, Ivy Manor's Olivia, and four nursing assistants who were devoted to my dad. The memorial service is simple, one that my father would have appreciated in spite of his anti-religious leanings.

Collecting my father's cremains the next day shatters the comfort I felt at the memorial. The Biblical "dust to dust, ashes to ashes" was shoveled aside when the funeral industry coined the word cremains. I hadn't thought much about this step when I kissed my father's cheek and said goodbye in the nursing home. I didn't see his white-draped body removed by the mortuary. I didn't see him put into the cheap casket made of particleboard, or "chippie" as it's called in the industry. I didn't want to visualize what happened in the cremation furnace. But I am brought back to reality when I have to pick up his cremains.

I have experienced making arrangements at funeral homes three times. Once with my mother-in-law, who was embalmed and viewed, and twice with international students who had died in car accidents, when my task was to arrange for embalming and repatriation of the bodies to Colombia and France. The same well-known funeral home took care of all three situations. It was a beautifully landscaped, churchlike building with an interior that resembled an upscale suburban house: pale-blue plush carpeting, a formal "living" room with wingback chairs, mahogany side tables, and porcelain table lamps. On the faux fireplace mantle were artistically arranged bronze and porcelain urns ranging from a classical Greek design to smaller teddy bears in blue and pink. Soft music was playing. The scent of wisteria was in the air. This is what I expect when Floyd and I go to what I thought was a funeral home to collect my father's ashes.

The address takes us from the suburbs to an industrial part of Denver. Gray concrete. No landscaping. No sign. An ominous black smokestack. Thoughts of Dachau and Nuremburg go through my mind. We check for the street number on the building but can't find one, so we park and walk to the only visible entrance. The windowless steel door has a small brass plaque indicating the name of the largest group of Denver mortuaries.

A narrow staircase goes to the second floor, where we find a closed office door. We knock several times. Finally, a short, pudgy man in a rumpled white shirt opens the door and ushers us in. After presenting us with several forms to sign, he goes into a back room to find the right cremains. I can see him through the storeroom door, looking for names and numbers on the shelves. He retrieves a plain brown cardboard box, plops it down on the desk, thanks us, and ushers us out. No wrapping, no handle, just a container the size of a serving box of cheap wine. This truly is the Wal-Mart of the funeral process.

I thought ashes would be light, but the box weighs about seven pounds. The sense of finality feels heavier than the box I place on my lap in the car. I didn't plan on being physically involved in the process of death, yet here I am grasping what remains of my father in my sweaty hands. When I loosen my grip, I can see the damp imprint of my thumbs on the tape that runs across the top of the box. I carefully unseal the tape, and pull apart the flaps. Inside is a heavy black plastic bag fastened with a red twist tie.

Floyd takes his eyes off the road and looks over at me.

"You're not opening the box, are you? I don't think you should do that."

Floyd has more propriety than I, and less curiosity. I sit for several minutes with my fingers on the bag considering my husband's caution. The contents don't feel like ashes or fine dust. There are bumps in the bag. I untwist the tie, sniff, and look inside. There's no odor, just gray and white ashes dotted with bone fragments. They remind me of the "clinkers" my dad used to scoop out of the coal-burning stove in the living room of our house on Cherokee Street. I can't help thinking he would get a chuckle out of ending up as a clinker. I pick up one of the fragments and turn it over in my fingers. This is as close as I can come to his physical presence in death. I place it back in the box, pull the bag together and twist it shut with the red tie.

I have closed the lid on my dad's life, and I can't go back to change this final event. As usual, I have made a quick decision—but probably the right one this time. The ugly cardboard box sitting on my lap fills me with sadness. My reason tells me that the decision to let my father die was the right one, and I must admit that it has relieved me of the burden of caring for both parents. My dad would have approved of my honoring the choice I made. He hated the idea of embalming with its cosmetic artistry, satin-lined caskets, and outrageous expense. I have done as he asked, although I regret the heartless process of cremation. Yet, deep inside, I realize that regret will only prolong the process of accepting his death.

Connie Lou Johnson, Multiple Contest Winner, Reviews Her Winnings.

Connie Lou Johnson Solves Quiz; Wins Treasure Chest Of Prizes

"Another April fool, huh," were first words when she read the telegram announcing her as winner on the Doctor IQ Junior Radio Show, Saturday, April 3.

As THE RODEO goes to press Connie has received two of the eight prizes she has won by answering a group of geographical riddles. The two prizes are a Benrus watch and a Parker pen and pencil set. Some of the other gifts Connie expects to receive in the "Treasure Chest" are a bicycle, a radio, and a pair of shoe skates.

Winning contests is not unusual for Connie Lou, for she makes a hobby of it. Connie won her first prize, when she was eight years old, on the Junior Genius Radio

since, Connie has been piling up win after win until the number of contests she has won equals about 86.

Coming from Baker, where she was head girl last semester, Connie has started making a good record at West. She is a member of student Council and her grades last grading period were all A's except for one B.

Connie is 14 years old; she is 4 feet, 1½ inches tall, and weighs 95 pounds. Her favorite song is "Four Leaf Clover" and Harry James ranks tops in bands. She enjoys baseball, football, and ice skating; and she could spend all her life eating strawberry short cake.

All Westerners can look forward to seeing Connie as a ____ that is ____

Mama, Connie, and baby Sonja

Mildred in Cesar Morganti portrait she won

At Eben Ezer sanatorium, little Millie with her mama and papa

Mildred and Jim, Brown Palace Presidential Suite

Mildred, Jim, and baby Connie

Mama and me

*Queen for a Day,
Mildred lifted to
auditorium stage*

*Mama with watercolors
displayed on bed at Ivy Manor*

CHAPTER II

QUEEN FOR A DAY

HALF-HOPEFUL AND HALF-GRATEFUL, I PAUSE OUTSIDE THE OPEN DOOR OF my dad's old room at Ivy Manor. His name has been removed from the brass holder on the wall and replaced by a hastily lettered note card that reads "Maxwell Timmons." The removal of my dad's name plate finalizes his death of more than a month ago, but it doesn't erase his presence from my mind. I still walk by this familiar room wishing he were there, so I could kiss his cheek and put my arm around his shoulders. Coupled with that desire is relief that the shell of a man occupied by Alzheimer's is gone, and now I can more clearly remember my father as a clever, intelligent, reclusive man who loved my mother and me in his own quiet way. Instead of looking at the details of his death, I'm able to wide-screen the event and put it into perspective. Occasional flashes of guilt obscure the broader view, but I realize now that my decision was the right one. To turn the final page of this chapter in my life, I step into the room, now vacant during the lunch hour, to look at the bed where my dad died. I see evidence of a very different occupant, Maxwell Timmons. Stacked neatly on the blue coverlet are a yellow legal tablet half-covered with small, precise writing and two hard-cover books: *The Poetry of Walt Whitman* and *A Tale of Two Cities*. The next time I visit this room, I won't be checking on my dad. I'll be getting acquainted with Maxwell Timmons, someone who may partially fill the void my father has left. . Just his name evokes my interest. He must have an intriguing story to tell and—if he's still able to read these books and take notes—the ability to tell it. Every Ivy Manor resident has a unique story. Encouraging them to tell me about themselves adds pleasure to my sometimes somber visits. I'm eager to talk to Maxwell Timmons.

Mama, not to my surprise, has settled into a comfortable routine that doesn't seem to be shadowed by grieving for my father. It's as if she has put the book of my dad's life on the highest shelf of the library, still there but impossible to reach. She has the habit of quickly putting upsetting events into the past, conveniently ridding herself of them because emotional upheavals cause her to suffer physically. Her "nervous stomach," as she described it many years ago, was triggered by any event that upset her. As far back as I can remember, she made frequent visits to the doctor and received diagnoses of colitis, ulcers, and generic bowel problems. After hearing her descriptions of Eben Ezer and the impact of TB in her mother's and grandmother's lives, I recognize the concern with her physical condition, but the fact that she hasn't mentioned my father in the two weeks after the memorial is harder to understand. Is it that she thinks about him but putting it into words would upset her? Is she so worried about just living through the ensuing days that she has put him completely out of her mind? Did my dad actually die to her several years ago, when Alzheimer's sucked away his personality, his awareness, and his mental capacity? I can understand the latter because I also experienced this demise.

It would bring us much closer if we could share feelings about my dad's death, but we've never been a family that encouraged expression of feelings. We simply never put words to our emotions. I've tried to break this barrier with my husband and children because it brings a comfortable intimacy, but I'm not going to try it now with my mother and possibly disturb this unstressed interlude in our lives.

If I said, "I miss seeing Daddy," she might reply, "Don't go there, Connie, it will just upset me." It's unrealistic to think she would agree and share her feelings of sadness with me. I'll tuck away this hope of talking about my dad for an appropriate time as we continue our life review. Delving into her past to retell the childhood experiences at Eben Ezer as "the best time in her life" seems to have adjusted her negativity. She's back in the schoolhouse of her mind, studying her Danish dictionary, memorizing geographical facts, writing letters, and painting landscapes and ships. All of these activities take her mind off physical infirmities, and the paintings are an actual product that she can give to others and that can be recognized as an achievement. Raheen has asked her for copies or originals of all her paintings to put up in the tiny visiting room, a gallery of sorts. It will feature a small, framed sign with her name on it, one that I have been asked to supply.

Having her art displayed has sparked her interest in venturing out to the Ivy Manor activity room, next to the visiting room where her pictures are displayed. In the past, her aversion to large groups of people kept her from visiting this room except to retrieve a glass of Lactaid from the refrigerator.

"I went into the activity room yesterday to play the piano when no one was around," she proudly told me. "I played 'I Don't Know Why I Love You Like I Do,' and Jo Ann and Lenny asked me to sing the words. They got a real kick out of the song."

So far, her socializing has been limited to me, if that counts; her favorite nurses and CNAs; and her lunch companions, the only residents she communicates with. Making friends with her table mates would fill a gap in her life and take some of the burden off me.

Today I've told her I'll meet her at the table with the lunch bunch despite her plea to "just bring me something to eat in my room." It's a high school cafeteria in Ivy Manor's dining room, except for the fact that everyone is in a wheelchair or a walker. Food fights are replaced by battles over who sits at which table. The small, four-person tables are segregated according to the popular "girls," residents who are high functioning like my mom; the jocks, men who still wear their Broncos and Nuggets T-shirts; and the outcasts, residents with severe dementia, who sit together at a table my mom's table mate Frances describes as the Misfit Table.

"Nobody wants to sit there," she says. "This place is cramped enough and bad enough that we need a few people to talk to who still have their wits about them."

Mama is talking to the popular "girls" when I arrive. I pick up four terry cloth bibs at the door: one for my mom, one each for Louise and Frances, Mom's tablemates, and an additional one for Gladys, who sits at an adjoining table. Frances and Louise are already seated and have pulled up a little rolling stool for me.

Louise, my mom's favorite, is inquisitive and intelligent, and doesn't tolerate any mistakes by the kitchen staff. She's packaged into a body that seems to shrink more each time I see her. Her cup-handle ears and small features give her an elfin look. Over the many lunch hours I've spent at the table, I've learned that she loves to read sexy Danielle Steele novels and that her first job was at "Monkey" Wards, actually Montgomery Wards mail order catalog center, for twenty-six cents an hour. Then she worked in a flour mill and, finally, for the *Sentinel* newspapers. Her husband died ten years ago. Because of what is rumored to be terminal cancer, she had to sell her house to her grandson, Stan, a local police officer, and chose to come to nearby Ivy Manor. Her only child, a daughter, lives in Oregon, but Stan takes good care of her, treating her to lunch once a week at a nearby Denny's restaurant, where she can smoke, and even taking her to her old house so that she can pick up things she needs.

Gladys walks slowly up to the next table, her oxygen tube wound around one leg and a dimpled I-don't-care smile on her plump face.

"What in heck are you doing, Gladys?" Louise scolds. "You should know better." She gets up from her chair, clucking her tongue, untangles the oxygen tube, and pushes the chair out, so that Gladys can settle her heavy body into it. Although eighty-five-year-old Gladys is almost blind, her sharp hearing picks up on everything said at our adjoining table. She always seems to be in good humor, probably because she has left her abusive, controlling husband behind in a separate assisted-living facility. "I don't have any use for him" is one of her favorite phrases. Gladys' current love in life is eating dessert. I always bring an extra piece for her when I treat my mom's table to lemon meringue pie.

Quiet, elegant Frances is the classiest member of the Lunch Bunch. Her permed, short white hair is always perfectly combed, and she smells faintly of Chanel No. 5. She sports a different pastel button-down-the-front cotton dress for each day of the week. Her fondest memories are of dancing in her high heels and drinking martinis at the Broadmoor hotel in Colorado Springs.

Mama introduces the first topic of conversation, one that is always on her mind because it involves a constant irritation.

"I spent most of the morning in the bathroom. I get so tired of this diarrhea," she says.

"You're lucky you're not Gladys," Frances counters. "She fell asleep on the toilet yesterday and then fell off."

"It was so comfortable, I couldn't help falling asleep," Gladys responds from the other table, turning in her chair so she can be included in the banter.

"That's like Frances, who sat on the patio furniture and had permanent lines on her bottom." Mama says.

"Yes, I had lines on my derriere. I guess that's the same as my bottom, isn't it?

"You could call it your ass," Louise suggests.

"Yeah, or your rear end," my mom laughs.

I join the laughter and rejoice in the fun my mom is having. This doesn't occur very often in our solitary visits in her room.

Louise puts her hand on my arm to pull me closer to her. "Connie, I want to ask you an important question," she whispers. "I've been reading my book and watching some ads on TV. There's something I want to know. Is it really possible for a man to have an erection that lasts four hours?"

I'm surprised and amused, and I think a minute before answering. Louise pulls me close to her right ear. I feel like I'm speaking into a horn that will magnify my whisper so the whole room will hear.

"It may be possible in a Danielle Steele novel, Frances, but I don't think it is in real life. I can look it up on the internet because I really don't know for sure."

I feel a tug on the back of my jacket. It's my mom. I scoot my stool away from Louise and turn toward her.

"I thought you came to visit with me," she says. "I want to talk to you, and it's not to tell you a secret."

Her voice becomes louder with each word. This jealous reaction dismays me. It has happened before when I've chatted too long in my mom's room with Raheen or Olivia. I like these women and enjoy their conversation as much as they appreciate mine. I don't want to be Mom's best friend forever. I just want to be a daughter she appreciates.

"I'm sorry, Mama. I was just trying to answer Louise's question."

She turns away from me and makes an announcement to the entire table. "You're still writing the book about me aren't you? I have a list to give you. It took me two days."

She reaches into the bag on her walker and extracts four pages torn from her address book. Louise, the only table mate who has heard my mom, turns her head slowly from side to side. She sighs, adjusts her bib, and taps her fingers on the table.

"These are all the contests I've won," Mama says. "I want them in the book."

She sits up a bit straighter and lifts her head with pride before she hands me the pages. I pat Louise's arm and mutter "excuse me." Then I reassure Mama that I'm still writing the book about her and thank her for the pages. Several months ago, we discussed her heritage and her childhood, and I asked her what other milestones stood out in her life. Evidently this question has encouraged her to produce material about her contest wins in the forties and fifties. I'll focus on this and table the erection question until the next meeting of the lunch bunch.

My mom had several motivations for entering popular contests during my growing-up years: the desire to achieve and be a publicly recognized "winner"; the opportunity to use her creative word-play skills; and the addition of luxuries to our modest, bare-essentials lives. The late forties and fifties, an era of "Mad Men" abundance and massive consumption in the U.S., tantalized the public with prize-winning advertising contests aimed at increasing sales of every brand from Chevrolet to Quaker Oats to Lucky Strike cigarettes. The word "contesting" became part of the vernacular, promoted through its own publication, *Contest Magazine*, where my mother and thousands like her could find upcoming contests, rules, deadlines, hints, and winning entries. Popular forms were naming contests; 25-words-or-less jingles (completion of a given set of phrases in a limited number of words); slogans (Campbell's "M-mm, M-mm, Good!"), and idea contests. For many housewives in this era, entering contests provided a sense of accomplishment not available in other ways.

My mother kept a roll of stamps and envelopes at her side because entries had to be sent via mail and include a proof of purchase. Prizes could be everything from small amounts of money to appliances to trips overseas. Advertising agencies were commissioned by the brands to set up the contests, advertise them, deal with entries, organize the judging, and distribute the prizes. My mom knew which agencies would be most open to clever, humorous entries and which ones were more interested in honest, down-to-earth submissions. Unfortunately for my mom and for others, contests of word skill lost ground in the sixties to sweepstakes entries, just a name in a barrel of names and a slim chance that it would produce a win.

I need to fill in the gaps in the list of Mama's contest wins, so I arrange to meet her the next day an hour before lunch. She is sitting on the bed with the tray table pulled in front of her, head bent over a piece of lined paper that she is industriously writing on.

"I've thought of some other good details about the contests," she says after greeting me. "I estimated the number of prizes I won, and it came to about 300."

Counting up her prizes was a validation of her achievements. Like many only children, myself included, she was an overachiever rewarded for good grades, spelling-bee wins, best essays, and any competition that brought accolades.

The lilt in her voice makes me smile. Reminiscing about contesting is bringing back the same "Guess what? I won first prize" excitement I remember when she would receive a phone call, official letter, or even a telegram announcing her win. She basked in the spotlight of news photos and articles.

I sit in a chair at the end of the bed with my own note pad while she finishes the paragraph she is writing. She puts down her pen and pad and pushes the table to the side, ready to begin our conversation. No rubbing of her aching tummy—she just folds her arms and searches her memory. I lean forward to ask the first question in my mind, but she is there before I say a word.

"You know, Connie, when I think about it, winning contests

started with my mother."

She tells me that her mother was always at the top of her class during the eight years that school was offered in Lyle, Minnesota. She had provided my mom with books about other countries and maps of the world when they were living in Brush, and especially loved to teach her geography, grammar, and spelling.

"I remember my first geography book when I started second grade," Mama says. "We had just moved into the new house that Papa had built. On the first day of school, I got three new books: geography, spelling, and a reading book. I had only been to school for a few months in Minnesota, but they put me in second grade. I loved my new teacher, Miss Bleasdale. She had been a patient at Eben Ezer, just like my mama had. I was always sitting at the kitchen table with my books when Papa came in from work at the Brush creamery. He could never find room on the table for the bottles of milk and the butter he brought from the creamery. He would laugh and say, 'Which is more important—the butter or the books?'"

Picturing my mother as a little girl opens my eyes to the sweet, eager child she must have been and the warm family she experienced with her mama and papa. It also shows me the direct path to her career in contesting. I think it became a vocation from that day in elementary school when she won the county spelling bee. When I read through her list, I recalled many of the prizes she had won, everything from a live Easter chicks to international trips.

Besides fulfilling her own need to compete, achieve, and be recognized, she had visions of her only child being a super achiever, a big-time Winner. Just like the blue eyes and high cheekbones, the impetus to achieve was passed down from my only-child mother to her only-child daughter. From the time I was in grade school, mama pushed me into entering quizzes, spelling bees, and writing contests.

I started to enjoy winning the competitions that I achieved by myself, but then there were the times she was so enthusiastic that she put my name on an entry she wrote. Multiple entries in different names gave her more of a chance to win. Embarrassing to me and rather unethical, but it was a common practice among passionate contesters.

My most embarrassing involvement in her contest career came from an entry my mother submitted in my name. I was fourteen and at that stage had no interest in my mom's contests. My most pressing concern was saving money for a poodle skirt and a new sweater to attract one of the boys in my eighth-grade class. When my mom had told me that she had won a prize in my name, I didn't even bother to ask what it was. When it arrived, I was in the side yard of our 1890s house in West Denver practicing my baton twirling in preparation for lessons my dad had arranged; he wanted to encourage his bookworm daughter to do something slightly athletic.

Mama called to me from an upstairs window. "Go wash your knees and put on a dress, Connie. Don't you remember I told you about winning a bicycle? The *News* photographer will be here in a few minutes."

A photographer? I was excited about the bicycle, but I didn't know I'd have to face a photographer. I grudgingly interrupted my baton twirling and trudged into the house to wash and get dressed. As I brushed the tangles out of my long brown hair, I took a thoughtful look in the mirror above the bathroom sink. Would they know I hadn't written the contest entry? When my mother entered in my name, was that the same as lying?

My mom had given me the chance to solve the geography riddles in the "Dr. IQ, Jr." quiz by myself, but, like most fourteen-year-olds, I had better things to do: playing "Some Enchanted Evening" on our old record player while I dreamed of dancing with the West High quarterback, meeting my friends at the corner drugstore to drink a chocolate short after school, or holing up in my bedroom to read the latest *Calling All Girls* magazine. So I said "no" to her "Connie, you really should do this" request. Now I was faced with pretending to be the winner. I swallowed my smidgeon of guilt and shook hands with the photographer when he arrived. It wasn't hard to smile and say "thank you" when I saw the result: my first and only bicycle, a blue Schwinn with a portable radio on the handlebars. I would be a happy, but guilty, cyclist, and my mother would look forward to trying another contest in my name.

By the time I was in high school, my mom was the queen of contesting. She was President of the Denver Contest Club and had more than 300 wins to her name. Contests were in the newspapers, in magazines, and on the radio. This was the heyday of 25 words-or-less essays, rhyming "jingles," and radio quizzes, and she was good at all of these. At the time, I didn't fully appreciate her skill and playfulness with words, but now as I recount her achievements, I'm proud of her persistence, energy, and creativity, and I recognize how much she cared about enriching our lives with the cash and prizes she won. I also remember how proud of her my dad was and how much he enjoyed every prize, even the silver Ronson cigarette lighter he placed in honor on the coffee table although he had recently quit smoking

Our middle class post-Depression lives were embellished with prizes ranging from a box of baby chicks to a console record player and a trip to Argentina (my mom took cash instead). Not all her prizes were gleaned from writing. Spelling bees for adults and children were favorite radio shows during this era. On the KLZ "Three Bs" show, My mom tied in the spelling bee with an elderly teacher. The tiebreaker was a word contest that required contestants to list as many words as possible beginning with a given letter in one minute. The winner was the one with the most words. My mom had practiced alliterative sentences for each of the letters.

"What kind of sentences are you talking about?" I ask.

She leans forward, puts her elbows on the tray table and closes her eyes. A slight nod of her head tells me that she's going back forty years to retrieve her winning words. "I remember the sentence I'd memorized for the letter B: Big bad boy bought beer barrel, baseball bat, bread box..." she rattles off the words and stops with a sigh.

I shake my head in disbelief.

She closes her eyes and starts to give me a string of words that start with the letter C.

Mama tells me that trips were her favorite prizes. Although she took cash instead of the trip to Argentina, she is proud of her entry to *Argosy* magazine, which posed the challenging question: "What can you do with used beer barrels?" As my mom frequently did, she submitted several entries in her name, my dad's name, and a friend's name. I was safe this time because I wasn't old enough to drink beer. My Dad's entry was the winning idea: install a record player on top of the barrel, with a door in the side and shelves for record storage inside. My mother crowned this clever idea with a written statement: "We'll all dance to the "Beer Barrel Polka."

In 1950, a local KOA radio contest, "Free for All," awarded her a trip to Hollywood to appear on the "Double or Nothing" quiz show. My parents had never traveled to California and, of course, had never dined at the Mocambo nightclub with movie stars, nor visited Paramount Studios. A twenty-five-word statement won them a trip to Las Vegas in 1967 to stay in the new Caesar's Palace and to see the Tammy Grimes show emceed by Tony Curtis. In 1974, my mom received the prize of her life from the Peter Heering Company: a trip to Denmark to see the relatives she had been writing to since she was eight or nine years old. This win came from providing a last line to a four-line Valentine's Day jingle. She remembers her winning lines but not the original poem:

"You are the one I hold most dear.

In the bank of love, you are my cashier."

When Peter Heering found out that the winners were Danish (My dad was a mix of Danish, Swedish, and Norwegian), he escorted them in the limousine himself to the tourist sights in Copenhagen, out to his cherry orchard and factory, and to the old factory by a canal where his parents had started the business.

Mama settles back onto her rumpled pillow and sighs.

"He really liked us," she says with a wistful smile, "so he paid for extra nights at the Arthur Frommer Hotel, just so we could spend time visiting all the relatives I'd never met before."

We were living in Egypt at the time, so I hadn't heard these details of the trip, but I'm there with my mom and dad now, feeling the joy my mother must have felt to be where, in a sense, her life started. Pleasure for her fills my heart and feeds my love for her. Learning more about her positive experiences balances the frustration I often feel when she is negative and critical. I see her as a person in the whole perspective of her life, not just as a ninety-three-year-old resident of Ivy Manor focusing on herself, her aches and pains and fears.

When I suggest that the trip to Copenhagen must have been the highlight of her adult life, she agrees and tells me that she learned to write Danish as a child just so she could write to her grandmother and aunts and uncles, but she never thought she would see them. In the early days of the twentieth century, immigrant families didn't take back-to-the-roots trips to their home countries as many of their descendants do today. They had to work hard to support themselves in a new country, and a journey by ship was expensive. When my Grandfather Grondahl said goodbye to his family, it was forever. He never looked back, but my mother always cherished the connection with her extended family in Denmark. I ask her why that connection was so important, and she replies, "I don't know, but I always wanted to see the people I wrote to." I think that, as an only child of an immigrant family, she needed to find her place in a larger family context. Actually meeting her relatives gave her a sense of belonging. This may also be the reason she loved being part of Eben Ezer, a Danish community that surrounded her with affection.

Mama was confident about the cleverness that brought her many prizes, but she never expected to win a contest based on looks and personality. I frequently pull her "Queen for a Day" photo album from my bookshelf to see how attractive she was in 1946 at the age of thirty-five. I remember her putting on a yellow picture hat that framed her blonde hair and high cheekbones as she got ready to go to the Denver Auditorium for the traveling broadcast of the popular "Queen for a Day" radio show. She was late arriving at the auditorium because a Hispanic friend who planned to go with her canceled at the last minute; her husband wouldn't allow her to go to a public place without a male escort.

"You'd never believe, Connie. When I got out of the streetcar, I actually ran the three blocks to get there before the radio show started. The door man said I was too late, but I was so out of breath that he finally let me in."

There were only two vacant seats at the back of the 12,500-seat theater. A woman in the second row saw her walking up and down the aisle and waved at an empty seat next to her. Before she could sit down, the host Jack Bailey shouted, "Would you like to be Queen for a Day?" He surveyed the waving, shouting ladies, and picked three. "Let's have that blonde with the yellow hat come up on the stage" was his invitation to my mother. Two assistants actually picked her up and lifted her onto the stage. That was the beginning of an astounding win that had nothing to do with writing but a lot to do with contest savvy.

The three chosen contestants had to explain to the audience "Why I want to be Queen for a Day." The winner would be chosen Queen, crowned, given a silver scepter and a red velvet robe, and granted her wish. When Jack Fitzgerald had established my mom's profile—name, housewife status, husband working nights as a radio engineer—he asked the big question: "Mildred, why do you want to be Queen for a Day?" My mom explained that my dad, who worked for United Airlines as a radio mechanic, went to work at 4 p.m. and returned home at 2 a.m. and crawled into bed to sleep until 9 or 10 a.m. This never allowed them time to go out or have any fun as a couple. Bailey added some sexual innuendo to the "no time to have any fun" and got lots of laughs from the audience. At the time, my mom had no clue what he was talking about. Her wish was a simple one: a night on the town with my dad. Evidently her explanation was quite enchanting and, when it came time for the audience to vote by applause for each of the women, my mom was at the top of the applause meter: Denver Queen for a Day. She was given a new hairdo and makeup, outfitted in an evening gown with long white gloves at the May Co., and taken for a night on the town with my dad, including an overnight stay in the Presidential Suite at the Brown Palace Hotel. My girlfriend and I, both of us in sixth grade, visited the stately hotel the next morning to see my mom and dad eating breakfast in the room that President Eisenhower always stayed in. Prizes, including a blond console radio/record player, kept arriving at our door in the months that followed her crowning as Queen for a Day.

Mama's energy is waning, so I ask a final question. "Why do you think you were so successful?"

Her eyes are closed and she doesn't respond for a few minutes.

Then she settles back on the bed. "I always felt I had a chance at winning, so I tried lots of times until I did win."

I realize more than ever that her attitude about trying until you achieve your goals was passed down to me. I've benefited from this inheritance in my college and professional life, and I owe this to her. Listening to my mother tell her story is causing me to replace my memories of failed attempts to please her with an acknowledgement of the gifts of time, creativity, persistence, and resilience she gave to me. She may not have expressed love with outward affection, but she and my father sincerely wanted me to be the best person I could be. So far, I'm just the listener in this process of storytelling, with the benefits of better understanding my mother and, in turn, myself. At some point, however, I'd like to turn the tables. I'd appreciate my mother asking questions about my life and discussing troublesome events we shared in the past. This seems to be the only way we can develop depth in our intimacy.

CHAPTER 12

ACROSS THE MILES

ON THIS DECEMBER DAY OF BLUE SKY, SUNSHINE, AND MELTING SNOW, my canvas, go-to-Ivy-Manor bag holds the usual items plus a small, tattered album of Queen for a Day photos and the chapter I've just written about Mama's contest career. Mama has asked me to bring the album, which I've saved from my parents' downtown apartment. Both items should be good conversation starters, along with the newly printed collection of my poetry, *A Last Good Night,* which I gave to my mother several days ago. The title poem bemoans the fact that my grandfather died of a heart attack in his bedroom, locked from the inside, while my grandmother, wordless but worried about him, was in her bedroom on the other side of their house. Other poems in the book were written during the last twenty years. Many are from *Ma'alesh: Verses from Egypt,* which was printed by American University Press and sold in Cairo hotels, and some are about life in the small Michigan town where we lived during Floyd's Ph.D. study. At Christmas, I'm planning to send copies of the book to close friends in the many places we've lived. The parts of my mother's life story that I've put down on paper have affirmed the value of her life, and my book of poems is an affirmation of the oft-neglected creative part of my life. I'm hoping she'll have read some of the poems and will want to share her reactions with me. I don't get much response from my mom when I mention family events or what's happening at school. That's partly my fault. Even as a child, I was more of a listener and a problem solver. I always felt that my father was observing me and understood my moods, but he never said anything, and when I tried to share with my mother, she usually diverted the conversation to her problems and needs. It became a habit for me to put my emotions into writing in the Big Chief tablets that I hid under my bed.

My one-sided relationship with my mom has led me to encourage openness of communication with Sonja, Missy, and Troy. They seem to feel free to tell me about their lives without fear of judgment.

Today I'm hoping the album of old photos and my book of poetry will be an opportunity for a good two-way conversation. It has been a long time since she has shown real interest in my life. Few chances are left to create a shared connection.

With an energetic hello, I enter the now too-familiar room. Mama is hunched over an open drawer in her bedside chest. She's wearing a red blouse and a navy blue skirt that gaps in the back as she bends over. She would be more comfortable wearing one of the knee-length dusters in her closet, but the skirt and blouse signal the pride she still has in her appearance. My poetry book is on the bed next to her glasses and the Kleenex box arranged with holes for pencils, the flowered address book, stationery, envelopes, stamps, and hearing aid batteries.

When she hears my voice, she closes the drawer and sits down on the bed. She rubs her right eye with a Kleenex to open the lazy eyelid. I sit on the end of the bed. No hello. This may not be the best time to build connections, I think, but I forge ahead and place two items on the bed between us: the contest chapter of the book about her life and the accompanying photo album.

"I brought the chapter about your contests and your Queen for a Day photos, Mama."

She glances at the items on the bed. "Just put them in the drawer of the chest."

What an unpredictable reaction. I thought she would love to see the old photos. It's as if I stepped into the elevator to go up to the top floor, and it suddenly shot down to the basement. Just last week, she was so enthusiastic about writing down all her prizes, so I could collect them in a chapter for "her book." What is the problem today? She answers my question as she pushes the book toward me over the fold of the bedspread.

"I really got upset when I read that poem about Grandpa. I felt lousy all night and couldn't sleep."

This unexpected remark deflates the hope that she would be interested in my poetry and maybe even be proud of my writing. I know which poem she's talking about and realize that I was naïve not to think about its effect on her. I thought she might talk with me about the distance between her parents and shed some light on a relationship I've never quite understood. Her method of dealing with difficult life events is to see only the surface, ignoring the sometimes disturbing meaning of what has happened. She frowns down at the book and gives it another shove.

"Are you going to send this book with your Christmas letters to Denmark?"

Now the puzzle is solved. It's not just about what I said in the poem but what the relatives might think about my grandparents.

"I had thought about sending it to Benedicte because she gave me a book of Danish poems when she visited us here, but I'm also sending it to friends who might be interested in the other poems."

"You shouldn't do that." She emphasizes with a limp slap of her hand on the bed. "I really have a problem with the poem about Grandpa and Grandma. It's just not fair to them."

I take a minute to mull over her criticism. At least she was interested enough to read "The Last Goodnight," but she certainly isn't proud of the poet. I pick up the book and hold it close to my chest. The picture I describe in the poem trails through my mind: my grandfather's tiny, unheated bedroom across "the miles of cook stove warmth" from my grandmother's room. He has just latched the door from the inside and labored to settle himself on the creaky iron bed. Wearing a white sleeveless T-shirt and gray work pants, he is propped up on the iron head of the bed, quilt pulled up so far that his felt slippers are visible at the end of the quilt. His pulse is thudding as he recognizes the pain in his arm and chest, reminiscent of the heart attack he had two weeks ago. He is thinking about the many years he and his wife have been isolated from each other. She, raising their only child after recuperating from TB, and he, escaping from the house to indulge in the "cigars and beer and bickering" that she hated so much. The last verse of the poem says:

"It's all just part of the routine," he mused.

The latch, the clothes, the light, the bed, and death.

She'll hear and think that I'm all right.

Or does she even care?

No, not enough to say a last goodnight."

No matter how many times I have envisioned this scene, it always brings a swell of sadness to my heart. With both hands, I pick up the book and hold it out to my mother, an offering I know she won't take.

"I didn't mean to be unfair or untruthful, Mama. It's written from my perspective and my concern that they were so far apart, even when Grandpa was dying. It's no secret that it's difficult to have a close relationship, especially in their generation." I could have added, "In your generation and mine, too."

My mother summons her waning strength and pronounces, "Those things happen, Connie, but you don't tell the world about them."

I realize now that she may not accept the evolution of the book I'm writing about her life into a book that "tells the world" about our family relationships and the emotional legacy I have received from my parents and grandparents. "Those things that happen," the disappointments and trials of marriage, are at the heart of the emotional distance between husbands and wives throughout three generations of our family, and it's important to explore them. Not only does this help me to understand my own parents, but it also sheds light on my own sometimes distant relationship with Floyd. I realize, from my mother's life stories, that the past is present in all marriages. If we don't understand its influence on our lives, it may be too late to build a closer relationship with our spouses. Would she be able to understand the larger picture?

I lean in closer and put my hand on her arm.

"I know the poem is personal, Mama, but it's just one scene that shows how barriers can build up between couples as the years pass. This is something that happens all the time."

"That may be, but it is personal. And it's sad."

I wonder if the sadness she feels is a reflection of the lack of emotional and physical intimacy between her and my father.

She moves her arm from under my hand, wipes her watering eyes, and lies down on the bed. Her right hand begins kneading the knots in her stomach. I shelve any plans I had to connect with my mother today. This visit represents a disconnection, a rift.

"I'm sorry this upset you, Mama. I don't need to send the book to our Danish family. It's really not that important."

My mouth makes the expected, obedient response, but my mind repeats a refrain of disappointment: *I wanted to share my book with you. I wanted you to appreciate the poems.* She withdraws her hand from her skirt and points to the poetry book.

"You can keep your book. I'm tired now, so you should go home. I'll see you tomorrow."

I'm the five-year-old who gets sent to her room because she has banged too hard on the piano keys. Mama needs a nap, so I have to take one, too. Rejected, void of hope, but obedient, I stand up, say goodbye, pack the book in my bag, and retreat to the privacy of my car. I sit in the sunlight coming through the windshield and take one of my comforting chocolate chip cookies out of the bag to munch on while I reread the offending poem.

What would my Danish relatives think if they read these words? Would it destroy the fantasy of their immigrant relative's perfect life in America? Or would the poem cause them to reflect on their own or their parents' relationships? Although they'll never see it, I hope that it would simply remind them of the sadness of dying without a loved one at your side.

I haven't thought much about my grandparents' estrangement since I wrote the poem almost twenty years ago, but now in the light of my mother's stories about her life, I'm beginning to see a pattern passed down through the generations in my family. It's no secret that any couple can easily slip into separate lives devoid of the intimacy of shared feelings, especially when they have no parental role models of the very relationships they need. Once this has happened, it's difficult to take down the bricks in the wall they've built, so that they can regain the closeness needed to face the demands of daily life. Reading "A Last Good Night" again forces me to look at my own marriage and the lack of communication between Floyd and me, two people who truly love and respect each other but seldom express the thoughts and feelings that build emotional intimacy. A picture from twenty years in the past comes to mind.

It was nine o'clock on a Wednesday evening. I was propped up on our bed with a stack of research paper drafts on my lap and Shadow, one of the family cats, curled up next to me. A burn on my index finger, the result of hurrying to take the meat loaf out of the oven before it dried out, made it difficult to hold the red pen. I squinted my eyes to clear the blur of handwriting on the first paper and counted the remaining essays. Twelve papers in total. I sighed, put down the pen and stroked Shadow's silky, gray fur. "Can I really do all of this?" I asked her. "Can I cook dinner, clean house, help with homework, be a good wife, and work, too?" She responded with a rumbly purr. The sound was reassuring but not as good as a human voice. That human voice belonged to Floyd, who had had a long day at the Denver University's Research Institute, a job that focused on research rather than his teaching talent, but one that had brought us back to our Colorado roots several years ago. Each evening, as soon as dinner was finished, he retreated to the basement to de-stress by watching TV with Troy, our eight-year-old. Sonja and Missy, fourteen and fifteen, usually settled comfortably into their evening routine in their own rooms.

I had a routine, too, but I wasn't comfortable with it. This was my first year of working full time since before our three children had been born. I loved my job with international students and was pleasantly challenged by helping to establish a new ESL institute and by writing my first textbook. But I was also challenged to keep up my Super Woman image. Why couldn't I be the perfect mother, excellent cook, good housekeeper, devoted teacher, and loving wife all wrapped up into one glamorous, youthful, slim woman? What was wrong with me? Since I'd been a child, I'd had the compulsion to use the time God gave me in a worthwhile manner. That was one of the reasons I made lists and prioritized. What better way to use time than by organizing it and doing what was most important? But at this point, my priorities were clashing. I'd run out of time to devote to the demands of a new job, running a household, and paying attention to the needs of our three children. I needed help and support.

Floyd yawned as he came into the bedroom, and emptied his

pockets on the top of the chest of drawers. He took off his glasses, rubbed his eyes, and headed for the bathroom. Maybe there's time now, I thought.

"Could we have a few minutes to talk?"

He took a quick glance at the bed, the papers, and me. "Aren't you busy with your paper grading?"

The avoidance in his words brought a rush of warmth to my face. I moved the stack of papers off my lap, and sat up on the edge of the bed, close to where he was standing. He moved back a few steps.

"We never have a chance to talk or share how we're feeling. I want to know how you feel about your new job, and I want you to know what's going on with me."

He turned back to the dresser and rearranged the billfold, keys, and glasses in a straight line. Then he looked over his shoulder at me but didn't meet my eyes.

"Everything's okay. I'm just getting used to the research side of things."

He walked around the bed toward the bathroom. I could tell he was hurting, but the "just ignore her and it'll be all right" reaction outweighed the empathy I had with his situation. My fingers clenched and my pulse raced.

"Can't you just talk to me for a minute?" I shouted.

I could hear him humming a tune as he quietly closed the bathroom door. Avoiding confrontation was a common response in our marriage, but the added hum was the final insult.

"I hate it when you ignore me. I hate it," I repeated as the tears started to flow.

I felt like I'd been beating on a wall between us until my hands were bloody. I loved this man I'd been married to for more than 25 years, but I couldn't seem to break this impasse. I knew the anger would dissipate if I just opened the bathroom door, put my arms around him, and told him I loved him. But I just couldn't bring myself to do this, maybe because this reaction would give him the power and control in the relationship. It was just as hard for me to express love and affection as it was for him to discuss a problem. We shared the same values, the same goals, the same bed, but we didn't share times of closeness, our innermost thoughts, our feelings. We didn't even share feelings in times of sadness. The stillborn birth of our first child, a Down syndrome baby, was a difficult event in my life and, I would guess, in Floyd's, but we never discussed how it affected us or comforted each other. We just "sucked it up" and went on with life.

How much of our difficulty with emotional intimacy was passed down to us by our parents? Some hints at this were recorded in a journal Floyd and I shared at a Marriage Encounter weekend that I cajoled him into attending soon after we celebrated our twenty-fourth anniversary. In writing about the masks we wear, he told me that he appears to be Mr. Imperturbable, always calm, never angry, always in control, never showing emotion because to do so is to lose self-control, which is a bad trait according to the example and teachings of his father.

"To be silent," he said, "may frustrate, but it can't personally hurt you."

When I replied through my journal, I told him that the silence hurts more than any words. It means I'm not worth conversing with, my concerns not valid enough to pay attention to.

He further explained that his father, whom we both admired, rarely showed any strong feelings and believed that to be a man, one must set his emotions aside. To admit one has problems is to admit lack of ability or confidence to deal with issues. It's admitting weakness. This made sense to me, because Floyd's father was a physically and mentally strong man with Cherokee Indian heritage, a man of the Old West who wore a well-worn Stetson hat and cowboy boots. Driving cattle, slicing testicles off bulls, building fences, milking cows, raising four boys during the Depression, always working two jobs in order to get ahead. Floyd's mother, Harriet, was a positive, loving woman who worked beside her husband in all the ranch and farm tasks and always showed affection in their later years by grabbing his hand and holding it tight, even as they lay in bed together when she died. She initiated the affection, a good role model for me and the other wives who joined the family.

The barriers I bring to a close emotional and physical relationship are just as strong as Floyd's. My dad knew how to build a radio and an electronic organ from scratch, play a ukulele, figure which dog would win at the track, type 120 words per minute, lead a Boy Scout troop, and fix commercial airplane radios, but he didn't know how to show affection or any strong emotion. He had been a sickly child who spent time resting and reading by himself in his own room while his two step brothers and a sister went on with their own lives. His role model was a shy, quiet father who used his pipe smoking as a shield, so that he wouldn't have to interact with other people. I never had a conversation with my grandfather that lasted more than one minute. My dad's mother was a striking, heavyset woman with snapping, dark brown eyes and hair that turned white when she was thirty, possibly because of a bad first marriage. She loved to talk, especially if she could spread gossip. I wasn't around this set of grandparents often enough to know the details of their relationship.

On the other hand, my mom was outgoing and talkative, and needed a confidante. She shared her thoughts and problems with me instead of establishing intimacy with my father. I was the focus of her life: confessor, achiever, psychiatrist, and overall substitute for my dad's attention.

"All Daddy does is sit and read, even when company comes," Mama would complain. "He doesn't even look up when I try to talk to him."

My dad's intense occupation with the written page, his ability to ignore what was going on around him, especially when my mother wanted to talk to him, is a trigger for my frustration and anger when Floyd ignores me. My exit from the family when I married and moved out of state encouraged my parents to become companions as they shared more activities together. "Going to the dogs" was what my dad called their weekly trips to the dog races, where he enjoyed gathering data; he had a mathematical formula for choosing the winning dog. They also watched TV basketball and football together. My mom knew the names of all the players and could converse knowledgeably about the games. When my dad retired from television/radio station KOA at sixty, they chose to live in a subsidized apartment in the heart of downtown Denver just walking distance from the Denver Public Library, the museums, and the shops on the Sixteenth Street Mall. All of these sites in my mom's beloved Denver brought interest into their lives and an intimacy they had not shared before.

However, this short period of closeness was fractured by signs of dementia five years before my dad had his stroke. He knew he was losing his mental acuity long before we did, and it angered him. The idea that he would be lucky and win lots of money led him to answer every piece of mail and every telephone call that solicited a purchase with the chance of winning cash prizes. With their one credit card, he ordered magazines, jewelry, whatever was offered in the mail or on the telephone. The amount owed on their Visa card grew to the point that they could never pay it off with the meager $1100 a month they received in their Social Security check. My mother never mentioned these problems until after my dad's stroke. Then she told me that she had been afraid to leave him alone because telephone solicitors called all the time.

"When I answer the phone," she told me, "I tell them that we are an old couple with no money. Stop bothering us."

They argued frequently. Daddy threatened to leave her and the apartment and "live with the bums in the Burns Hotel" several blocks away. His disintegrating personality was developing jagged edges of anger. After his death, she told me what frustrated her the most. "He was always pestering me for something sexual." This was one of the reasons she didn't want to stay in the same room with him at Ivy Manor. It was separate rooms again and strangers to each other, a situation that was particularly poignant to me. I'd always wanted them to end their lives together as true companions. I have the picture of Floyd's aging mother and father holding hands when they walked together and even when they lay together in the same bed when she was close to death. It's too late for my mom and dad but not for Floyd and me.

CHAPTER 13

PERMISSION

MY MOM'S WINTRY REJECTION OF "A LAST GOOD NIGHT" HAS BEEN
nudged away by the greening of springtime . It's a season of new
beginnings and time for me to tell my mother about a possible trip
to Cyprus for a new project that I'm involved in. Since canceling the
marketing trip to Belgium because of her broken femur, I've grown
stronger in my ability to draw boundaries. I can still feel that prickle
of apprehension about her reaction, but I'm much more confident
about her care now that Olivia has a firm friendship with her and a
commitment to take good care of her.

As Ivy Manor's automatic doors open, a burst of lemon-scented
Lysol engulfs me. Francis is sitting in a straight-backed chair next
to the bird cage, watching the entrance. Her oxygen tank is on the
walker, tubes neatly threaded behind her ears and into her nose. Her
china-cup ears are trained on any passing conversation.

"Connie," she wheezes, "I've been waiting for you."

She motions me over to her chair and presses her hand down
on my arm to draw me down to her level. I'm wondering what the
secrecy is about. Something must have happened since I visited two
days ago.

"The inspectors are here," she whispers. "They surprised
everybody and came yesterday. It's been crazy."

I pull up a chair next to her, so she can continue her report. She seems excited by the change in routine and the secrecy. She pushes the oxygen tube deeper into her nose and leans toward me.

"Somebody must have known they were coming because yesterday one of the nurses came into my room..." The words trail off while she takes a deep breath. "And looked through the drawers in the chest next to my bed. They found some cigarettes I'd hidden there and threw them away, and they snatched the Oreo cookies that I was going to eat for lunch..." Another pause and a breath plus a thump of her fist on the front of the walker. "I was really pissed off."

I acknowledge her frustration at losing her private stash of pleasures but don't mention the safety factor of oxygen and lighted cigarettes.

"You'd better go see what's happened with your mom. I'm staying right here out of the way."

I put my hand over hers on the walker, put the chair back in its designated space and head for the elevator, thinking that this may not be the best day to tell my mom about the trip. But I need to get it out of my mind. The usually neglected inside of the elevator door has been scrubbed of its finger marks, and when it opens to the second floor, I pause a moment to take in the changed atmosphere: a vase of fresh white and yellow daisies is sitting on the top of the nurse's station, half obscuring nurse Madoline's head as she sits next to a gentleman in a business suit who is thumbing through a medical-records book. The usually busy hallway is empty of residents. Evidently the wanderers and the ones with a tendency to nudity have been sent to their naughty corners. All the doors are uniformly opened to the halfway mark. The newly polished floor reflects the ceiling lights; even the burned-out light on the call board next to my mom's room number has been replaced.

Supposedly, nursing homes are not warned in advance about a visit from the state inspectors, but the staff must have had enough time to clean, polish, fix, and dispose of offending items. This inspection is crucial to the continued operation of Ivy Manor. State governments oversee the licensing of care facilities. In addition, each state has a contract with the Centers for Medicare and Medicaid Services (CMS) to monitor facilities that want to be eligible to provide care to Medicare and Medicaid beneficiaries. The majority of Ivy Manor's residents receive aid from these agencies. Nursing homes must meet more than 150 regulatory standards. If there is a problem, CMS can take action against the home by fining, denying payments, assigning a temporary manager, or installing a state monitor, depending on the nature of the problem.

During the five years I've been visiting almost five days a week, I've never been present on the actual day of inspection. I feel loyalty to Ivy Manor's good caregivers and continued exasperation at the careless and poorly trained ones. I'm hoping the inspectors will note the improvements I've seen since the facility was sold several years ago: a new furnace boiler, new paint and reception furniture, an updated kitchen, more attention to resident cleanliness. Most important will be their interviews of residents. Are they comfortable? Do they feel well taken care of? Do they feel respected? I don't think the question of happiness will be addressed. How many people in their last years truly feel happy to be out of their familiar homes and away from family and friends? If my mother were asked the question at this point in time, I think she might say "Happy? No, but I'm okay." Her painting and the work we've been doing on her life stories has brought her some real satisfaction.

When I poke my head inside Room 214, I see Elinore, my mom's roommate for the past two months, asleep in her wheelchair next to the windows on the far side of the room, oblivious to the events. My mom is standing, propped against her walker, hunting for something in the four-drawer chest next to the bathroom. The inspection has hastened a change in her usual uniform. Today she's wearing a red blouse, a small red-white-and-blue scarf around her neck, and her old navy blue skirt that's at least two inches too large. I knock on the open door, so I don't frighten her.

"Hello, Mama. It's Connie."

She leans on the walker and inches it around to face me. It takes her a few minutes to focus on my presence. When her sight has cleared, she raises her hand from the walker in acknowledgement, but turns back to rummaging in the top drawer of the chest. "You'll never believe what's happened," she says.

I move closer and start to move my arm lightly around her shoulders in a semi-hug. She shakes her head to stop me.

"That new head nurse Madoline came in and went through every drawer. I can't find my soda crackers and the extra batteries for my hearing aid, and she took my mouthwash and extra Imodium out of the Kleenex box on my bed. She said another resident might come in and get drunk on the mouthwash or take the pills."

I understand her frustration at the invasion of her only private space and can't fathom any one drinking her mouthwash, but I know that I've encouraged the contraband of Imodium pills hidden in a baggie in a corner of the Kleenex box. At least three times in the last few months, the nurse's station has run out of Imodium when my mother was desperate for relief from diarrhea It takes almost two days for the over-the-counter pills to be sent from the pharmacy.

Tom, a wheelchair-bound resident who always wears an orange Broncos shirt, startles us both when he bumps into the wall by my mom's door. Evidently his driving ability has been impaired by a search of his room.

"I told her to get out of my room and stay out," he mutters to himself. "That was my only *Playboy* magazine."

Raheen comes down the hallway to whisper in his ear that she has his Playboy and will return it when the inspection is finished. She turns Tom around, gives his chair a boost toward his room, and opens our door. She takes one step inside, offering no greeting, just a pronouncement. "Mildred, the inspectors saw your paintings in the visiting room and were horrified when they came into your room and saw that you didn't have a place to use when you paint. They told me to give you another bedside table even though there's really not room for it."

"I don't really need another table," my mom responds.

"You'd better take it and keep it or I'll get fired," she shoots back. "What the inspectors say is the law."

Evidently Raheen, as activities coordinator, took credit for my mother's painting and was then held accountable for not providing better conditions for creating the artwork. No easel, no table, just her lap and a heavy piece of cardboard with paper clipped on it. Mama shrugs her shoulders in acceptance but with a proud tilt of her chin. I can see she's glorying in the attention she's getting. She moves her walker over to the bed and sits down.

"Do you know what happened next?" she says. "One of the examiners, a nice young man, gave me that mental alertness test we get every few months. They asked the usual questions about who's the President of the United States, what's today's date, what's your birthday. You know, all those simple things. Then they asked me if I could spell "world" backwards."

"And you could, I'm sure."

She smiles as broadly as she can, showing the missing teeth and the dimples that I'd almost forgotten she had.

"Of course, I could. Then Kingsley, the new guy from Uganda, came in after the test to bring me some water. I asked him if he could spell "world" backwards. He said, 'I can't even spell "world" forwards.'"

I laugh with my mom, something that doesn't happen often enough. I'm astonished that a forbidding inspection can turn into a positive experience for my mother, one that puts her in the spotlight she has always enjoyed and affirms that she is still sharper than most ninety-four-year olds. Then I remember the two topics I wanted to discuss with her today, one about relationships in our family and the other about an impending trip I want to take. But is the middle of an inspection the right time?

With an unusual burst of energy, she cuts through my thoughts. "Could we go down to my gallery and visit for a few minutes?"

I quickly agree, help her to step into the arms of the walker, and together we slowly navigate the empty hallway.

Since our December disagreement about the poem that revealed the gulf between my grandparents, I haven't wanted to disturb the calm routine of my visits by asking my mom about her own marriage and the problems she faced in her relationship with my dad. However, I have continued to ponder the lack of intimacy between husbands and wives throughout our family history. I know that being Scandinavian is a factor—that old, unexpressive Nordic coolness. Or it may be these couples shared a closer relationship than I was aware of. Then there are the cultural differences between generations. This intrigues me the most.

From what I've read and mulled over in the past six months, couples in my grandparents' generation (early 1900s) and my parents' generation (1930s) had lower expectations of what a marriage should be, and sharing thoughts and feelings wasn't part of what was expected. They also had fewer options in marriage partners, so the idea of soul mates wasn't a factor. My grandparents married acceptable Danish, Lutheran partners that they had met in the small immigrant community in Minnesota. They did not have the opportunity to know much about each other before the wedding. Their roles in marriage were rigid. My grandfather supported the family and my grandmother stayed at home to provide a clean, safe environment for their only child.

My parents also married Scandinavians but had a wider choice that included partners from their hometowns, their churches, and the college they attended. They dated for a year in college before my mother became pregnant. She had planned to become a teacher, an accepted profession for women, along with secretarial work or nursing. But marriage intervened, and few women worked after having children. Life just happened in those days. You did not look below the surface to reflect on a life event. You accepted it and went on. To be a good wife or husband, you were not expected to be a good friend. In the mid-1950s, when Floyd and I were married, gender roles were still fairly authoritarian. A woman went to college to pursue her M.R.S. (Mrs.) degree, and college was an ideal place to find a husband, preferably by the time she graduated. Her husband's career came first. Floyd and I were married in our senior year after dating for almost four years. We had the advantage of knowing each other's goals and dreams and working together as editors of the college newspaper in our first year of marriage. In our minds, marriage included a close relationship. I postponed a career in journalism for a teaching job to support my husband through his master's and Ph.D. studies. In addition to my teaching job, where a strict dress code prohibited women from wearing pants, I fulfilled the role of the expected "happy homemaker": house-cleaner, meal- preparer, and husband-encourager. As time passed, career goals, three children, and multiple moves from one home to another allowed little time to nourish the closeness of our dating years.

Today, in our children's generations, more intimacy is expected, and couples are encouraged to share their thoughts and feelings. I see this, particularly, in Troy and Diana's marriage. They are Generation

Xers who are outwardly affectionate, say what they think and feel, and also look at marriage as a friendship.

Instead of just speculating about my parents' relationship from the complaints I've heard from my mother, I'd like to hear what my mother thinks. How would she describe her relationship to my father? Was it what she expected when she married him? If not, what did she think marriage would be like?

We sit down in the tiny visiting area just off the Ivy Manor activity room to see the paintings displayed there. Thanks to Raheen's request, I have framed ten of mama's watercolors and created a nameplate identifying her as the artist. Mama settles into one of the small armchairs I have donated for the space. She smooths the folds of her navy blue skirt, adjusts the catheter bag on the front of her walker, and leans forward to survey her watercolors.

"That picture of the lighthouse is crooked, Connie. Would you straighten it a bit?"

I get up and adjust all of the paintings, so they are aligned in the two rows on the wall to meet both of our standards of perfection.

She gives a "that's good" nod of her head. "I'm about finished with the painting of the gazebo. Can you frame it for the gallery?"

I agree and take advantage of her reference to the TB sanatorium. "You've told me how happy you were at Eben Ezer and the good times you had in high school. I'd like to write about your twenties and thirties, marriage, all those moves during the war.

She looks up at me with eyes that are trying to open as wide as possible, takes her hands off the front rail of the walker and folds them across her waist. "I don't know. There were hard times in Longmont … pregnancy … the Depression. And it was hard to leave Papa and Mama and move to Fort Logan. I loved Denver, though."

I affirm what she's told me and try to steer her back to marriage.

"So you had some difficult times in Longmont and Fort Logan, but Denver, where you lived the longest was probably the place you liked best, right? What were the times in Denver that you and Daddy really connected and did things together?"

She gives me a sidelong glance, suspicious that I'm going to a place she doesn't want to go. "I don't know what you mean by "connected," she responds with an edge to her voice. "We did things together: built furniture, gardened, went to the dog track. Actually, the happiest times were when we did things for you. You know, Connie, we decided just a few years ago that you were the best thing we had done with our lives."

I'm overwhelmed by the compliment and the fact that Mama has shared it with me. I can visualize my parents sitting together, intimately talking about the meaning of their shared lives, a closeness I didn't know existed in their marriage but one that I had hoped was there. I breathe in the moment and swallow several times to keep the emotion from bubbling up into my voice.

"Thank you, Mama. I really appreciate that and what you did for me."

She scoots back on the chair and rests her head on the back, so she can review her paintings. We're quiet for a few minutes, relishing the shared moment. Then she pulls her walker closer to her and starts to get up.

"Let's stay here for just a few more minutes, Mama. I want to tell you some news. I just found out about a chance I have to spend some time in Cyprus."

"Oh, dear," she says and sits back down on the chair. I'm waiting for usual response of "If you leave, I may get sick," but she just looks at me, waiting to see what I'll say.

I recite the details: "Our school has been chosen for a State Department grant. I'm going to have to make several trips to Cyprus, and so will Vicki, our Arkansas director. We're going to establish an

English language program for journalists, government employees, and other professionals on the Turkish part of the island, the north of the island. Floyd can come with me on some of the later trips. And we can stay in the Greek part, the south, with Sonja and her family. She can help with the project when Vicki and I aren't there. I'm excited to cross the Green Line and work in the north."

Mama taps her hearing aid, takes it out of her ear, and then puts it back again.

I repeat my opening statement. "I'm really excited…."

"Does this mean you have to be away for a long time?" she interrupts, proof that she heard me the first time.

I decide to level with her. "The first visit will be about three weeks because we'll visit the stakeholders, do a needs assessment, and hire teachers. After that, it will be a short visit every four to five months. I can do most of the work from home."

She doesn't respond for a few minutes, maybe because she hasn't heard anything past "three weeks." She grasps the arms of the chair and tries to turn her head to see directly into my face, but the stiffness in her neck won't allow it, so looks straight ahead. "It's such a long time, Connie, and I haven't been feeling good at all."

The illness mantra was expected, but I'm not going to back down this time and, amazingly enough, I don't feel guilty about leaving as long as I know she'll be taken care of. I counter her statement in a rush of words. "Missy will come visit you several times each week, and Floyd will come, too. And don't forget that Olivia will take good care of you."

"By the way, did you type my poem, so I can give it to Olivia?"

I'm confused by the quick change in subject, but I assure her that the poem is in my bag, ready to place on Olivia's desk. A few weeks after rejecting my poetry book, she began to write some short poems of her own, reminiscent of the winning "jingles" she wrote as contest entries. Her "Ode to Olivia" summarizes the good qualities of "a nurse who gives tender loving care, one who is strict but always fair. A more versatile nurse you've never seen. She can do the polka or walk like a queen...." The poem "tickles me," as she would say. It reminds me that she is the source of the bit of creativity I enjoy.

She nods and unclasps he hands. "I'm sure Sonja will be happy to see you."

I inch forward on the chair to be sure I've heard her. A positive nod of her head tells me I have. I'm amazed at this softening. It's part of a change I've seen lately as she reminisces about her life. Just last week Olivia called me over to the nurses' station as I was leaving and related a conversation she'd had with my mother. "I was surprised, Connie. Your mom told me that she worries about all the demands she makes of you. She said that she's afraid her aches and pains have been more important than your life. 'I've just been too selfish' were her words."

Mama clears her throat and, in a strong voice, says, "I'll try to get along without you, Connie. Will you make sure that Missy understands exactly what I need for lunch? And please talk to Olivia."

I'm speechless. Mama is actually giving me permission to leave her in the care of Missy, Floyd, and Olivia. Unbelievable. It must have been difficult for her to respond positively. Her left hand is nervously fingering the folds in her skirt but a slight upturn of her lips responds to my relief and excitement at the prospect of working in Cyprus. Her interest in geography and the letters she and Sonja have exchanged have sparked her fascination with the tiny island. Not only does she keep a small map taped to her Kleenex, box but she also knows that it is 66,000 miles away and has memorized all of its important cities. A pleasant sense of relief sweeps over me. I can spend time thousands of miles away from my mother, with her blessing. As an old Greek proverb states: "As long as you have the blessing of your parents, it does not matter even if you live in the mountains."

Chapter 14

Mama's Own Decision

Is ninety-six years of life enough? Mama has greeted each birthday during the last three years with disbelief that she has lived this long. The Cyprus project is in its third year, and each trip, made with her continued consent, has marked changes in her physical condition. When I returned from my last trip, she was unable to lift her legs up on the bed to lie down. When I put my arms around her to help her scoot up on the bed and lifted her legs, I realized how light and tiny she was, probably no more than ninety pounds, instead of the usual hundred and five.

"Olivia used to help me get settled on the bed," Mama said, "before she was fired."

I was shocked. Olivia fired? How did mama get along without her friend and caregiver while I was gone?

"Olivia hasn't been here for two weeks," she said. "When I asked the nurse who took her shift, she looked kind of funny and said 'maybe she's sick.'" Then Lenny came in to change my diaper and told me that Olivia had been fired because she treated Bertha with ingrown toenail medicine without a doctor's order. Isn't that ridiculous? She was the only nurse who really cared about me."

Mama plucked at the ridges in the bedspread as if to smooth the bumps in her life.

I was upset, too. I felt the loss almost as much as she did. Olivia defied the proprieties of the straight-laced nurse, but she had more practical knowledge than most physicians have. I remember her telling me that sometimes she had to "stick her finger up the ass of a patient to see if she's constipated" rather than being like Judy, the nurse practitioner, who "prescribes an enema for everybody even if they're dying." Besides that, she added a positive note to Ivy Manor, taking it from the doldrums of death and dying to the humorous heights of laughing and loving every moment of life. What was going on that she would be fired? One time I heard Madoline scold her when I was at the nurse's station. "Remember you're just another nurse, nobody special," was her comment. Maybe jealousy was at the root of the problem.

Losing Olivia has multiplied the burden of Mama's advancing age. That, and the fact that all but one of her friends from Minnesota, Brush High School, Colorado Teachers' College, and the old West Denver neighborhood are gone. My father died six years ago. The only ones left to write letters to are her distant Danish cousin, Linna, now ninety years old; Mabel, her best friend from high school; and Sonja in Cyprus. However, her letter-writing habit lives on. She writes notes to me at least twice a month with new reminiscences for the story of her life.

She hands me a six-page letter today, written in large, cursive script on the small, lined note paper I gave her for her birthday.

"I scribbled because I can't see the lines very well. Would you sit down and try to read it aloud, so I know if it's legible?"

I unload the chair where she's displaying some of her paintings and move it closer to the head of the bed, so she can hear me better. She closes her heavy eyelids and folds her arms across her chest.

I begin reading: *"I'm going back to my high school days because my whole life was affected by the two most wonderful teachers at*

Brush High, namely Miss Wolfe and Miss Erickson (Latin and English). I decided I wanted to be a teacher. The others in my group went to business schools…."

The back-and-forth nods of her head affirm her pleasant memories. She has told me that the influence of these teachers led her to substitute-teach in Latin and art, but she never held a full-time job because, as she says, it was too stressful.

I stop a minute after I read the name "Harry Madsen," because it has recurred several times in recent conversation. When I ask if this was her first boyfriend, she responds, "I liked him a lot. We had so much fun together, but that ended when he went away to a Lutheran college in Minnesota." I speculate about how different her life might have been if she had married the son of a minister. She smiles and unfolds her arms as I continue to read about her college life.

"I went to Greeley to college as I got a scholarship there, and my folks moved to Greeley…. I didn't really know how to dance as we had no dancing at Brush High, but I began being asked to frat dances. The Sigma Mus were the high-grades-no-athletes bunch…. A friend of mine, Verna, first saw Jim up by Traylor's Drugs and thought he was so cute. He had coal black hair and a light tan suede jacket (on which I later painted his fraternity logo, the Pi Delts). Grandma got me a dress for the formal dances, a long black chiffon, with or without a jacket. It went to a lot of dances…."

My eyes skim over the page, eager to see if she will talk about her pregnancy and the hasty marriage that she revealed in the hospital.

"I didn't really know Jim well until we had an art metal class together. We got acquainted there and he lived just a few doors from me in the big apartment house on the corner…. He wanted to date just me, so he broke off with his old girlfriend, Wilma Brooks. My folks didn't care for him. He didn't talk much and made a poor impression. He had joined the Pi Delts, a good fraternity, so he gave me his pin

and that night at the frat house, the orchestra played "She's the Sweetheart of Rho Delta Pi," and each of Jim's frat brothers took turns dancing with me...."

I pause here to see if her face reflects any of those distant romantic feelings for my dad. A trace of a smile is there. She pulls the knit comforter up to her shoulders. I shuffle the pages to find the final one and skim ahead before reading it aloud. It appears that she has edited out the secrets about pregnancy and changing dates on the marriage certificate.

"Go on, Connie. Can't you read my writing?"

I nod. *"Later Jim and I were married and lived in Longmont. He worked in the office at Kuner Empson canning factory. Connie was born in 1934."* I squint my eyes to make out the final sentence slanting upward at the bottom of the page: *"We loved her so much!"*

The words blur as I reread them to myself. This is the first time she has expressed her love for me in a full sentence. When I look up at her, I see a tear escaping from her closed eyes. She wrote those words for me and wanted to be sure I would read them. I reach over to hold her hand.

"I love you, too, Mama."

She seems embarrassed and wiggles her hand away from mine. Then she quickly changes the subject. "When do you think you'll finish the book?"

I want to hold onto the emotion and ignore her question, but she has lifted the lid of her good eye to peer at me. I consider that I have pages of notes for two books. Would it be disappointing if she knew I was not only writing a book about her life but also one that focuses on our relationship? Is it all right to be critical of my mother in print? Can I tell the truth from my perspective when she can't defend herself and her truth? These are questions I need to deal with before I continue writing.

"I don't have a lot of writing time right now," I say, "but I try to journal some each evening before I go to bed."

She unfolds her hands and pushes the palms against her stomach. "You try to do too much, Connie. People always ask me why you're still working."

The truth in her words scrapes like a sharp fingernail on a blackboard. It hurts and it's valid. I do fill my plate too full, trying to please too many people. I also recognize that my mom would like to be the primary focus of my life. But if she were, I think I would shrivel up and die when she died. My work is the oxygen in my life. I breathe in the joy that comes from contact with students from around the world and the support I receive from my colleagues. This helps to balance the frustration and sadness of my mother's situation. My hand covers my mouth to prevent me from retorting, "You've just ruined your message of love."

"Mama," I say, "I'm working because I love the school, and it gives balance to my life."

The shrug of her shoulders expresses "I knew you'd say that." It's followed by a long sigh of resignation. "Well, I hope you can finish the book while I'm still here. I think something serious is going on with my stomach. Not just the usual irritable-bowel stuff. There's been some blood in the toilet for a couple of days. I told Jean, the weekend nurse, but she didn't do anything about it."

Now she's clenching her hands at her waist. I wish she had told me sooner. It's possible that she was trying to spare me this additional concern, or maybe she was withholding the information to make me realize I haven't been paying enough attention to her condition. No matter what the reason, the symptoms could mean a serious problem that needs some immediate attention.

"Edefina is here today. I'll tell her right now." I lay Mama's letter on top of my bag and hurry down the hallway to the nurse's station.

Edefina's smooth, coffee-colored face is set off by a red-and-yellow headscarf tied in knots around her hair. That hint of her Ghanaian heritage is countered by her plain, cream-colored nurse's scrub and the stethoscope around her neck. She is an excellent nurse who may replace Olivia in my mother's estimation. When I tell her the situation, she immediately goes into problem-solving mode. She takes a stool sample and sends it to be analyzed. Then she calls Dr. Terry, who suggests giving my mom Prilosec, a drug that inhibits the production of stomach acid, until the sample is analyzed.

Several days later a new Evercare nurse practitioner, Kim, calls me at my office. Dr. Terry is away on vacation. Kim reports that the analysis showed blood in the stool and severe anemia, probably from the blood loss. There is no softening prelude to what she blurts out next. "You have three choices. We can give your mom a transfusion at the clinic and see what happens, or we can try to find out where the bleed is by admitting her to the hospital for a protoscope and an endoscope. And, finally, we could just let nature take its course with no treatment at all. She could get better or she could die."

Her directness startles me. I must have been dozing through the last few days, not realizing the possible outcome of my mom's condition. My mind races to keep up with my heartbeat. For more than a year, my mom hasn't even wanted the bother of leaving her room when I've suggested lunch at our house or a trip to Denny's restaurant nearby. I know she would definitely refuse to go to the hospital and probably would feel the same about having a transfusion in the clinic. Does "nature take its course" really mean there's a chance she could get better, or does it mean she would die without treatment? The decision to not treat my father replays itself with all the numbing questions. How can I make a decision that sends my only remaining parent to death? What if it's the wrong decision and she could get better? I guess I had naively hoped my parents would just die in their sleep, no decisions necessary, but this gentle death probably doesn't happen very often. I had hoped I wouldn't have to go through this again with my mother.

I ask Kim about the possible causes of the bleeding. She tells me that it could be colon cancer or colitis or any number of things, but it would be necessary for her to be hospitalized to find the real reason.

"What if nothing is done and she continues to lose blood?"

There's a pause in the conversation, and I hear Kim breathing into the telephone.

"She would get weaker and her heart would have to work harder. She'd have some breathlessness and then a possible heart attack, but we could keep her comfortable with medication."

My mind records snapshots of each of the steps in Kim's description and prints them next to the stages of my dad's death from pneumonia. There is a difference in the decision-making that sets the steps in action. I had the sole responsibility for withholding medication for my father because his mind had already been stolen by Alzheimer's and my mother did not want to be involved in the heart-wrenching outcome. But my mother is still alert and in control of her life, as much as is possible in a nursing home.

I hold my breath for a few seconds before responding to Kim. "Trying to get her to go to the hospital or clinic. Not treating her and hoping for the best. These are the only alternatives? This needs some consideration, Kim. I want to talk to my mother. I also need to talk to Dr. Terry when she comes back."

When I arrive at Ivy Manor later that afternoon, the bathroom door is closed, and I hear my mother whispering, "Oh, dear. Oh, dear."

I knock on the door, open it a few inches, and poke my head inside.

"Are you okay, Mama? Do you need help?"

She's standing up with her back to me, but she recognizes my voice. "I'm OK, Connie. I'll be out in a minute. Just close the door."

I do as she asks and stand by the door for several minutes before she opens it.. Her blue cotton duster almost reaches the floor because she's bent so far over her walker. She's looking down at the old felt slippers she has modified with shoestrings that tie around her ankles. When I put my hand on her elbow to steady her, I can feel a tremor in her arm. Together we shuffle slowly to the bed where I help her to sit down on the bottom sheet, lift her legs up, and encourage her to use her elbows to push her body up on the pillows. She doesn't have the strength in her arms to do this, so I try to help her by cupping my hands under her arm pits and gently pulling her up.

"Don't do that, Connie. You don't know how. Only Lenny can help me."

I don't respond to the slight at my abilities. I'm focused on her deterioration and the decision that has to be made as soon as possible. I leave her lying almost flat on the bed with just a thin pillow under the back of her head and pull up the blue blanket to cover her. She puts her arms over the blanket and looks up at me.

"I'm surprised," she says in a loud whisper. "I didn't think you were coming today."

I sit down on the chair next to the head of the bed and search for words that she will accept. "I wasn't going to, but I needed to talk to you. Is your hearing aid working okay?"

She mouths a silent "yes."

I slowly tell her about the test results and start to tell her what the physician's assistant has told me about the choices facing us.

She interrupts me as soon as I reiterate the first two choices, the hospital for tests or the clinic for a transfusion. "I don't want anyone poking me at the clinic. It wouldn't do any good anyway," she says. "Definitely not!"

I'm surprised at the strength in her voice but not surprised at her refusal. "I just want to stay in bed," or "in my room" are recent responses to suggestions that she go down to lunch with her friends. "I just don't want to be bothered," she always says.

"Think some more about the transfusion, Mama. It might work and it would relieve the discomfort you're feeling. We'd only have to go a few blocks to the clinic next to the hospital. I'd go with you and it wouldn't take very long."

"No, Connie. Clinic or hospital, I don't care which. Both of them are horrible. Having those tests would kill me if nothing else would." As she speaks, she seems to fold into herself like an origami bird, arms crossed with her hands under her chin and her knees pulled up. "I'm too old, and I've had more pain lately than anyone knows."

"Pain" is a word she seldom uses. When I encourage her to have a medication stronger than the six or eight Tylenol she takes every day, she always says that she's not in pain, just discomfort. "Those strong pills make me see things that aren't real," she explains. She has a fear of drugs that would make her hallucinate or lose control of her mind.

"The main thing I want, Mama, is that you don't have to experience more pain. Kim said they could keep you comfortable with medication if you decide not to have any treatment and continue to lose blood." I pause and search my mind for a gentle way to verify that she understands the outcome of no treatment. I reach over and put my hand on her arm. "Do you realize what this means? If you don't have treatment, you'll … you'll …"

She finishes the sentence for me. "I know. I know. I'll die."

The tightness in my shoulders dissolves, and I'm able to take a deep breath. It's a relief that she understands and is able to make her own decision, whatever it may be, relieving me of the burden. Both of us are quiet for a few minutes. Then she unfolds her arms and straightens her legs.

"I don't think I'll do anything."

I'm surprised at her decisiveness. She's always had definite opinions about day-to-day events, but this choice isn't what I expected. Having medical care for every ache and pain was common for her when I was growing up. But then there was that decision twenty-five years ago when she said, "No more chemo," to the doctor who was treating her for ovarian cancer. As far as we know, the cancer did not return.

"You don't have to decide right now, Mama. Let's talk to Dr. Terry about it when she comes back tomorrow."

"No, this is what I want," she affirms.

She lifts her chin, takes a deep breath, and musters the strength to give me some directives. "I want you to take the money from that drawer. I just got my fifty dollars for the month, and there are three envelopes with money in them. You can give them to Ben, Jesslyn, and Kayla."

She has actually planned ahead. Organizing her final days has given her some control. I know that it won't do any good to argue with her, so I retrieve the envelopes of cash for her grandchildren and put them in my purse. She continues to give me directions, just as she did when she regularly cleaned out the closets and cupboards in their apartment to take unused items to Value Village. For her, this marks the beginning of a new chapter in her life, the conclusion.

"I want you to take all the pictures and paints out of the chair and take them home."

I can't accept this. They're so important to her. I don't want to take them home. "Don't you want to keep some to look at?"

"No, I've memorized the pictures, so I don't need to look at them. It would be nice to have that chair empty, so someone can sit on it."

She's clearing her life of unnecessary items. She's preparing the room for dying. Her directions are clear, but I'm reticent to follow them because I'm not ready to accept her death. I question my ability to stop the routine of the seven years we've spent together here at Ivy Manor, yet I have no words to counter her decision.

Still the commander, she says she is tired and I can leave now. I do what I'm asked, kiss the top of her head, and tell her I'll be back tomorrow.

The next day I call Dr. Terry. She is angry that the nurse practitioner has presented options to my mother without first discussing it with her. She also seems surprised at my mom's decision. "Are you sure it's her time? She seems so vibrant. Still painting and writing letters."

I tell her that this seems to be what my mom wants, and Dr. Terry confirms that it would be senseless and debilitating to send her to the hospital for tests. She assures me that not treating the bleeding and palliative care are an option if the ultimate outcome is understood. Then she points out the other choice, a transfusion. "It could be just a one-time thing. It might help if this is a small ulcer and not cancer or some other problem. There's also a slim possibility that healing could happen without any treatment, although the continued bleeding is not a good indication."

Dr. Terry has clarified the choices, but the information still complicates the decision. When I confide in Floyd, he quickly weighs in on the side of a transfusion. He reminds me that in three weeks we have tickets for a final trip to Cyprus, an opportunity he's been looking forward to for months. I realize that I haven't paid any attention to him in the past few weeks. I'm sorry about this, and I do want to go together so he can visit Sonja while I finalize the project in the North. But I also know that this time is crucial in my mother's life. I need to concentrate on what's happening now before I can think about three weeks from now. Is the transfusion the best choice, not because it might allow me to leave for a short time, but because it could provide her with an extended and more comfortable remainder of her life? My mom has always taken chances on contests or lottery tickets because she believes in the chance of winning. The transfusion is like a lottery, and she might be the winner, but does she want to be? I'd like her to take a chance. I'm not sure I can convince her, but I will try.

When I enter my mom's room the next day, I see a woman in Dockers and a checked shirt sitting on the bed next to my mother. When she turns to greet me, I recognize Dr. Terry, casual, comfortable, and friendly. I haven't seen her since my father's death six years ago. Dr. Terry has always liked my mother and given her postcards that she can use as ideas for painting, and told her about her travels. This personal attention from an important person has perked up my mother. Her cheeks have a bit of color and her voice is stronger than usual. I stand at the end of the bed to listen to their conversation.

"Mildred, did you make your decision because you weren't satisfied with the care you're getting here on a day-to-day basis?" Dr. Terry asks.

This is a perspective I haven't considered. Dr. Terry knows what my mom thinks of Ivy Manor.

"No, that's not why," my mom responds. "But you know they're always closing the door when I ask them not to. And when I ring the buzzer for something, it takes them half an hour to respond. I never get tea in the afternoon either."

My mom just can't resist getting in her complaints in spite of the seriousness of the conversation. Dr. Terry goes over the implications of not treating her bleeding.

"I've thought about it," my mom says, "and I know I don't want to be poked or prodded or taken to a clinic. I just want to be left alone."

"That's okay, Mildred. We'll do what you want and keep you comfortable. What do you think, Connie?"

She turns to me for an answer. In a rush of words, I say, "I think it would be worth trying a transfusion. There's a chance it would help."

My mother responds with a quick frown. "Come on, Connie, let me have my way. It's my life."

Yes, I think to myself, it is your life but it's also mine. I've always let you have your way even though it affected me. A transfusion seems right to me. We have so many unfinished stories to talk about and questions I'd like to have answered.. I'm not ready to let you go. This seems too personal for me to say in front of Dr. Terry, so I remain quiet. The doctor gives my mom a kiss on the forehead and tells her she'll come back tomorrow. We walk together down the hallway to the nurses' station.

"She's a hardy lady with a mind of her own and a good mind at that," Dr. Terry says. "Her vital signs are still maintaining. We'll just have to wait and see."

She gives me a hug and whispers, "We'll take good care of her."

The night of my mother's decision, I dream I'm driving a car skidding out of control on an icy mountain road. In front of me is a cliff with no guard rail and, no matter which way I turn the wheel, I can't stop the car from sliding off the edge. When I wake up and recall the dream, I panic at the thought that I've set in motion the events leading to my mom's death without being able to halt their progression. But then I consider that my mother is the one who freely chose to "let nature take its course." And you can't stop Mother Nature, right? I am both proud of her bravery in taking responsibility for her life and uncertain about letting her go without trying a transfusion. She may still have some quality of life, unlike my father had, and may be able to bring her reminiscences to a positive conclusion She could affirm the accomplishments of her paintings and foresee the hopeful futures of her grand- and great-grandchildren. These are all plusses, yet I dread an extended life for her with more pain and increasing helplessness. I want her to have a pain-free death, whenever it comes, and it could be in a few weeks if the bleeding doesn't stop.

During the next week, I alert Missy and Troy and their families about her condition. Missy, Mark, and Ben stop by, as well as Troy, Diana, and their daughters. Mama enjoys the attention as long as she can tell them when to leave. Visits to Ivy Manor are just as difficult for the kids because they are surrounded by reminders of the mortality that we all face, no matter what age. Just walking in the door today is traumatic for Missy. She is met by Alta, a Hispanic woman whose dementia has trapped her in the past. Tears are running down Alta's face and she grabs Missy's arm.

"Help me. Help me. My baby. Where's my baby?"

Her flimsy gown is pulled up to her hips, and she is shivering. Missy tries to help by picking up the blanket she has dropped and tucking it around her bare legs. Alta continues to beg for help. Missy pats her on the back and asks how she can help, but she keeps crying.

An aid passes by and laughs off the situation. "Don't worry about her. We're trying to find her baby doll."

Missy has to pause outside my mom's door until she can compose herself.

Later, Mama calls me to report on her visitors. She can't hear clearly on the telephone now, so she just begins talking when the ringing stops.

"It was good to see Missy, but I was trying to sleep. Troy and Diana came, too. The girls are really cute. But it was hard on me to visit with them. It just took too much energy."

I'm not surprised at this bit of self-centeredness, but I wish she could have said, "It was nice to see everybody." Then I realize that dying is a self-centered business.

As the days pass, Mama's anemia becomes worse. She's exhausted. She can only drink water and a bit of Ensure. Everything hurts. The bones in her crooked neck crack so loudly I can hear them.

This isn't the comfort Dr. Terry promised. Janet, a bright, young RN has begged her to go to the clinic for a transfusion.

"She shouldn't give up," she tells me. "I've been encouraging her to get a transfusion because it will give her a chance."

Floyd goes with me to an appointment with Dr. Terry, and we talk together about the possibility of a transfusion.

"It will make her stronger," Dr. Terry, says, "but she'll still have the pains that she has now. Also it's a one-time procedure. If the bleeding doesn't completely stop, we won't do another transfusion."

It's excruciating to not be able to do anything. It's like having a leg crushed by a boulder with no hope of extricating yourself. I'm still trapped in the car in my dream.

In the next few days, the strength of her stubbornness weakens in the face of an aching body, severe stomach cramps, and diminishing energy. She can't rub away the stomach pain that makes her clench her fists, and Tylenol, the only drug she will accept, doesn't relieve her pain. Both Janet and I encourage her to go to the clinic for a transfusion.

In a weak whisper, she agrees. "If it will help with pain, I guess I'll try it."

We schedule the procedure the next day, with Ivy Manor's bus taking her just four blocks to the clinic. When I hurry from work to meet her, she's her old complaining self, which encourages me. She may have the strength to endure the transfusion.

"The bus was uncomfortable. Dr. Terry should have told them I needed a wheelchair. It scared me to use a walker. I don't think I should have agreed to this."

"You're really doing well, Mama. I'm proud of you." I repeat these phrases throughout the five-and-a-half-hour process. I bring her water, tea, and crackers while the first bag of blood is emptying into her veins.

"I don't think I can sit here any longer," she whispers as the nurse is adjusting the second bag. "My toes are numb, and I'm afraid I may have to go to the bathroom."

I remove her shoes and rub her toes. Then quickly run to the pharmacy to get some Imodium. I offer her a hot cup of tea and a cracker with the pills. She closes her eyes and tries to keep from fidgeting. I keep up a patter of conversation about the family and my work. She endures my conversation and the final moments of the transfusion.

"You've made it, Mama. We're finally finished."

She whispers, "I can't believe it."

The Ivy Manor bus takes us back to the nursing home, and I spend another hour getting her settled in her bed. Her eyes close in fatigue, but she manages to say a sweet "Thank you, Connie."

A tiny, crackly voice singing "I don't know why I love you like I do" is the greeting I receive when I walk in the door the next day. The follow-up to her song is "Why did you take away my drawing paper and pencils? I want them back because I have an idea I want to sketch."

Mama is back! An amazing transformation in just 24 hours. If this continues, we'll have more time together. Niggling at the back of my mind is the realization that I will have to face similar life and death decisions in the near future.

CHAPTER 15

"YOU LOOK LIKE YODA, GRANDMA"

THE LATE AFTERNOON SUN IS OUTLINING THE STALKS OF DEEP PURPLE IRIS between the two walkways leading to Ivy Manor. It has been two weeks since my mother's transfusion. I notice two wheelchairs side-by-side in one of the white gazebos. "Big Bruce," his broad shoulders stretching out his orange and blue Broncos sweatshirt, has an arm around the shoulders of Tasha, a buxom Russian-born resident with hair dyed a deep russet color that clashes with her tight red sweater. Tasha is the only resident who still wears lipstick and mascara. She is slumped forward and snoozing. As I get closer, I can hear her snoring.

"Hi, Bruce. How are you today?"

He keeps his hand on Tasha's shoulder and looks up at me.

"I love her. She said 'yes' to me. We're going out tonight in my car." His hand travels down toward Tasha's bosom.

Tasha, roused from her sleep, pushes his hand away.

"I don't think she wants you to do that, Bruce. You'd better behave yourself," I say.

He looks up at me quizzically, takes his hand away from her shoulder and puts it on her knee.

I decide to interrupt the love fest by changing Bruce's focus. "Let me move you over here by the flowers, Bruce. Have you seen the new birdbath that Raheen put here?" I roll him out of the gazebo a few feet and go inside to alert the receptionist.

She laughs and comes out to move both of them inside. "Bruce is always like that before dinner. He goes hunting for Tasha and 'feels her up.' He thinks she's his wife or girlfriend, I don't know which. When the sun starts to go down, the craziness begins."

In Bruce's case, it is probably confusion about who Tasha is and where they are. On the few afternoon visits I've made lately, my usually sharp mother has been confused about what day it is and what items she's asked me to bring her. Her bedtime has also inched up to five o'clock, because she's completely tired out. Today I had final grades and a graduation party, so I'm later than usual.

I peek through the door that is open to her prescribed eight inches. She has a pad of lined paper on her lap and is trying to push her crooked middle finger in a position to grasp a pencil. She greets me with a weary smile. "Next time, I hope you can come earlier. I really needed you this morning when everything was going wrong."

Mama has returned to life and also to criticism.

Like a mouse who spies cheese in a trap, I take a fatal step and unnecessarily defend myself. I'll never learn. "I've only come in the afternoon a few times, Mama. But anyway, how are you feeling? It's been two weeks since you had the transfusion."

"I feel okay, and I'd be even better if the care here improved. One good thing is that Edefina told me this morning that there was no indication of any more bleeding."

"Thank God! I'm so relieved. I'm glad that you're writing again, too."

She shows me the writing tablet with the title "My New Project: Happy Timer" looping up and down at the top of the first page.

"The worst time of the day for me is between five and six in the evening," she says, "waiting for my pain pills. Trying to get comfortable with my catheter and my pillows. I decided to find a good memory to think about and write down some of my thoughts."

I read the first paragraph to myself: "Fairmont elementary school is my first thought. A lovely new building Connie got to attend. Teachers best—gave students appreciation of many things. She got some great basic training at Fairmont. She loved the library—always mentioned the King Arthur paintings there."

As I skim over the three pages of shaky penmanship, I find memories of our old neighborhood in West Denver and our good neighbor Nancy, who Mama encouraged to try contests with her. My mother is full of surprises. After being near death, she has revived and is looking for ways to lift her spirits and occupy her mind.

She puts down the pencil and rubs the fingers of her writing hand. As usual, her middle finger is stubbornly raised above the rest again, an obscene gesture that doesn't fit the situation. She asks me to put some lotion on her hand. I find a small tube in the Kleenex box next to her elbow and begin to gently massage the back of her hand. It's difficult to distinguish my hand from hers. Both are thin and crowned with average-length fingers. Her forefinger has a smudge of blue paint, a reminder of the Little Mermaid painting she was unsuccessfully trying to touch up yesterday. Her nails, carefully trimmed by me, are longer than mine, but our knuckles have the same circular ridges, like smiling faces above a more serious and startling topographical maze of swollen rivers, valleys, and ridges. The blue veins on the backs of our hands are ready to burst through the surface of the thin, taut skin. Her wrist bone protrudes like a whorl on a tree trunk. Mine is not as noticeable.

I remember when Cody, my then four-year-old grandson, came from Cyprus on one of his family's regular August visits. Sonja brought him to visit Ivy Manor to see his great-grandmother. After politely shaking her hand, he continued to stare at it. Then he laughed. "You look like Yoda, Nana." Fortunately Nana didn't know who Yoda was.

Just last week my five-year-old granddaughter, Kayla, stroked my hand with her smooth little fingers, her nails dotted with pink polish, cruising over the bumpy veins and bones as if she were tracing a color book maze with her crayons.

"Why are your hands like this, Nana? They look like Great-Grandma's."

An unspoken response trailed across my mind: *Yes, sometimes I can't tell which hands are hers and which are mine. It's hard to know where I end and she begins. Who's dying and who's alive.* Instead I told Kayla that it's just a sign of getting older.

Each month that passes makes it more difficult to differentiate myself from my mother. In the mirror, I see the Scandinavian cheekbones sharpening over my sagging jowls and my upper lip creasing into deeper wrinkles. I feel young mentally, but age is stealthily sneaking up on me. I can also observe it in the faces and actions of my children and my colleagues. Not as many compliments on how I look and many more offers of help in lifting heavy objects. Although I'm still working at a job I love, I feel twinges of yearning for a time when I can just sit in the sunshine and enjoy the beauty and goodness of life. "I'm the co-founder of a school and semi-retired as the director" is still my answer to "What do you do?" However, there is a dawning awareness that the things I have to do are consuming my entire life. I'm working twenty hours a week at school; spending another fifteen hours on curriculum and e-mail monitoring of teachers' lesson plans for the Cyprus project; visiting my mother almost every day; doing the cooking, laundry, and bill-paying; connecting with my adult children and grandchildren; volunteering with immigrants; and trying to write. I would like a taste of just "being" without completely abandoning myself to retirement. I'm certainly not yet ready for old age.

Mama pulls her hand away from mine. "That's too much rubbing. You can stop now."

Her middle finger has relaxed, and her right eye is open and searching on the bed for the writing pad that I'm holding in my hand. When I hand her the "Happy Timer," she clasps it to her chest. "I need to think of more good times before I get ready for bed and have my pills. The nights are so long now, but I try to fill them with pictures in my mind. Sometimes memories of things I regret creep in there and upset me."

I pat her arm and lean forward to give her a quick kiss on the forehead. "I wish you good memories tonight, Mama," I say, wondering what those regrets are. Do they relate to the secrets she told me or a hurtful experience I still want to discuss with her?

CHAPTER 16

EXPLORING OLD HURTS

MY MOM'S MANTRA TO "JUST LOOK IT UP IF YOU DON'T KNOW SOMETHING" runs through my mind. Before the encyclopedia of her memory disappears, I want to explore what she referred to last week as "regrets" that creep into her mind during sleepless nights. The rejuvenating effects of the transfusion three months ago are waning. The eight Tylenol she takes every day aren't enough to dull the aching of her bones, and her appetite has dwindled to just bits of cake and sips of vitamin shakes, not enough to give her energy. I'm afraid there may not be much time left for conversation about the secrets she revealed to me in the hospital and about the time she intentionally hurt me by writing to Floyd's mother about my selfishness. This injury isn't the kind that requires stitches or even band aids, but it keeps surfacing in my mind like a buoyant bit of balsa wood. I don't want to upset her by talking about it, but I need to know if she even remembers that time and knows how much it hurt me.

Eight years ago when she was recovering from her broken leg in the hospital, she tearfully told me that God would never forgive her for "having many men." I've never re-visited this confession, and I wonder if she was telling me the truth or just imagining these encounters with other men.

An opportunity presents itself at my next visit. Our greetings have become a ritual of "Hello, Mama. It's Connie" followed by Mama touching her hearing aid, pushing up her eyelid to better see who it is, and then acknowledging me with "Oh, I'm so glad you're here." Then I bring a chair as close as possible to her position on the bed, and learn over to give her a peck on the cheek. Sometimes she accepts the affection and sometimes she doesn't.

Today the response is "Don't bother with that. It's too awkward."

I still want to make some physical contact with her, so I carefully brush away the thin wave of grayish blond hair that always slips down to her right eyebrow. In the last twenty years, I've broken the initial awkwardness of hellos and goodbyes in our family because I wanted to encourage the physical affection that I missed as a child. It wasn't difficult for Floyd to give goodbye hugs to our adult daughters and grandkids, but at first he avoided hugs with Troy by putting out his hand for him to shake. In Floyd's family, firm handshakes were typical male greetings and farewells.

Mama adjusts the newly placed oxygen tube behind her ear and responds with a slight reprimand in her voice. "I know you think I'm a cold potato, but we don't need to kiss. We know how we feel about each other."

I chuckle to myself at the "cold potato" analogy and tell myself that habits are hard to break when you're ninety-eight years old.

As if to defuse the frigid image, Mama begins to reminisce again about Harry Madsen, the young Danish man she "liked a lot" in high school. Maybe this will answer my question about other men in her life. She tells me he was the son of a well-known pastor who established All Saints Church and Eben Ezer. I've seen his photo in the tattered album I have at home. He's a tall, strikingly blond eighteen-year-old with broad shoulders filling out a white shirt open at the neck. Next to the photo Mama has pasted an invitation to the Brush High School Junior-Senior Banquet with Harry's signature and "Please come with me" written in the corner.

Mama pauses to refresh her memory and her dry mouth by taking a sip of Ensure from the plastic straw attached to a Disney princess cup that I found in the baby aisle. She can no longer manage a loose straw in an open cup.

"Harry had the only car in our group of four or five. We had so much fun driving around in that car with the rumble seat in back. He invited me out one evening to go to a speakeasy outside of town. I told him that Papa wouldn't allow me to enter a place like that, so we just sat outside and talked."

I ask my mother what happened to Harry.

"He went away to a fancy college back East, and we moved to Greeley, so I could go to Teachers College. I only saw him one other time, at an Eben Ezer reunion several years later. He introduced me to his fiancée." She stops for a few seconds, then continues in a barely audible voice. "Later when we were alone, he whispered 'I'm sorry' in my ear."

The fact that she still recalls Harry's apology tells me that he must have been her first love from high school into college, where she met my father. She may even have hoped to marry him. The sweet teenage innocence of her story tells me this was a significant event in her life, but not an affair. If extra-marital affairs are one of her regrets, it might ease her mind to tell me about them, and it would resolve my curiosity, but at this point in our relationship it's not necessary for me to know. I've grown to understand that that both of us are imperfect human beings, vulnerable women who sometimes make bad decisions.

She surprises me by continuing the conversation about boyfriends. "I learned to dance in college and went to a lot of fraternity dances with different boys. Then I met Jim and he asked me to be 'pinned' to him at a Pi Delta party. That was it."

Here's an opening I didn't expect. I clear my throat and decide to ask an indelicate question. "In the hospital, you told me about some other romances, other men that you cared about. Were there others?"

A mental voice tells me that I'm being disrespectful and intrusive, but it's a matter I've wanted to verify. For eight years.

Mama raises her head from its resting position on her shoulder and tries to open her eyes enough to see my face. "What's that? What did you say about the hospital?"

Now that I've stepped into this interview, I can't get out of it. I repeat what I said.

With her head back in its resting position, she mumbles, "I don't remember saying any such thing."

"Just forget it, Mama. It isn't important."

She may have been telling me the truth in the hospital, or her confession may have been affected by the anesthesia or her missing drugs. That's enough. I won't bring it up again. Mama is quiet but still alert. She doesn't seem disturbed by my question. I can't brush away my hurts as easily as my curiosity about her secrets. I need to confront her about the nasty letter she wrote to Floyd's mother. Then maybe I can let it go.

I go over the details in my mind, trying to search for a way to ease into discussing the unauthorized trip with Floyd's family to meet President Eisenhower. Floyd's brother Rollin had won a national leadership award through his work in 4-H and the family was invited to accompany him to Washington, D.C. His brother Gene couldn't go on the trip, so Floyd's mother invited me to come along. I was excited at the opportunity, but Mama had wielded the big stick of "I'll get sick if you go." When I rebelled and went anyway, she retaliated by writing Floyd's mother a note that detailed my faults: a bad daughter, selfish, uncaring, and disobedient. Evidently, she thought one way to keep me in line was to hurt me. Before that incident, she had bruised my feelings—but never intentionally. To me, the letter was the same as saying "I don't love my daughter and I want to hurt her." It also revealed that she didn't want to share me with another family. I saw her action as complete rejection and meanness.

Mentally reviewing the event fuels my need to talk with Mama about the trip and the letter, but to do it without anger, to help her search her memory. She is always interested in Missy's hockey-playing son, Benjamin, and his travels. Maybe some family news will introduce the topic.

I say, "Ben just came back from an ice hockey game in Texas. His team won second place in the tournament. They didn't have enough money to fly, so they had a long, uncomfortable ride in a school bus. It reminds me of that long road trip I took with Floyd's family when we went to Washington, D.C., to meet President Eisenhower. We all squeezed into their big, old Buick and drove for hours. Do you remember that? I think I was eighteen or nineteen."

She pauses a few seconds, wrinkling her brow, trying to bring up the memory. "I remember you going. I think I was sick then."

I rush ahead, eager to get to the point yet fearful that she won't remember the letter. "You didn't want me to go with his family, did you?"

Several minutes pass without a response. I repeat my question.

She takes a deep breath before answering. "I know that Daddy thought it was a good idea for you to go. We didn't agree and argued about it."

My dad never told me about this. He just said he'd leave the decision up to Mama, an easy way out of confrontation.

A wisp of damp hair over her ear demands her attention. She tries to push it back with her bent middle finger but can't quite reach it. Then she puts her hand to her mouth, trying to rub the soreness from her tooth away.

I'm starting to regret the physical effects of this interrogation on her, but I forge ahead anyway. "You wrote a letter about me to Harriet. You told her that I was selfish and uncaring and a bad daughter. She didn't want to keep the letter, so she gave it to Floyd, who showed it to me."

Mama struggles to open her eye wider, so she can look at my face. I meet her glance with concern, not anger. She closes her eye and turns away from me. "Oh, my goodness, I don't remember any letter."

I'm not sure I believe her. Was this such a trivial event that she's forgotten or was it a mistake she just doesn't want to acknowledge?

I push myself to accomplish the final step. "It really hurt my feelings, Mama."

These are the words I should have said many years ago, but it was easier to swallow them down and avoid a confrontation. I was a coward. But I've said them now. I've expressed my resentment. I relax and look directly at my mom. Both of her eyes are closed now and her head is turned away from me.

"I was so hurt by what you wrote, but I never told you so."

"I don't think that ever happened," she whispers. She groans and wraps her arms across her waist.

In spite of her discomfort, I want to finish this episode. I tell her that Floyd's mother gave the letter back to me and told me it didn't change her opinion of me.

A knock on the door interrupts our conversation. It's the Nigerian nurse, MoreGrace. "I know you've been having more pain lately, Mildred, so I brought your Tylenol a bit early."

Like a TV channel-surfer, Mama quickly changes from the topic at hand and moves on. She opens her eye and smiles at MoreGrace, welcoming the comfort of a pain pill and singing, "I don't know why I love you like I do...." Has she completely forgotten our conversation, or does she just want to ignore it?

When the nurse exits, my mother's last shred of energy leaves the room with her. No more words about our conversation, just a whispered "I'm tired now, Connie."

I'm tired, too, but comforted in the fact that I've said what I should have many years ago. Just confronting my mother and telling her she hurt me is an achievement in itself, but I still can't put my resentment to rest. To think that she doesn't remember the letter may add another bruise to my emotions. As I leave Ivy Manor, I mull over my mother's motivation for writing the letter. I know she was jealous of my affection for Floyd's large, dynamic family and their affection for me. She didn't want to lose me to them. The letter was an effort to lower his mother's estimation of me. Maybe she didn't think that Floyd's mother would show me the letter, so I would never know. Then again she may have wanted to hurt me as punishment for not obeying her. I can only guess at this.

A surprise phone call greets me the next morning. It's Mama. She hasn't used the telephone for weeks because she can no longer hear my responses.

She's already speaking when I lift the receiver. "...that I hurt you, Connie. Please forgive me."

I can hear her sniffling into the phone.

"I hope you're there, Connie. I'm so sorry I hurt you with that letter. I hope you'll forgive me."

I'm flooded with appreciation for these words. They're the final release I need. "I forgive you, mama. I forgive you."

CHAPTER 17

HER BED IS A BOAT

FIVE MONTHS, MORE THAN 100 TRIPS TO IVY MANOR, AND A FEW CRISES have happened since Mama offered her apology and I forgave her. At the end of my visit today, I hear Madoline's blue Crocs slap against her heels as she charges down the hallway to catch me. Her demotion to assistant head nurse hasn't altered her in-your-face personality nor her ability to intimidate. She's almost six feet tall, with large breasts and muscular arms that protrude from under her short-sleeved, beige scrub. Her narrow, nearly black eyes snap, and she waves a finger under my nose. I can smell her sweaty armpits.

She issues commands, emphasizing them with a swing of her arm. "Your mom has to get out of that bed. She'll get bedsores if she stays there. She needs a shower. We need to change her bedclothes. We need to get her downstairs to eat her meals. You talk to her and make her get up."

What is this? What authority does she have to command me to do these things? Now I have even more reasons to dislike her than her vendetta against Olivia. Granted, my mother hasn't left her bed for more than a week. Madoline's attitude might put most residents on their feet, but not a stubborn woman like my mother, whose goal is to control her environment.

Three weeks ago, Mama had the Norwalk virus. Ivy Manor

was quarantined for the second time in five years while congestion, diarrhea, and vomiting spread among the residents. Even though a warning was posted, "Please do not enter if you have a cough, cold, or sore throat," I came to visit and observed that all doors were closed, meals were served in individual rooms, and staff members were wiping sanitizer over doorknobs and all surfaces touched by human hands. No one died, but many suffered dehydration and lingering coughs and weakness. My mother was ill for six days. On the sixth day, having recovered enough to use her walker to go to the bathroom and to navigate her room, she noticed that someone had completely closed the draperies on the other side of the room, disobeying her instruction to leave them open a foot. She used her walker to cross the room, tried to pull open the drapes and lost her balance. She fell to the floor, and her walker landed on top of her. Two of the aides lifted her back into bed. No broken bones, just a bruise on her forehead. In accordance with nursing home protocol, I was informed of the fall and immediately came to see how she was.

She allowed me to pull back the bedcovers to check her arms and legs for bruises, scratches, or cuts. I didn't see any visible signs of damage, but when I brushed that wisp of hair from her forehead I could see the beginning of a dime-sized bruise. I was relieved and said, "You're lucky you didn't break any bones. Hopefully, you'll feel better in a few days."

My words didn't comfort her. She responded with a whimper. "I may not have broken anything, but I really hurt myself. I can't even move my legs. I need to stay in bed now. Please don't ask for any physical therapy. I just want to stay in bed."

I reassured her that she could rest as long as she needed to, but I worried that she might not recover from this event as quickly as she did from the transfusion that brought her back to life several months ago.

As I step back to avoid Madoline's accusatory finger, I feel a wave of heat like a hot flash. I reach out and move her offending finger away from my face. The physical action brings back a time in Cairo when a taxi driver waved his hand in my face, saying "You pay now" after double-charging me. I whopped his hand with my rolled-up two-month-old Time magazine, and he backed down. That's when I first learned I had some power to confront an offensive person.

I take a deep breath and lift my head to look directly into Madoline's eyes. "Wait a minute, here. I've encouraged my mom to try walking. Demanding that she get up just won't work. If you knew more about her you'd realize that she has always bathed herself and hates showers, and also that she hasn't eaten in the dining room for the past two years."

In a voice that can be heard on the entire second floor, she steps back a few inches and repeats her demands, ignoring what I've just said. Her tirade is drawing attention from the other nurses and the gathering residents who have their hearing aids turned on.

In spite of my anger, I purposely modulate my voice to give me an edge in the dispute. "Madoline, you're not listening to what I just said. I'll continue to encourage her to sit up and to walk, but I'm not going to treat her like a bad child."

In chorus with my emphatic words I hear another, smaller voice praising me: "You've done it, Connie. You've confronted someone in authority and told them just what you think. Congratulations."

I can criticize (usually reserved only for my husband), coax, and cajole, but I've seldom threatened any one, not even my children, because it just doesn't work for me. And it definitely would not work with my mother. Besides, it would be cruel to threaten someone who has very little time left to live.

Madoline backs away, eyebrows raised in surprise and mouth open, possibly to shout at me even louder. But then she tucks in her chin and is quiet. With an embarrassed look at the people who have observed her loss of temper, she busies herself reviewing the pill bottles in the med cart. I'm pleased at her reaction.

I turn my back on her and walk down the stairs rather than waiting for the elevator. My car and a chocolate chip cookie await me.

Later in the day, my mother calls. Her words are interspersed with little sobs and sniffles.

"Madoline said that you're mad at me because I won't get out of bed. She says you've told her that I have to get up tomorrow morning. I'm sorry, Connie, but I feel so terrible all over. My legs don't work well. I'm so afraid of falling again."

I'm shocked that Madoline has lied to my mother, and to what purpose? To coerce her into doing as she asks? To get even with me by upsetting my mom?

"I'm angry at Madoline, not at you, mama. It'll be okay. Don't worry. I'll talk to her tomorrow."

I repeat these words over several times, but there's no response. I can hear her breathing more evenly into the receiver, but I'm afraid she can't hear the actual words because of her aggravated hearing loss. Even if she can't hear me, the tone of my voice seems to have comforted her and stopped her crying. I hear a faint "thank you" and then a sharp clack as the receiver misses its cradle and falls to the floor.

When I arrive the next morning, Madoline and two of my mom's favorite aids, tiny Lenny and Joe, a muscular young Korean, are waiting for me at the nurse's station. Why the reception committee? What's going on here?

Madoline looks up from the chart she's holding. "There she is," she announces to Lenny and Joe, who both smile weakly, with sidelong glances at Madoline, as if to say, *We don't want to be part of this.* "Let's get this done," she adds and starts to stride down the hall.

"We want you to be here while we lift Mildred out of bed, so we can change her bedclothes."

Acid rises in my throat, but I've had practice, so I'm ready for her this time. I clear my throat and call her back to where I'm standing at the nurse's station. Lenny and Joe remain by my side. "I certainly will help you with my mom, but we need to talk first. You told her that I was angry with her and had demanded that she get up and walk. That was a lie, Madoline. You really upset her and you know that I didn't say that."

Madoline steps back and holds her clipboard up to her chest. She looks down at the floor instead of meeting my eyes. No apologies but a complete change in her stance. She's now the compliant employee and I'm the boss.

"I'm just thinking about what's good for her," she says in a small voice. "We can't let her lie in bed."

I see an opening here both for some wisdom and a practical approach to my mom's fears. "The best I can do is encourage her to try. Let me see what I can do to prepare her for the change of bedclothes."

The four of us file into the room.

When my mother sees Madoline enter the room behind me, she starts crying and trembling. "I'm afraid of her, Connie. What does she want?" She pulls the bed clothes up to her chin.

I move close to the head of the bread and stroke her cheek. "Don't worry, Mama. Lenny and Joe just want to help you out of bed to sit on a chair while they change your sheets."

She burrows into the bed like a mole trying to hide itself from a predator. Her voice is almost inaudible. "Can't they make the bed around me? Lenny did that once when I had the virus."

I'm wracking my brain trying to think of a way to erase the fear she feels. "Let's try it this way. Lenny and Joe will be very careful."

I glance at Madoline and nod my head toward the door. "I think Madoline has other things to do, so she won't stay."

Madoline doesn't react for a few seconds. After considering the situation, she backs out of the room but with a final retort. "Don't worry about me, Mildred. I'll be back later."

"I hope not," my mom whispers.

I step back, and Lenny moves into my place. She smiles at Mama and puts her left arm under the sheet. Then she slips the arm behind her bony shoulders to help her sit upright. Mama begins trembling and whimpering as Lenny lifts her legs around and to the edge of the bed. I'm holding tight to the end of the metal at the end of the bed, wishing I could help but knowing that Lenny and Joe will do their best.

"I can't stand up." Mama raises her voice in a thin, raspy plea. "You'll drop me. Oh, no!"

Joe steps in, and, arms linked together, they smoothly lift her into the bedside chair. Her trembling turns into a full-blown panic attack. She's gasping and can't catch her breath. I'm afraid this reaction is a harbinger of a declining quality of my mother's remaining months. How does she hang on? It isn't through strength in her physical body. She has poor nutrition, little muscle power, and numerous ailments that we'll never know about. Her brain power must be the energy that keeps her going. It's also possible that a fear of death gives her strength. I'm at the point where I wish she would just say, "Enough! I'm ready to die." But then, again, how does one get ready? According to the death-and-dying books I've read, reviewing one's life is part of the preparation that she has accomplished. Saying goodbye to your loved ones is another step. A strong belief in an afterlife would hurry things along, too. Her Catholic table mate, Francis, always said, "I wish Jesus would take me today." I could tell my mother that she can look forward to an afterlife with her own mama and papa and my father, but my own doubts about heaven would be obvious to her. Several months ago, I brought her a book of meditations and prayers. She put it in the hold-everything tissue box and told me that she still says the childhood prayer: "Now I lay me down to sleep. I pray the Lord my soul to keep. If I should die before I wake, I pray the Lord my soul to take." This may be the only expression of religious faith that she will ever share with me.

Lenny holds my mother's hand while Joe retrieves an oxygen tank from the other side of the room. I step to the side of the chair and put my arm around her shoulders. Lenny says, "It's okay, Mildred. Just breathe. Breathe in. Breathe out."

Joe hooks the oxygen tubes around her ears and into her nose. They lift her back into her bed. In about fifteen minutes her breathing is normal, but she's still shaking. Luckily, Dr. Terry is in the building making her Wednesday rounds of Evercare patients. To my relief, she stops in to check my mom's heart and pulse rate.

"I'm sorry that you've had such a bad morning, Mildred."

"It was terrible," she whimpers. "They expect me to get out of bed. I can't do that. My legs don't work. And that Madoline. She's always shouting. She scares me!"

Dr. Terry strokes my mom's forehead and gives her a quick kiss. "It'll be all right. We'll let you do what you think is best. I'll stop by tomorrow to see how you are."

God bless, Dr. Terry. My mother respects and trusts her. It's easy for me to give up the decision making to her.

Later I find out that the good doctor has asked Ivy Manor's newly appointed head nurse, Caroline, to remove Madoline as my mom's primary nurse and to put someone else in charge of her care. She has also left word that my mother can remain in bed if that's what she wants, but the staff need to continue to gently encourage her to sit up and to exercise her legs. In the next two weeks, at each visit I try to coax her into just sitting up on the side of the bed, hoping that from there she may try to use her walker again. But to no avail.

That's it. My mom has "taken to her bed," a phrase I've heard applied to elderly aunts or grandmothers several generations ago. They would decide to go to their upstairs bedrooms to wait for death while the family cared for them. Mama's life has narrowed just like the vision in her one open eye. Changes of bedclothes are done in the bed with the expertise of an aide who, like a magician, pulls out the old sheet and slips in a new one without lifting her. No more swinging her legs over the side of the bed to use the tray table to drink a glass of liquid or eat some buttercream cake. No more trips to the hairdresser who comes to Ivy Manor several times a week. I now shampoo my mom's hair in bed. After two weeks of requests by me, sponge baths are given in her bed, too, but only by Carly or JoAnne, the aides my mom demands. And the most difficult adjustment of all: no more attending to her own toileting needs. Now she must rely on diaper changes by the staff. It's more difficult for me to accept these changes in her life than it is for her. She is comfortable with her decision to be bedridden. I'm not. I know that she wasn't injured in her fall. I can still see evidence of strong muscles in her legs, muscles she used to walk all over downtown Denver. She insists she cannot move her legs other than lifting the knees a bit and flexing her feet up and down.

This is a dilemma for me. I've repeatedly asked her to try some physical therapy, but she gets even more defiant and dissolves into tears. "Just leave me alone" is her frequent response. Dr. Terry's advice is to let her do what she wants to do in her last few months but, judging from her ability to survive almost ninety-eight years, I'm not sure it will be only a few months. Dr. Terry has even requested that no other resident be placed in her room. This makes it very easy for the staff to ignore her, so the small tasks of care fall to me in daily visits: shampoos, face and hand washing, nail care, eye drops, mouthwash, food, and uplifting conversation. Can I last as long as she lasts?

My mom's bed has been her sanctuary throughout her life. When I was a child, I remember her reading in bed, writing contest entries and letters in bed, and retreating to her bed when she was upset or nervous. I'm sure my dad had to have a special invitation to join her under the covers. Security, renewal, retreat were always there in her bed. I'm reminded of "The Land of Counterpane," a poem by Robert Louis Stevenson that I memorized as a child when I was sick with scarlet fever. I still have the book, *A Child's Garden of Verses*. Mama gave it to me while I was recuperating in quarantine. The first and last verses were important to me as an only child:

> My bed is like a little boat;
> Nurse helps me in when I embark;
> She girds me in my sailor's coat
> And starts me in the dark....

> All night across the dark we steer,
> But when the day returns at last,
> Safe in my room beside the pier,
> I find my vessel fast."

My bedroom was the center of my very quiet life. My father frequently worked at night and slept during the mornings, and my mother valued her quiet time to paint and write contest entries. She regularly rested in the afternoon because of real or imagined illnesses and made me go to my room to nap or rest. I was happy to prop myself up in my bed, reading for hours, dreaming up imaginary scenarios with the stuffed animals I adored, and writing diary entries and poetry in my notebooks.

On the left side of her bed, within easy reach, Mama has fitted empty Kleenex boxes with holes for pens and pencils, places for stationery, stamps, fingernail scissors, a comb, and lip balm. At the foot of the institutional blue bedspread are her brushes, paints, and finished or partially finished watercolors, kept there in the false hope that she will be able to paint again. On her left is the tray table with the telephone taped down so she can't drop it, a water pitcher, wet wipes, and soda crackers. The tray table that was a gift of the state inspectors who admired her paintings sits across the middle of the bed, so she can pull it toward her for her meals. It also holds another Kleenex box. This one holds a small flowered address book that contains the addresses of friends she has corresponded with. The address book also has notes that test her memory of geography and incidents in her life that she wants me to record in this book. To an outsider, her world is a mess, but to her it is her independence. Using the items within her reach, she can take care of her needs. She doesn't need clear eyesight or muscular arms to reach these things. But if the cleaning staff moves something, she is lost. She is the commander of her ship, so they suffer her wrath.

Her spiritual needs seem to be fed by the paintings that I have put on the walls around her bed: the Little Mermaid in the Copenhagen harbor, the Viking Ship, the gazebo at Eben Ezer, the pond lilies unexpectedly blooming in a winding creek with a background of wintry, snow-covered mountains.

"Looking at my paintings is a comfort," she tells me. "I feel like I've made something of my life here in the nursing home."

Dr. Terry still has the hope that my mother will venture from her bed if she realizes that her fear of falling and, as the doctor interprets this, her fear of death, is unfounded. This fear is common in the elderly and is associated with decreased quality of life, increased frailty, and the notion that falling equals death. I'm touched by the strong motivation Dr. Terry has to help my mom..

"Do you think Mildred would visit with a nice, low-key psychologist?" Dr. Terry asks.

"I doubt it" is my quick response. "She doesn't want any new people in her life. It's possible that she might show her paintings or one of her scrapbooks to someone who's interested in her. But it would never work if we say that this is a psychologist who would like to talk to her about death."

Dr. Terry grabs at this straw. She arranges for Dr. Peg to visit with my mother to learn about her life. I mention this to my mom and suggest that she show the visitor her Queen for a Day album and talk about her contest wins.

"Well, maybe, but she can't stay more than a few minutes," my mom says.

The next day, just as I'm saying goodbye, Dr. Peg knocks on the door. Dressed in neatly creased jeans and a purple sweater, she's in her fifties, petite with salt-and-pepper hair and a very gentle, quiet manner. I set up the folding chair close to the head of the bed.

"Thanks so much for letting me come, Mildred," she says. "I'm really interested in getting acquainted with you."

Mama pulls her eyelid up a bit to get a glimpse of this stranger who has come to visit. "Hmm, I'm really tired, so you can't stay very long. Connie's writing a book about me, so I don't want you to steal any of her material."

I laugh to myself. Mama values her life story so much that she wants to protect it from being told by anyone but me. I didn't realize she was so possessive of the material and who might publish it.

"That's wonderful, Mildred. Don't worry. We'll just visit for a few minutes."

I leave to return to the office. About an hour later, my mother calls with the announcement that she was excited about Dr. Peg's visit. Evidently, they talked about her paintings, her childhood, and her contest wins.

"Would you believe it? Dr. Peg was here for an hour, but the time went by so fast," she recounts. "She's going to come again next week, so I can tell her about Queen for a Day. Would you bring that little brown photo album you took home? It'll be easier for her to look at that and ask me questions."

She tries to hear my response but gives up after a few seconds and says goodbye.

Wonders never cease. Mama enjoyed an hour's visit with a psychologist. She's telling the story of her life to someone other than me. She's still in charge.

CHAPTER 18

MOTHER'S DAY

I'VE NEVER BEEN A GOOD SLEEPER, SO I VALUE THE FEW DREAMS I CAN remember. Since my mother decided to finish her life in bed, I have vividly dreamed about her. In one of these dreams, I carefully pluck her from her bed like a dry, curled leaf that can crumble at my touch. My hands are cupped around her tiny body as I carry her into the sunshine outside the nursing home. I pause to let the warmth permeate her body and warm my shoulders. Then I raised my hands high. A breeze lifts her and carries her away. In another snatch of a dream, my mother is a doll that I cradle in my arms. We go to a restaurant where music is playing, and I hold her close while we happily twirl around the dance floor.

Remembering each of these dreams, I've felt a warm pleasure. They reflect three wishes I've had in the past few years: to hold Mama close to me, a gesture she would never allow; to whisk her out of Ivy Manor into the beauty and warmth of the outdoors; and to have her pass away as gently as a wafting breeze.

I don't have to dream to carry Mama with me in my mind all the time. When I see the snow-tipped mountains outlined against a cloudless, azure Colorado sky, I think, "Mama would love to see that, so she could paint it." Even a ride on the light-rail train from the suburbs to downtown Denver prompts me to think how excited she would be to take this new form of transportation after riding streetcars and buses for seventy-five years. Each time I travel overseas, I look at my surroundings and wish that she could see through my eyes: Her granddaughter's house in Cyprus with its peach stucco walls and red tile roof. The fields of red and yellow tulips in Amsterdam. The imposing Dubai tower in the Emirates. This yearning to have her experience the wonder and beauty of life touches me in a tender place. It hurts to be so close to her, to know what she enjoys, to know her thoughts so well that I can finish her sentences when she can't find the word or phrase, and, finally, to know that I cannot give these experiences to her.

Then I remember what happens when I show her a photograph of her granddaughters or a colorful postcard from a place she has never traveled to. She'll study it for a few minutes with her good left eye. Then she'll send it to her memory bank, where it will stay forever. Weeks later she will comment, "Sonja's hair looks better long. She had such short hair in the photo" or "Floyd looked so funny wearing that little Egyptian cap when you had your anniversary party. Why did he want to wear such a crazy thing?" I used to look at the quick return of my photos as a rejection of my gifts, but now I know they are filed away in her mind to serve as a diversion for her in the solitary confinement of her bed.

When I visit today, two months after she's retreated to her bed, she's in the same, predictable position, like a doll that has been placed carefully in a crib. She is lying on her back because the catheter she's had for eight years makes it uncomfortable to lie on her side. Her skeletal, eighty-pound frame hardly makes a bump under the bedclothes as she dozes. I decide not to wake her up yet. I sit in the chair at the end of the bed, next to her useless feet propped up on a rolled towel to prevent bed sores.

With a little groan and some rattling, she clears her throat. She lifts her head up and down as if the motion will open her eyes. I stand up and move to the head of the bed.

"I'm here, Mama. It's Connie." I touch her shoulder and repeat the words.

She mumbles, "Connie?" I follow the routine of placing a soft pillow behind her back, using a cotton ball with eye wash to help open her good eye, and cleansing the eyelid that's permanently shut. She's wide awake now, trying to turn her head to better look at me, actually to stare at me as if she's committing to memory as much of my face as she can see. I smile at her.

"It's crazy, Connie, but I can't remember what day it is."

"It's Sunday and Mother's Day, Mama. I brought you a few little presents, some hand lotion, some purple iris from our yard, and a Thomas Kincaid card with one of those pretty cottages surrounded by flowers."

She directs me to put the card on her tray table so she can look at it later and to put the flowers on the chest as far away from the bed as possible, commenting, "They're pretty, but I don't like the smell." I put the vase of iris on the chest in the unoccupied part of her room and bring her the hand lotion.

She is struggling to pick up the card with her crooked fingers. "Now I remember that it's Mother's Day. MoreGrace wished me a happy day this morning when she brought my pills. I have something there for you, too," she adds, pointing to the table tray table that holds her water glass and the Kleenex box. "More found it in the drawer when she was looking for a new hearing-aid battery."

I pick up a folded piece of lavender stationery. It says, "To Connie on Mother's Day." Mama must have written it last year and forgotten to give it to me. I unfold the page and silently read the uneven lines of cursive writing that she could still produce a year ago.

> To a Daughter from Her Mother:
> Mother's Day is for daughters, too,
> and there's none other like you!
> Always giving—so kind and true,
> Although many depend on you,
> from students to teachers—the whole crew
> you take time for all—be it problems big or small.
> If I knew how, I'd write an ode right now
> but words can't express
> the joy and happiness you've given me.
> I'm so thankful and proud to be
> mother of a special daughter, Connie.

My throat is tight with emotion. Her verse is not only an expression of her respect and love for me, but it also shows that she knows something about me and my life outside of the nursing home. I've always thought she wasn't interested in what I was doing because our conversations were focused on her life and her needs. I'll treasure this poem. It's an expression of love and gratitude that she would find difficult to share directly—although lately I've noticed that she has coupled "Do this, do that" with "Thank you for doing so much" or "You've been so good to me." In return for the verse, I try to reach over the tray table to kiss her but can only take her hand and brush my lips over its cold and bumpy surface.

"This is beautiful, Mama. Thank you."

I see a slight depression in her cheeks, where her dimples are, as she tries to smile. She squeezes my hand. "That's OK, Connie. It's too hard to reach across all this … What's that word? This stuff … this para …"

I try to help her out. "Do you mean 'paraphernalia'?"

As if darning a hole in a sock, she repeats the lost word over and over, syllable by syllable, trying to stitch together the edges of her memory. What she normally recalled in fifteen seconds now takes five minutes at best, and, as a result, her speech has slowed and her words are sometimes slurred. Her deafness adds to the confusion. It's sad, because words have been a treasure chest for her. She has always played with them in her everyday speech and used them to write winning rhymes and essays. I still remember one of the sentences she rattled off in the last round of a radio spelling bee to win the competition for number of words beginning with the same letter: "bouncing baby boy burst blue balloon beside Bob's bed...." Difficulty in retrieving words is natural as one ages, but for my mom it's like losing a limb. Defeat is not an option. While I arrange the items I've brought her, she begins reciting the vocabulary homework she has assigned to herself:

"Para ... fin. No, para ... fi ... nal ... ya."

My pronunciation of "paraphernalia" in a loud voice helps her to repeat the word correctly. I can imagine little Mildred, the third-grader in Brush Elementary, repeating words before spelling them correctly to win a spelling bee.

"Missy," she says. "Can't think of real name. What is it?"

Melissa, I tell her.

"My tooth. You wrote it on a card for me to remember. A, B, C, abcess."

I applaud the mnemonic device. I'm proud of her will to keep her mind alive which, in turn, seems to keep her heart pounding and her lungs working. The note card reminds me to check on the antibiotic prescribed for her abscessed tooth, one of the three teeth left in her mouth. She refused to have dentures and didn't want a visiting dentist come to the room, and now, of course, she can't leave her bed to travel to the dentist who previously extracted her crumbling teeth.

This is just one of the problems I can't solve, even though I'm the Heloise of simple solutions. Her tooth should be pulled, but she couldn't withstand the surgery. The antibiotic is a holding pattern until the plane runs out of fuel

Last week, I took these problems to a quarterly Care Conference. Usually, the meeting is attended by the head nurse, the social worker, and the activities coordinator, but this one was limited to just the new boss, Caroline, and me. I like Caroline, a pleasant, buxom blonde (my mother would appreciate the alliteration) in her mid-forties. She reminds me of Olivia who wore bright aqua scrubs decorated with an assortment of pins given to her by the residents. As we sat in the familiarity of the tiny conference room lined with my mom's paintings, in chairs I had donated, some of my apprehension about discussing my mom's physical condition dissipated.

Caroline propped a large spiral notebook on the coffee table and riffled through the six inches of pages that represented my mother's nine years of records.

"Mildred has been here for such a long time," she said, "and you've been such a good daughter, caring for her in all those visits."

I mumbled my thanks at the compliment.

Caroline pulled out the most recent report and her check list. "There's not much to report this time, Connie. We have no status on weight or height because she won't get out of bed to be weighed or measured. Her nutrition seems to consist only of the vitamin shakes and what you bring her from home. The transfusion she had last year brought about an amazing recovery, something we didn't expect. Then the bout of Norovirus led to her fall. I don't believe she was injured, was she?"

"No," I said, "but she refused to get out of bed, and she didn't want physical therapy. I think she was afraid of falling again. She just resigned herself to finishing her life in bed."

Caroline nodded, consulted her list, and added that my mom's blood pressure was quite high and her oxygen levels just below the acceptable level. She noted that keeping her on oxygen would make her more comfortable. As she turned the page in the notebook, a half-sheet memo fluttered to the table. She retrieved it and read it to me. "Allow Mildred to do as she wishes. Respect her in the time she has left." It was signed by Dr. Terry.

I knew that Dr. Terry had requested that the staff encourage, not force, my mother to leave her bed, but I had never heard her actual words.

"Your mother is really a special case, isn't she?" Caroline said with a slight smile.

"Yes, she is, in many ways."

Mentally I delineated why she was special: the length of time she'd spent in Ivy Manor; her stubbornness; the respect she'd engendered among many caregivers because of her intelligence, her memory and her creativity; and the frustration she'd caused others with her many demands and criticisms.

Caroline asked me to sign off on the checklist. "Just one final thing," she said. "You also need to review and okay Mildred's end-of-life decisions. Here's a copy of her Declaration as to Medical or Surgical Treatment that she approved when she first came to Ivy Manor."

Mama's signature of nine years ago in perfect Palmer method writing put the stamp of authority on a document stating that she did not want any life-sustaining procedures. In other words, no resuscitation, surgery, or artificial nourishment. Only medical procedures or interventions that would provide comfort and pain control would be allowed. The bottom of the page was heavy with two witness signatures in addition to the notary public's name and the state of Colorado seal.

I rubbed my arms to warm away a slight shiver. Mama's death

was staring at me from the official page. I paused for a minute before initialing the box on the checklist that said I had reviewed the document. Caroline passed the Medical Durable Power of Attorney page to me. My name, written by my mother, was the only line I could focus on against the small, dense type of the document. I was the designated agent who had "the power to consent to giving, withholding or stopping any health care, treatment or diagnostic procedure."

I would never forget that I had wielded my power in hastening my father's death when I told the staff to withhold antibiotic treatment for his pneumonia. My awareness of that power was as constant as my own heartbeat.

Caroline asked: "Would you like to put your mother on Ivy Manor's hospice care?"

I shook my head, not understanding. Hospice care? I started to ask for her to repeat the question.

She quickly added, "It might be easier for us to care for her in these final days if she's under our hospice care."

A cool breeze swept into the room. I put my arms into my sweater and buttoned it. In an attempt to ignore Caroline's words, I stared at the paintings on the wall in front of me. These were proof of my mother's life, products of her imagination. Would they take them down when she was gone? Then what would be left of her presence here? I'd resisted the fact that my mother really is dying and that this may happen at any time. The routine of almost ten years of visits was so much part of my daily life that I couldn't imagine it ending. We were just now becoming closer than we'd been for most of my life, and I was not sure I wanted this budding relationship to end now. During the past year, we'd developed a friendship on equal footing, instead of the old lopsided connection of a demanding mother and a dutiful daughter. Granted, we both had habits that were difficult to break — my desire to please and her need to control — but underneath these responses was a respect for each other's strengths and an acceptance of our weaknesses. For me, the most significant realization was that I didn't have to be perfect in my mother's eyes to receive her love.

Caroline reached across the table and put her hand on my arm. "I know it's difficult to accept her passing, Connie, but it's evident that her health is deteriorating day by day. I promise that we'll make her as comfortable as possible."

I completed my signatures on the end-of life paper work and placed it on the open notebook in front of me. Caroline closed the book, shook my hand and left me sitting in the conference room. I surveyed the pictures on the wall: stark white lighthouses with beams at the top shining against blue skies; snow-capped mountains and water lilies that didn't belong in winter streams; an Eskimo village surrounded by totem poles in honor of grandson Troy's Alaskan Inupiat heritage; Viking ships sailing on white-tipped waves; the Little Danish Mermaid; and a lacy white gazebo. These were products of Mama's creative life that would remain in my heart when she died, a death, that was necessary for both of us. She had survived several near-death episodes, and, like the dry leaf in my dream, her body was curling in on itself and quickly losing its connection to any life-giving force. I prayed that she'd be gently carried away. Her body was ready, but I wasn't sure she was prepared. She was stubborn and didn't want to give up, but in spite of her attempts to regain her mental acuity, she had little quality of life. And, in spite of the closeness we were developing, I was just plain tired of caregiving. There was not much left that I could do, and I needed to move on. I had my own bucket list of goals for my senior citizenship: quality family time, travel, writing about cultural experiences, Egypt, and, first of all, finishing "our book." These years at Ivy Manor had taught me many things about my mother and myself. The recounting of Mama's life stories had helped me understand the negative parts of her personality: the self-centeredness, the critical and controlling attitude, and her difficulty in showing love. I'd also learned to appreciate her positive aspects: her sharp mind, her creativity, her encouragement of any talents I had, and her ability to carve out a life in a nursing home like Ivy Manor. I'd tried to react to the things I didn't appreciate by choosing to be a positive person, trying to love unconditionally, and giving of myself to others. Granted, I'd gone too far in some of these areas, but there was still time to modify my people-pleasing behavior. I would always be my mother's daughter, but our relationship would continue to grow in strength through my memories, and the writing of our book.

CHAPTER 19

THE BEST OF HERSELF

TWO MONTHS HAVE PASSED. MY DAY PLANNER IS OPEN AND CENTER STAGE on my desk in the crowded office I share with a part-time instructor. I've cut my hours at work to about twenty per week. This change is reflected on my business card, which describes me as "Co-Founder and Director Emerita." Holding on to my professional identity in the face of aging is like clinging with all my strength to my handbag as a purse snatcher tries to escape with it. Although I'm neither teaching nor directing the center, I still relish the spice of cultures that season each day and the warmth of friendship that my colleagues provide.

Like a checker board at the beginning of a game, the filled squares in my planner are neatly lined up, with some space in the middle waiting to be filled. The college International Day I initiated thirty years ago is coming up this Wednesday. With Missy's help, the mariachis and belly dancer will highlight the twenty cultural booths manned by students from each country. A deadline for the student writing magazine I publish each term is penciled in for next Monday. I'm training some new Conversation Partners today at one o'clock after the International Club meeting. My volunteer position on the board of a community immigrant initiative will fill another square in the middle of the month. Outlined in red is an appointment at Ivy Manor with Dr. Terry. Because they have become part of my daily life, the visits to my mom are not on the calendar. A yellow sticky note on today's date reminds me of the groceries I need to buy for a cookout for the kids and grandkids this Sunday. I shake my head as I survey the tasks. I'm still that child trying to win a contest for person with most activities.

I push the planner to the side of the desk and ponder the visit Floyd and I made to my mom yesterday. When we entered the room, I loudly announced our presence.

To my surprise, Mama responded immediately. "I'm so glad you're here, you and Floyd," she said, emphasizing each word, so we could understand her breathy voice.

The way she was lying on the bed reminded me of the Tutankhamen sarcophagus: a rigid body stretched out, with her head on a thin pillow and her feet propped up a few inches on a smaller pillow. The back of her hair formed a gray crown matted down on the back pillow. Her one good eye was open just a slit, and the other eye was permanently closed. An oxygen tube threaded into her nostrils and back over her ears. Her arms, crossed at the wrist, lay outside the rose-colored spread. This vision of my mother, immobile for the last five months, will forever remain in my mind. I had naively imagined she would still be able to sit on the side of the bed, writing notes to me and sketching ideas to paint. I blinked my eyes to stop the tears and took a deep breath as I sat down at the head of the bed. Floyd unfolded the visitor's chair and sat at the end of the bed, just out of my mom's sight.

As if she had planned what she would say long before we arrived, Mama began to speak. "I've been counting my paintings on the wall. They're blurry, but as long as I can tell there are five of them, I know I'm not blind." Her struggle to remain alert and positive was touching. This was my mother, the best of my mother, the mother who was grateful and satisfied with the life she had lived. Floyd turned in his chair to look at the familiar paintings, nodded his head, and, when he turned back to the bed, started dusting the wood on the footboard with his fingers.

We sat in silence for a few minutes. Then Mama adjusted the oxygen tube that had slid out of her nose and continued her monologue. With a slight lift at the corners of her mouth, she described a scene from her childhood. "Last night I thought about Eben Ezer and Sister Sine baking ginger cookies. I could see that big black oven and smell those cookies. I took a walk around the lily pond and went into the tent where Grandpa and I slept."

As if to close the distance from the past to the present, her left hand started moving back and forth over the rose-colored bed spread. She hit the Kleenex box with the back of her hand and knocked it out of reach. "Did you move my paper and pencils, Connie? You know I need them. I have an idea for a sketch."

"They're right here, Mama, on your left side." I showed her where the pad of paper was tucked under a fold in the spread.

Although she could barely hold a cup of water, she still had the will to draw, not realizing that it would be impossible to grasp both the pencil and the pad at the same time. She fingered the edge of the pad and turned her head toward the wall. "I can't see the calendar. What day is it?"

Floyd, who had been a quiet observer until now, cleared his throat and replied, "It's the twenty-eighth of April."

With a sigh that whistled softly through her oxygen tube, she declared, "April is almost over. I've made it another month." She paused to calculate the months. "And I'm almost ninety-nine." She licked her dry lips and paused for a few seconds. "You know ... I've had a good life."

Her pronouncement was the "happily ever after" I used to wait for when my grandmother told me fairy stories. Mama wouldn't have said this at the beginning of her stay at Ivy Manor. Her life, as she knew it, had changed for the worse: no familiar home, a husband with Alzheimer's, her own body failing, and no one but her daughter to rely on.

As if she sensed what I was thinking, she said, "I can never thank you enough, Connie. I haven't been easy to live with, I know, and I'm sorry. You've done so much for me." A tear slipped from her good eye. She tried to reach her cheek but touched her chin instead.

I swallowed several times to stop the swell of emotion. She was saying goodbye. I learned forward and wiped her wet cheek with my finger. "I'm glad I've had these years with you, Mama. You know I love you."

She nodded her head slightly in affirmation, and the bones in her neck cracked. I stroked her arm until she moved it to her lap. Her throat made a rattling sound when she tried to clear it. She was determined to say more in spite of the effort it took.

"I don't know what I would have done without you, both of you. I know one thing. I wouldn't have lasted this long. Maybe that would have been better for you."

It would have been easier for me, I thought, but I wouldn't have had the opportunity to repair our relationship and to better understand myself. I'd gained perspective on the stumbling blocks in our relationship and had discovered the importance of the building blocks she'd provided me. The greatest understanding I'd gained was the recognition that my self-worth was not based on how much I pleased my mother and others. It was based on who I really was, being true to myself. I didn't have to be validated by others if I valued myself.

Silence settled in on all three of us. We needed time to absorb the important words that had been said. Mama's shoulders relaxed and her arm slipped back to her side. The oxygen tube magnified the raggedness of her breathing. She was asleep.

It's difficult for me to bring myself back to the present as I sit at my desk, remembering the importance of yesterday's visit. What will today bring? Will these days be her last? I hurry through a few of the tasks at my desk, put my day planner in my briefcase and tell Missy that I'm going to visit Grandma. She gives me a hug. "Tell Grandma I'm thinking about her."

I linger for a moment in the reception area of the nursing home to look at the new faux wood flooring and the rust-colored armchairs that flank a polished mahogany side table, all part of the renovation of the first floor. A blot on the newness of the lobby is the "not working" sign on the elevator. I take the interior stairway to the second floor and down the hallway to Room 214, now as familiar as my own bedroom. I knock on the door to alert my mother.

She appears to be sleeping, but it's difficult to determine these days because of her closed eyes. I would guess, from her perspective, there's not much difference between sleeping and being awake, much as there is not much difference for my aging cat, who appears to be dozing all day long although her twitching ears reflect alertness.

I knock gently on the table across her bed, but there's no response. "Mama. It's Connie!"

She stirs. I repeat my announcement. Her eyes remain closed, but she groans as she tries to move up a bit on her pillows. She can't achieve this because her propped-up feet are rigid. She clears her throat and, thinking I'm one of the nurses, asks in a whisper, "Has Connie been here?"

"It *is* Connie, Mama. I'm right here, and it's ten o'clock."

She repeats the usual affirmation. "I'm so glad."

Her hand tentatively reaches for her eye but ends up on the tip of her nose. "I can't get my eyes open."

I ask if I can put a damp washcloth on her right eye, the only one that will open slightly. Without waiting for an answer, I get a washcloth from the bathroom, fold it, dampen it with warm water, and carefully press it against her eye.

"It's so cold," she complains trying to turn away from my hand.

The process is repeated with warmer water in hopes it will dissolve some of the matter that's holding her eye shut.

"It's too warm," she says.

A final step may solve the problem. With the forefinger of my left hand, I pull up on her eyelid while my right hand finger pulls down slightly on her lower lid. The eyelids part and I reach for the eye drops, squeeze in several drops, and ask her to roll her eye around. All I can see is the white of her eye, but she confirms that she sees me, a fuzzy replica of a daughter. I lift her head, turned rigidly toward the right, and as gently as possible put a thin pillow behind it.

She groans again. "Only Lenny can do that," she says. "You don't know how."

She seems fully awake now and in need of some sustenance.

Lenny has refilled the blue Cinderella cup with water. I put it in her right hand and try to cup her fingers around it. Her knuckles are too rigid to hold it.

"How do I do this?" she asks.

I know she wants to hold the cup by herself, so I put it in her left hand and prop it against her other hand.

She tries to move the cup to her mouth. When she feels the drop of water from the straw, she's on the verge of tears. "Oh, no, it's spilling! I don't understand. I was able to hold it this morning."

When I ask her if she can move her right arm up to the table, she struggles to lift it but is unable to move it more than an inch. Something has happened since Floyd and I visited yesterday. I know she can't stay the same, but I didn't expect her to deteriorate so quickly. I hold the cup to her lips while she takes a single sip. Our limited conversation is punctuated by my mother's "I don't know ... I just don't know." After fifteen minutes, she tells me it's time to leave because she's tired. I lift her right arm and kiss her hand.

"Be careful going home," she whispers.

I stop at the nurse's station to tell Janet about the sudden change in my mom's physical abilities.

She nods her head in recognition of an event that's part of every nurse's daily life. "I'm sorry, Connie. It may have been a small stroke, something that's expected at this stage. There's really nothing we can do."

Doing nothing is hard to accept, but prolonging a life that is without quality is just an extension of pain and suffering. It has been long enough.

CHAPTER 20

I Don't Know Why

THE NEXT THREE WEEKS ARE A SERIES OF STILL SHOTS. WHEN THUMBED through quickly, they compose a moving picture of my mother's refusal to succumb to death. In the first scene, Floyd and I are just sitting down to dinner when Edefina calls to inform me that Mama has a fever; they're testing her urine for infection. She suggests that I call Dr. Terry for more details. Dr. Terry tells me that a urinary tract infection is an expected part of a downward spiral. Impossible to stop the descent, I think. Then I remember that Mama's death was predicted twice before, but she rose above her ailments and came back to life. Will this time be final? No more physical resurrections? Although I experienced my father's inevitable steps toward death, it's different with my mother. My dad's dementia took him away from me several years before his actual death, but my mother is very present in all the memories we've shared and all the understanding I've gained during these ten years. I need to stick with her in this final chapter in her life.

I've tried to be a realist when I've talked about the deaths of other people. I've used "died" instead of "passed on," "passed away," or "crossed over," because I'm not sure that there is a destination we pass on or cross over to. Yet I have a strong belief in a Supreme Being, God, Allah, Spirit of Life—all good words with the same meaning. I see the goodness and beauty of this Spirit in human beings of all cultures and religions, in nature, and at work in the world. I've studied Christianity, Buddhism, and Islam as a member of an eclectic group in church, but I don't know if there's an afterlife, and I'm beginning to believe we create our own heaven right here on earth. In spite of these beliefs, it's very difficult to say "death" when talking about my mother. It's just too final. Too stark.

I'm reminded of a conversation I had with Raheen several days ago. I was sitting next to my mom's bed while she slept. The tap of the activity coordinator's high heels and the brightness of her fuchsia kameez added life to the somber room. She propped herself on the end of my mother's bed, something she would never have done if my mom had been awake to scold her.

In her strident voice, she declared, "Mildred will join Jim when she passes. That will be lovely."

I was surprised by her directness. I stopped for a minute to think about an appropriate response. I could affirm her statement and say that I could already see Daddy with angel's wings and beckoning arms, or I could be truthful.

"That would be wonderful, although I'm not sure she believes in an afterlife. She's been apprehensive about death the last year. It would be comforting to believe in a heaven, but I don't know what happens after death any more than she does."

Raheen raised her eyebrows in surprise. "Oh, my God, really? But maybe it's easier for people like me to believe. I haven't been as educated as you have."

She told me that she had been brought up with strong Christian beliefs even though Pakistan is a Muslim country. Her brothers and sisters married Muslim partners, but they still attended the Christian church and sometimes prayed in the mosque. This melding of Christian and Muslim beliefs was as much of an asset to Raheen as my education was to me.

Our conversation was brought to an end when Mama lifted her arm slightly and wiggled her fingers as if to say, "Shoo Raheen away." She had always resented it when I talked too long with Raheen, Lenny, or other workers. I thanked Raheen for her concern and told her I would talk to her later. My mother's hand relaxed as soon as she left the room.

I wish I could know my mother's thoughts about an afterlife. She was brought up in the Danish Lutheran church and then slid easily into membership in the Methodist church because, for her, church wasn't about doctrine but about relationships. She was never interested in exploring or expanding her beliefs. When I was about eight, she took me to Sunday school in our West Denver neighborhood because she enjoyed the companionship of the adults there. From third grade on, I was intrigued by religion and what it could teach me about being a good person. When I began reading, I pored over books about knights on crusade and characters on a mission for God. In the fifth, sixth, and seventh grades, I spent time in each church in an eight-block radius of our house. I loved the symbols, incense, and ritual of the little stone Episcopal church. I went through catechism in the German Lutheran church, and I enjoyed sitting at the back of the empty but awe-inspiring St. Joseph's Catholic church. As I continued my search in junior high, I read and reread all the popular Christian books: Fulton Oursler's *The Greatest Book Ever Written* and *The Greatest Story Ever Told* and Peter Marshall's collected sermons in *A Man Called Peter*. I believed every word of the Nicean creed: "Jesus, son of God, born of the Virgin Mary...." I wore a mustard seed necklace and repeated Norman Vincent Peale's positive-thinking meditations each morning. These experiences enriched my life and, at the time, provided comfort when I had problems. I've grown past these childhood beliefs. Now I see them as the beginning of a path that has widened to include the experiences of having close friendships with

Muslim and Coptic friends in Egypt; of finding the goodness innate in my Buddhist, Muslim, Christian, and non-believing students from around the world; and of studying philosophy and religion with close friends within the institution of an open and liberal church.

In a second scene at Ivy Manor two days later, I find my mother with a normal temperature and a mind that is struggling to function. As if she's putting a key into the ignition and getting just a few sparks, she keeps trying and then gives up. She tries again and her brain is energized. As the morning parade of nurses and aides comes into the room, she studies them carefully through the tiny aperture of her one good eye.

"Lenny," she says. "More. You're MoreGrace."

She notes the names of every caregiver. After she has gained some mental power, she starts working on her body. She is able to lift her right arm but not to use her fingers. She hasn't eaten anything since Sunday morning, when she took a sip of water, but today at three in the morning, she stopped Edefina when she came in to check on her.

"Mash potatoes," she said. "Want mash potatoes."

This morning, I am able to give her bites of runny mashed potatoes and sips from a cup of Lactaid.

"Wha … happen?" she asks. Her words are slurred.

I lean my elbow on the bed next to her head, so I can hear her better. "You had a stroke, Mama, and an infection of some kind that gave you a high fever."

She moves her head slightly in response. I can tell she is grateful for the explanation. "My…little…book…address? Where? Box. Who took?

I have removed the Kleenex box that held her address book, and the CNAs have taken away the box she adapted to hold her personal-care items. Basically, we have taken away the world she is familiar with so that the aides and nurses can care for her more easily. If she had the words, she would scold us. Instead she stutters, "I ... don't ... know. I don't know ... why...."

I know what she's trying to say. "I don't know why I love you like I do ... I just do," I repeat. "Do you remember that little song you sometimes sing to Lenny when she changes you? I do know why I love you like I do. You're my mama. You took good care of me."

She practices the familiar phrase. "I don't know...love...like I do."

"That's fantastic, Mama. Your speech is much better."

Edefina comes in the door to report on my mom's 3 a.m. revival. "She's much better, Connie. She's been asking for some white cake, too, but I couldn't find any."

Next Rebecca, the Ivy Manor administrator, comes in to greet my mom. Mama calls her by name. She knows each of the aides and nurses who come to see her and welcome her back.

In the third scene, the spiral that paused for a day has begun its descent again. I find my mother awake but lying flat in bed with no pillow behind her head. Her blue pajama top is twisted around her chest. She has a plastic straw grasped between the knuckles of her twisted hand. The call button, usually pinned to her pillow, is hanging over the side of the bed. She looks so alone and helpless. I'm relieved that she's still alive but worried that she has been neglected by the staff and by me. She seems to sense that I'm here.

"Who's there? Is that you, Connie?"

I touch her shoulder and stroke her empty hand. "Yes, it's Connie, Mama. Are you okay?"

"Not okay ... but glad you're here ... need water."

I prop her up on the pillows that have slid to the side of the bed and hold the sippy cup up to her mouth.

Instead of drinking, she begins shivering. "I'm so cold," she says.

I get a light sweater out of the closet. When I wrap it around her shoulders, I can feel her upper body trembling. Then her hands reach out in front of her, grasping for some invisible hold in the air. I hear a gurgling in her throat.

"Help me, Connie. Help!" she whispers.

I jump up and run to the nurse's station to get Edefina, the nurse on duty. "It's my mom. You need to give her some morphine or do something."

We rush down the hallway to the room. I hold both of mama's hands in mine to try to stop the shaking while Edefina takes her vital signs. Her blood pressure is 195, temperature 101, and pulse skyrocketing.

"She's probably had a stroke," Edefina says.

Mama tries to push the blood pressure cuff away because it hurts. I continue to hold those frail but violently shaking hands for what seems like an hour, until the trembling has calmed.

This must be the end, I think, a frightening and awful end. I've read about the final stages of death but realize that each case is unique. This is not the way my father died.

After the nurse puts a small morphine pill under her tongue, I sit next to the bed for several hours, focusing on mama's face: cheekbones emphasized by sunken cheeks, eyes that look sewn shut, and a mouth that's slightly open exposing two bits of worn teeth. The oxygen tubes are still in place, and regular breaths are interspersed with ragged ones. Then her left arm moves slightly back and forth across the spread. Her head nods and her lips move to form silent words. At first, there's only a soft moan and then the words emerge.

"Wha' now?" she asks.

Those two words are heavy with meaning. I don't know what happens next. I guess that she's asking what physical crisis comes next, but it's also possible that she wants reassurance about life after death. It might be reassuring to her if I could speak about heaven and meeting her loved ones there, but I'm afraid she would see through these words to my own doubts. What should I say?

Before I can provide an answer, she clarifies her need: the facts of her present situation. "Hospital? Where am I? People coming in … I don't know them."

I reassure her that she's here in her bed at Ivy Manor, and I'm right here beside her. She relaxes a bit and slips into sleep again. An hour later, when nurses' shifts change, MoreGrace suggests that I go home. She assures me that she will keep watch over my mother and call me about any changes. That little voice in the back of my mind says, "A good daughter would sit vigil with her mother no matter how tired she is or how long it lasts." The voice at the front of my mind says, "I'm so tired, and I've been vigilant at her bedside through several near-death events over ten years. That qualifies me as a good daughter."

The final scene takes place when I return the next morning, a Saturday. I can smell the dirty diaper before I enter the room. There's mama asleep with feces on her nightgown, on the sheet, and on her hands. Cookie crumbs and a half-eaten granola bar are at the end of the bed. There is no ice water in her glass. I'm furious. I ask for an aide to change her. She's had diarrhea. Have they given her Imodium? No, they ran out of Imodium, I'm told. I get the bottle I've hidden in her drawer and ask them to give her two pills. What happened to the pledge to keep my mother comfortable? Apparently comfort does not include the smallest decencies. And who would have the gall to take a snack break in her room?

By the time, my mother and the bed are cleaned up, she is awake and parting the fog in her mind. With every neuron in her damaged brain, she's struggling to make sense of the past three days.

"I'm not … same person. I don't know … who I am."

I again explain the stroke. I ask if she remembers Daddy's stroke, the lightning bolt that tore their lives apart twelve years ago. A slight movement of her chin affirms her answer. I can feel her searching for the clarity of mind that has been her trademark. She's trying to swim toward a shore she can't find. I just don't know how to help her. I need to touch her to show my love in some way that she can feel. I stroke back the wisps of hair trailing across her forehead and smooth her warm brow. She doesn't resist my touch as she usually would. My fingers trail down to the still-smooth cheeks, now sunken as if she were taking a long sip through a straw. I kiss her cheek. The only deep wrinkles on her face are around her mouth. Both eyelids are matted shut. Asking her approval first, I remove the matter from her lids with a damp cotton ball.

"I love you, Mama. Is there anything else I can do to make you comfortable?"

She lifts her left arm a few inches and lets it drop limply to her side. "Love …," she whispers and turns her head slightly on the pillow. "Sleep."

Those are the last words I hear before she drifts into unconsciousness. The word "love" is palpable, the first time she's ever said it aloud to me. I can feel it radiate warmth through my tense body. It will connect us through life and death.

QUESTIONS FOR BOOK CLUB MEMBERS

1. How does Sophocles' quote "Don't judge a life good or bad before it ends" fit the narrative of the book? Have you had similar experiences in judging a person earlier in life and changing that opinion as he or she nears death?

2. Describe Ivy Manor. Was it a suitable place for the author's mother? Why or Why not? How did the physical environment and its caregivers affect the mother's life?

3. Olivia was one of Mildred's favorite nurses? What characteristics did Olivia have that helped the two to develop a close relationship?

4. Balancing her professional life and her care-giving life was difficult for the author. How did she cope with the tug between her two lives? Were there any similarities between her international student work and her care-giving?

5. Describe the author's father and his place in her life, both as a child and as a parent with Alzheimer's.

   How did this disease affect their relationship?

6. What was the relationship of the author's mother and father early in the daughter's life? After the daughter left home? How did the mother and father relate to each other in the nursing home?

7. What were the secrets Mama revealed in the hospital? How did this revelation affect her relationship with the author? What doors did it open for both of them?

8. In what ways did being an only child determine the kind of relationship the daughter had with her mother? Do most only children have a tendency to be people pleasers? Why or why not? Do the author's people-pleasing ways change during the narrative? Why or why not? Mama frequently repeats the story of the author's birth by saying, "You almost tore me apart." How does this affect the daughter?

9. How did the author's experience of living in Egypt for four years make her better able to cope with caring for her parents? What experiences have you had that strengthened your ability to cope with difficult changes in your life?

10. What life and death decisions did the daughter have to make? How did she handle these? What did she learn from these decisions?

11. What did the author learn about her mother as she facilitated her life review? How did several generations of mothers with tuberculosis have an impact on Mama? On the author?

12. What did the author learn about herself during her mother's life review? How did this change her relationship with her mom?

13. The author's parents were born in 1910 and 1911 and experienced surviving the Great Depression. On generational charts, they would be categorized as traditionalists (1900 to 1945). How did living in this era affect their education, work lives, and married lives? In addition, they shared Scandinavian roots. How did this heritage affect their choices and attitudes?

14. The author and her husband were influenced by both Traditionalist and Baby Boomer attitudes. How did these influencers affect their married life?

15. Why was it important for the author to be a good daughter? Was this a problem or a benefit in her relationship with her mother?

A SELECTION OF QUESTIONS FOR LIFE REVIEW.

What are the major turning points in your life? *Turning points are experiences, events, interactions with people or places that affected the direction of our lives.*

Who were the important people involved in this turning point?

What were your feelings and emotions at the time? Now?

How did your life change because of this turning point?

How would your life have been different if this had not occurred?

CHILDHOOD

When and where were you born? What were you told about your birth and infancy, and who told you?

What are your earliest memories?

Where did you live when you were a child? Describe the house and neighborhood.

Who were the people in your immediate family? Extended family?

What were your parents like? What were their weaknesses and their strengths?

Did you have siblings? What were they like?

What family members had a major impact in shaping your life?

What were the rules in your family?

What did you have to do to be "good"?

What were some of the things you wanted to do but could not?

What was the best about your family? The worst?

What family member were you closest to?

Did you have any pets?

Did someone close to you die when you were a child?

Did someone important to you go away?

Do you remember being sick when you were a child?

What are your memories of elementary school?

Did you like school? What did you like best about it? What do you remember learning?

What was difficult or frightening?

Who was your favorite teacher? Shy?

Who were your childhood friends and what did you like to do with them? Who was your best friend?

ADOLESCENCE

Where were you living when you were in middle school and high school?

What was happening in your family at that time?

Who was your closest friend when you were a teen?

What did you usually do together?

Why has this friendship continued or diminished through the years? How do you feel about that now?

How did your relationship with your mother and father change at this time?

Can you recall times you spent with your father? Your mother?

Picture yourself walking through the door of your high school. What and whom do you see?

How do you feel? What specific memories come back?

Can you think of times when you were encouraged by teachers? Discouraged?

What were you involved in other than classes?

What goals did you have? What did you want to do after high school?

What were the rules from parents or other adults about dating, sex, alcohol, drugs, and smoking?

What were some of your experiences?

Did you have a crush on someone? Describe a first date with someone you liked. Did you get into any trouble as a teenager?

What was most important to you at this time?

EARLY ADULT YEARS

What were the most important events in your life in each of these decades?

What kind of person were you in contrast to the teenage you? What did you enjoy?

Did religion play a part in your life at this time?

What was it like to leave home?

When did you begin to feel you were an adult?

If you were in college or university during these years, what major did you choose?

Why did you choose this field of study?

Would you make the same choice today? Why or why not?

Tell about a teacher who inspired or encouraged you.

Which classes were a struggle and which were easier?

If you were working, tell about your job and why you chose it?

How much were you earning? What expenses did it have to cover?

Which of your skills were most helpful in your job?

If you were to turn back the clock, would you have made the same choices?

Did you marry?

If you did, what kind of person was your spouse? At the time of your marriage, how were   you alike? How were you different?

On the whole, would you say you had a happy or unhappy marriage?

Were you married more than once?

What were the most difficult issues to deal with in your early married life?

How were the tasks of home life divided between you and your spouse?

What do you think are the keys to a good marriage?

If you divorced, what do you think were the behaviors that led to the break-up?

How did your family react?

If you had children, how did they react? How did you try to help your children handle the divorce? What worked? What did not? How would you do it differently today?

What people supported you during this period?

How did your life change after the divorce? How was your life better? What did you learn about yourself during this experience?

What message would you give your ex-spouse today?

Did your spouse die?

How long had you been together? What were the circumstances of the death?

What do you remember thinking and feeling? What helped you get through this time?

How did your beliefs help you cope?

What would you like to have had other persons do at this time?

What advice would you give someone during the first few months of a partner's death?

If you did not marry, why not?

What skills did you develop as a single person? Who were your closest friends?

How did you spend your free time?

Where did you live?

PARENTHOOD

How many children do you have?

How old were you when your first child was born?

What were the special characteristics of each child?

What was your partner like as a parent?

Who did which tasks of parenthood?

How did your relationship with your partner change when the children were born?

What were the major differences between the way you were brought up and how you raised your own children?

What did you carry on from your own childhood? What did you want to avoid from your own upbringing?

Were there any major crises you faced during this time? How did it affect your children?

LATER ADULT YEARS: 40S AND BEYOND

What are the difficulties you have experienced during these years? What are the joys?

What important events have happened during these years?

How are you different today from ten to fifteen years ago? What is good about being the age you are today? What is difficult?

If you are working, describe your job. If you have retired, tell about the transition from working to leisure time. What has been the most difficult adjustment? Are there any unexpected benefits?

What are you doing now that you've always wanted to do?

What part does religion play in your life?

What are the most important things in; your life today?

YOUR MAJOR LIFE WORK

Life work includes activities that have occupied the most time. It may include work as a parent, spouse or homemaker; the history of your career or lifetime job, or lifetime service in religion, community work, or politics.

How did you get into your major life work?

Did it just happen or did it seem destined to happen? Did other persons urge you to   pursue this work? Did any childhood interests or experiences ifluence your path?

Has your life work been one continuous path or have there been changes? What were the ups and downs?

Are you satisfied with your life work?

Is there anything you would change?

What personal strengths did you bring to this work?

Based on your own experiences, what advice would you give to a young person just entering this phase of life?

REFLECTIONS ON YOUR LIFE

On the whole, what kind of life do you think you've had?

If everything would be the same, would you like to live your life over again?

What changes would you make in your life? What would you leave unchanged?

Review the turning points in life from the first question in this list. Have any of them changed in importance during this review of your life? If so, why?

What have been the major satisfactions in your life? Why were they satisfying?

What have been the major disappointments in your life? Why?

Are there regrets about relationships that linger?

Can these be addressed now? How?

What is the most difficult thing you've had to face in life?

What was the happiest period of your life?